A HISPANIC LOOK AT
THE BICENTENNIAL

DAVID CARDUS
Editor

INSTITUTE OF HISPANIC CULTURE OF HOUSTON
P. O. Box 20387
Houston, Texas 77025

i

Library of Congress
Catalogue Card Number
77-73833

CONTENTS

PARTICIPANTS

Acuña, Hector, M.S., M.D. Director, Pan American Health Organization. Washington, D.C.

Azios, A.D. Harris County Judge to Criminal Court Number 9. Houston, Texas.

Campbell, Leon, Ph.D. Associate Professor of History, University of California at Riverside, California.

Cardus, David, M.D. Professor, Baylor College of Medicine. Houston, Texas. Chairman, Board of Directors, Institute of Hispanic Culture of Houston.

Durham, Harold, B.A. Graduate student, Department of Philosophy, University of Houston, Texas.

García, Juan, Ph.D. Librarian, Rice University. Houston, Texas. Consultant for the Library of Congress in XX Century Spanish History.

Giner-Sorolla, Alfredo, Ph.D. Associate professor of Biochemistry, Cornell University Graduate School of Medical Sciences. New York, N.Y. Associate Member and Head of the Drug Development Laboratory at the Sloan-Kettering Institute.

Hoff, Hebbel E., M.D., Ph.D. Dean of Faculty Affairs, Professor and Chairman, Department of Physiology, Baylor College of Medicine. Houston, Texas.

Malagón, Javier, Ph.D. in Law, Advisor, Secretary General of the Organization of American States. Washington, D.C.

Monsanto, Carlos H., Ph.D. Associate Professor of Spanish, University of Houston, Texas.

v

Quirarte, Jacinto, Ph.D. Dean, College of Fine and Applied Arts and Professor of History of Art, University of Texas at San Antonio, Texas.

Rodríguez, Louis J., Ph.D. Vice-Chancellor and Provost, University of Houston at Clear Lake City, Texas.

Ruiz-Fornells, Enrique, Ph.D. Professor of Romance Languages, University of Alabama, Alabama.

Rumbaut, Rubén, M.D. Associate Professor of Psychiatry, Baylor College of Medicine. Director, Day Hospital, Psychiatry Service, Veterans Administration Hospital. Houston, Texas.

PROLOGUE

The papers collected in this book were presented at a symposium held in Houston, Texas, October 8th and 9th, 1976. The symposium was organized by the Institute of Hispanic Culture of Houston in commemoration of the Bicentennial of the foundation of the United States of America for the purpose of creating a forum in which scholars pertaining to various disciplines would discuss the social, economic and political significance of Hispanic contributions to American life. Such contributions have taken place through the Spanish heritage of certain American institutions and the continuous influx of immigrants of Hispanic origin. Although a wide array of contributions in the multiple aspects of American life were suggested as possible topics for discussion only a few of them were addressed by the participants of this symposium. Topics relating to historical aspects were discussed by Drs. Rumbaut, García, Campbell and Malagón; concerning law, by Judge Azios; arts, by Dr. Quirarte; letters by Mr. Durham and Dr. Monsanto; economy, by Dr. Rodríguez; international relations, by Dr. Acuña; education, by Dr. Ruiz-Fornells; and science, by Dr. Giner-Sorolla. Most of these topics focussed on direct contributions to the United States of America. One of the suggested topics implied indirect contributions through universal values in the Hispanic arts, letters, and sciences. In this regard it was most rewarding to have the presentation by Dr. Hoff on Cajal, a man whose work has indeed profoundly influenced the field of medical science. In dealing with the topics of their own choosing, the participants were free to express their own views. The opinions contained in this book, therefore, do not necessarily reflect the Institute of Hispanic Culture position on any of the issues discussed. The speakers were also free to make their presentations either in English or Spanish.

The idea of providing an opportunity for presenting to the American public a variety of points of view on Hispanic contributions to the U.S.A. was discussed with Mr. Alan Reich, Deputy Assistant Secretary for International Affairs of the Department of State late in 1973. Mr. Reich received the idea with enthusiasm and in successive contacts helped us to establish relations with other groups in the country planning programs for the commemoration of the Bicentennial.

A steering committee constituted by Dr. James Castañeda, Mrs. Stella Cheesman, Dr. Carlos Vallbona and Mrs. Helen Worden assisted me in the planning and organization of the symposium. I would like to express now my deepest gratitude for their help. A great deal of gratitude also goes to all those who gave us financial support. In this respect, I would like to acknowledge the support of Mr. and Mrs. Keith Jackson, the Exxon Corporation, the Del Barto Foundation and the students Silvia Cardus, Josefa Castelli and Soledad Longoria who, headed by Professor Carlos Monsanto, organized the delightful folkloric show *Tarde Iberoamericana* which was presented at the Hamman Hall of Rice University on April 30, 1976, and whose proceeds were donated to the Institute of Hispanic Culture of Houston in support of the symposium.

David Cardus
Houston, January 1977

INTRODUCTION
A CONCEPT OF HISPANIC CULTURE
David Cardus

It suits an occasion such as the present to try once more to bring into the atmosphere of our thinking the concept of "culture" and the concept of "hispanic". What do we understand for culture? What do we understand for Hispanic?

As I see it, culture is a vital phenomenon which results from the interaction of three basic elements. These are: the past or history, the environment, and the individual's spontaneity.

Spontaneity is man's capacity to react before himself and to his environment. This reactivity is directed by intuitions that lead him, incessantly in the course of his existence, toward new and higher forms of life.

Environment is made of a physical world, man's perception of which is still expanding, and a nonphysical world made of ideas, feelings, knowledge, technical capacities and aesthetic and moral values, a world that Teilhard de Chardin called the noosphere, which is contantly remodeled by the spontaneity of each generation.

History is a legacy which contains in some particular synthesis the vital attitudes of past generations and the values they produced in facing, with their own spontaneity, their own environment and their own history.

Variations in the nature, and intensity and timing of each of these three elements result in different forms of cultural expression. It, then, becomes apparent that each cultural manifestation is a particular point of view of the universe and of the significance of life. One may ask then: Is there a *Hispanic* point of view?

In the cultural process that has been singled out as Western civilization, there has been a Latin contribution that Spain, more than any other country, was preordained to spread around the world. To a great extent Hispanic culture is Latin culture, a culture which embodies characteristic Roman and Greek components. Thus, the Greek supremacy of reason let to the concept that individual freedom is one of the highest spiritual values of mankind and the Roman supremacy of law and order led to the principles of social development and organization that prevail today.

But, one may still ask, is there a distinguishable "Hispanic" trait superimposed to this Latin background? In readying myself to express my feelings about this question the thought comes to my mind that it was in the old Iberia where more than anywhere else in the world a melting of multicultural elements, Greek, Roman, Jewish and Arabic took place many centuries ago. It was there that early in the history of Western civilization it was learnt that the preservation of spiritual values produced by different cultures is, in many circumstances, a vital imperative. The "Hispanic" is, then, understood as the epiphenomenon which results from the interaction of cultural traits brought by Spaniards and Portuguese with the autochthonous cultural elements which already existed in the American continent. At the time of discovery of the New World, the physical environment of man changed and new forms of individual spontaneity were added to those that Spaniards and Portuguese brought with themselves. It is not surprising, then, that the "Hispanic" acquires in this process constituent diversity and that through this diversity higher levels of cultural enrichment are achieved.

One of the characteristics of the Hispanic point of view is its profound humanistic realism. One cannot help thinking that as long as knowledge and technology constitute predominant driving forces in present cultural evolution, the Hispanic point of view must play an important role in promoting equilibrium among the forces which determine the destiny of the Western World.

Placed in the mainstream of Western civilization, the United States of America have been exposed historically to the influence of Hispanic cultural values. The vigorous presence of these cultural values is a palpitating reality today.

Traditional values in American life have characteristic expressions in religion, law, education, social behavior, economy, politics, science, art and in international relations. There has been a Hispanic participation in the gestation of these American values. More importantly, the Hispanic point of view is latent in this nation in approximately 6% of its population. Unquestionably, this imposes educational, sociologic, economic and legislative needs and demands, and social adjustments that cannot be disregarded for, from a cultural point of view, the "Hispanic" component of this nation has strong differential characteristics.

But, above all, the Hispanic point of view must be appraised in terms of its effective and potential contributions to American traditional values in each of their multiple expressions from religion, law, education, science, and art to international relations and its capacity to generate deep in the hearts of people the belief that this society possesses the resources to temper materialism with humanism and has the energy to sustain the imperishable pursuit of justice and happiness for all.

It is timely that Hispanic contributions to the birth and development of this nation be analyzed and made known to its people. In a limited way, this is what this symposium is about. It would lend much significance to this symposium if the ideas discussed would promote further studies along the same lines and would estimulate increased Hispanic participation in the cultural processes of this nation.

THE HISPANIC PROLOGUE

Rubén D. Rumbaut

What is Past is Prologue

A nation does not come into existence the day it declares its independence. First it is engendered; indeed, a long period of historical
gestation is needed for any healthy nation to be born. The Shakesperean
notion of "what is past is prologue" applies here also. The United States of
America declared its independence in 1776, achieved it in 1783, adopted its
Constitution in 1787, and elected George Washington its first president in
1789. Almost three centuries before George Washington was inaugurated,
Christopher Columbus had discovered, for history and western civilization,
the "New World", the American continent. The prologue to the birth of
the brand-new country had been long, painstaking, heroic and protean,
quite an extraordinary chapter in human history. For a long time and in
many important ways, that prologue was written in Spanish.

It is customary to refer to the Amerindians as "our natives", and to all
others who came after them as "immigrants". In reality, there are no
"native" Americans. Man is not native to the New World. The Amerindians are of Oriental origin, having come here from Asia, across the Bering
Strait, before everybody else. Thus, they should be properly called the
initial immigrants. However, it is undeniable that they were the original
inhabitants of the virgin lands and that, at the time of Columbus' arrival,
about 300 tribes (several hundred thousand people) existed and thrived in
the territory nowadays comprising the U.S.A. They, of course, also
represent a substantial part of the prologue. Positive and negative things
have been said about them. They had a priority in arrival and in land-rights;
their instinctive understanding of ecology, their love of nature, their sense
of identity with living things, their bravery, agility, endurance and artistic
sensitivity were outstanding. An accurate historical appraisal must,
however, be based on all the facts, due perspective and contemporary context. By the end of the fifteenth century, when Columbus' men landed in
the New World, the primitive inhabitants of what is now the U.S.A. were
still in the Stone Age, very fragmented, warring against each other,

5

sometimes even engaging in cannibalistic feasts. They did not possess a written language, not even a common oral language, because almost every tribe had its own. They did not form a political entity, nor a genuine nation, nor an empire. They did not constitute a civilization. They were mostly nomads who, having neither the horse nor the wheel, used as means of transportation the travois (an A-shaped contrivance of two trailing poles and a crosspiece) pulled by trained dogs or by their women. Women, by the way, were treated very harshly in many instances. Romanticizing and mystifying those realities would only contribute to confuse the perception of the complicated history of this hemisphere.

Common misperceptions about the Amerindians are the product of stereotypes, confusion and time distorsion. Indians are seen in western movies as inseparable from their horses. The Iroquois League of Five Nations is frequently cited as an example of political organization. The Cherokee language and syllabary are given as a proof of literacy. Those facts are true, but it is also true that in 1492 there were no horses at all in America, and there were none until the Spanish brought them. Only much later the Indians learned how to use horses. The Iroquois League was not founded until the end of the Sixteenth Century (almost by 1600) and only because of the persistent traveling and persuasive powers of Hiawatha (a real person, whose name Longfellow used mistakenly in his famous poem) as well as the war-like qualities of the five member-tribes. As for the Cherokees, Sequoyah was the hero of their literacy. He was the inventor of the Cherokee syllabary and the only man in history known to have conceived and perfected in its entirety a syllabary. Sequoyah, however, did all his work in the seventeenth century and is a classic example of cross-fertilization. He was the son of a white trader and an Indian woman. At an early age, attentively observing literate white men, he realized that there was a power in the written word that set apart those who could read and write. (His fame, by the way, is perpetuated by the beautiful giant Sequoia trees, named in his honor). The three examples are evidence that the rudimentary Indian cultures were radically affected and profoundly changed by contact with the European cultures, and since then they have never been the same.

Although some Indian tribes in this part of North America were more advanced than others — especially the Pueblo Indians of the Southwest — in general terms their levels of development and achievement at the time of the Discovery were not at all comparable with the ones reached in other parts of the continent by the great Maya, Aztec and Inca civilizations. Nevertheless, as human beings they deserved to be treated with respect, with understanding and without cruelty. Furthermore, in the last four centuries they have evolved and developed at a rapid pace, and form an integral, cherished part in the history, the present and the future of the U.S.

After the discoverers of 1492 came the explorers, the conquerors and the colonizers. The conquest was a tragic epic of cosmic proportions. No conquest in history has ever been pure, bloodless, compassionate. Even the ones that started as spiritual enterprises eventually twisted into adventures of war and exploitation. Unfortunately, this has been a universal fact of human nature at least until this point in history. No nation, race, society, culture or group is immune to the temptations of aggression, cruelty, greed and absolute power when embarked in a process of expanding and conquering. If all human beings were to admit it with sincerity and humility, perhaps then we would be able to find some preventive and lasting solutions, thus building a future of freedom, justice and peace. Until now, however, denial, rationalizations, scapegoating, blaming and creation of "black legends" have been the favorite mechanisms for projecting the evils of the world unto "them". Who is "them" depends only on whom is writing the history.

It will be naive and even dishonest, therefore, to look with different eyes at the Amerindians, the Spaniards, the French, the Portuguese or the English when studying the history of the New World. Raids, pillage and raping were systematically inflicted upon the Pueblo Indians by the Nomadic Indians. The conduct of the Conquistadores was frequently inspired by an unchecked thirst for gold, power, glory or sex. The "paleface" Anglosaxons subjugated, displaced, dispossessed, betrayed and even outrightly eliminated entire Indian tribes. Indians, and above all Africans, were enslaved for a long period of time; they, in their turn, had also used caste systems, slavery, exploitation and extermination of others whenever the circumstances were propitious. It appears certain, for instance, that no religion ever was more cruel and bloody than the Aztec's. No apologies or intellectualizations should be used to mask or deny the excesses or horrors of conquests and wars. No silence, distortion or subterfuge should be used, either, to suppress the myriad positive things brought about by the great convulsions of human history.

The gigantic, epochal movement spearheaded by the Spaniards that poured the occidental nations of Europe over the unknown lands of the New World was one of the greatest and deepest convulsions in history. The discovery broke the supposedly insurmountable barrier of the "Dark Ocean", and since then the Atlantic has laid wide open to an incessant crossing of people and cultures. Exploring, mapping, cross-fertilizing, developing, culturizing, civilizing, converting, teaching and growing coexisted with the negative features of the cutting swords and the raw power of the guns. Christianity, western culture, and the most advanced civilization and technology known to history until that moment also came on the peak of the oceanic tide.

When we travel today through this continent of ours, from the Artic to the Antartic, we can see splendid nations, thriving cities, wonderful peoples, and great urban conglomerates, like Montreal, New York, Ciudad de México, Río de Janeiro, Buenos Aires, Lima, Caracas, Bogotá, La Habana and many, many others. All this is the consequence of an incredible adventure, initiated less than five centuries ago by the Spaniards, under Spanish flags and titles, in Spanish ships, and led by an Admiral of the Spanish fleet. Whatever we are now, we owe it to them. The Discovery, as well as the immediate exploration, conquest and colonization were essentially Hispanic and later, when the Portuguese followed suit, a thoroughly Iberian enterprise.

By the middle of the sixteenth century — barely fifty years after Columbus' voyages — the Spaniards had already explored most of the coastal line of all South America, the entire Atlantic coast, and the Pacific coast up to Oregon; explored the interior of present-day Argentina, Bolivia, Colombia, Chile, Ecuador, Paraguay, Uruguay and Venezuela; all of Central America including the Antilles; all of Mexico; large parts of the southwestern and southeastern United States, including the valleys of the Mississippi, Rio Grande and Colorado rivers, and the California shores. They had also explored the Amazon and the principal river systems of South America; had discovered, named and crossed the Pacific Ocean all the way to the Phillipine Islands, and finally had been the first to circumnavigate the earth. Magellan, that towering figure, although born a Portuguese, did all his traveling for Spain, having adopted Spain as his country. After he died in the Phillipines, his ship "Victoria" completed the first round-trip around the world under the Spaniard Juan Sebastián Elcano.

In a short but excellent book, Gil Manilla adds another aspect of the Spanish saga during the Sixteenth Century: "They had made known," he emphasizes, "the doctrine of Christ and, though they had not brought the enterprise to a happy ending, they had founded the first European settlements in North America, and the first mission which attempted to preach the Gospel to the natives without any military aid... The first bloodshed in defense of Western culture, the cornerstone of the United States, was Spanish blood... When the French and the English appeared on the scene, Spain had already made her mark and shed her blood in one third of the present area of the United States."

Harold E. Davis, writing for *Collier's Encyclopedia,* judges the pioneer impact of the Spaniards in the New World, especially during the early decades, with the following words: "The sixteenth century was the Spanish Century in America, as in Europe. Indeed, history furnishes few parallels to the prodigies of arms and valor of the mere handful of Spanish soldiers and sailors of fortune in America, who carried on the conquest of the population... and the land. They penetrated thousands of miles inland through jungle and desert and across freezing mountain passes, defying tropical disease, starvation, thirst, and hordes of hostile warriors who often outnumbered them in a ratio of a thousand to one." Charles F. Lummis, an American historian, categorically sums it up in *The Spanish Pioneer*: "... no other mother country ever gave birth, as Spain did, to a hundred Stanleys... in a single century" ... "The Spanish pioneering of the Americas was the largest and longest and most marvelous feat of manhood in all history."

The Spaniards brought to the New World the wheat, sugar cane, olives, rye, barley and lemon; the horse, the cattle, the sheep, the goat; pigs, donkeys, mules, chickens. They taught plowing, irrigation and herding, built aqueducts and dams, and disseminated and improved the native crops, especially potato, tobacco, corn, and peanuts. They introduced iron, steel, metal tools and cooking utensils; wheel carriages; windmills; blankets and other forms of clothing; gunpowder, guns and other weapons.

They brought, of course, infinitely much more than objects, plants, animals and the necessary techniques for utilizing them. With the Spaniards came commerce and trade on an international scale, industry, mining, technology, banking, architecture; the fine arts, the basic and the applied sciences and the learned professions; the alphabet, the printing press, schools and universities. Spaniards introduced Spanish, the first European language to be spoken in this part of the earth and, almost simultaneously with it, Latin. They brought books by the hundreds, and then printed the first books this side of the Atlantic. Finally, with them came the immense Greek-Roman-Judeo-Christian tradition and accumulation of knowledge and wisdom.

Due to their daring spirit and superb use of ocean navigation techniques available to the Europeans at the time, together with the Portuguese they made possible communication and trading with the four corners of the world, joining all the continents for the first time in human existence. Thus, the human world was truly completed by the Iberians. As for the New World, through the trail blazed by the Spaniards the rest came later. The Mayflower sailed in the path opened more than a century earlier by the Santa María, the Pinta and the Niña.

There were more specific ways, however, in which Hispanic foundations were laid for the would-be nation of the United States of America. More than half of the present territory of the continental United States, plus Puerto Rico, were for centuries under Spanish rule. In twenty-four of the fifty states of the Union the Spaniards introduced Western civilization. Present witness to the long and large Spanish presence in North America are the innumerable U.S.A. states, cities, towns, geological formations and national monuments bearing Spanish names. There are some regions in the country in which almost every town and village has a Spanish name. Anyone traveling today coast to coast, from Florida through California, can see the first civilized settlements, houses, missions, schools, churches, ranches, public buildings and cities in U.S. history.

The first Christian martyrs, the first teachers, the first scholars and the first pioneers are no longer visible, but the places where they lived, worked and died are still with us. We cannot see the first naval construction sites in San Miguel de Guadalupe (1526-28), or applaud the first theatre play, presented in El Paso, Texas (1598). But we can visit the irrigation system built for the Isleta Mission near El Paso (1681) because it is still functional, or the Palace of the Governors in Santa Fe, New Mexico (1610), still open to the public, or, in the same city, the San Miguel Church, uninterruptedly used for worship since 1610. In that church, and in numerous others scattered all over the states, we realize that the Catholic Church owes above all to the Spaniards its present dissemination and vitality in the nation.

Charming Saint Augustine, in Florida, is the oldest city of the U.S.A. From its massive Castillo de San Marcos (a national monument) the visitor can see the Atlantic Ocean. Fragile ships brought over that ocean the expeditionaries led by the first white man ever to settle in North America: Ponce de León. He sought the Fountain of Youth, but eventually found an untimely death. He pursued, before anybody else, the American dream. El Morro National Monument, near Gallup, New Mexico, is a monumental rock that keeps for posterity, carved in its rugged surface by the very hands of the Conquistadores, the names of the ones who passed by, and the dates in which they rested under its shade and drank the water of its spring. In the beautiful and serene old missions of Texas, New Mexico, Arizona and California time seems to have gently stopped. Visiting any of those national monuments is like being suddenly immersed in an ancient sea of history. And all of it is Spanish history.

The Path of the Conquistadores

In 1513 Ponce de León discovered and named Florida (a Spanish word for Flowery land) and also the Bahamas Channel. Alvarez de Pineda, a great sea pilot, as early as 1520 explored the whole Gulf of Mexico from Yucatan to Florida and drew the first maps of the Texas coast. In 1521 Gordillo and Quexos reached Chícora, on the southern coast of North Carolina. Not long after, Quexos explored the northern coast up to Cape Hatteras, while Esteban Gómez sailed from Florida to Labrador, reconnoitering the mouths of the Connecticut, the Hudson and the Delaware. In 1526 Vasquez de Ayllón established a colony in the Carolinas, reached Cape Fear and postulated that the real wealth of those regions ought to be based on the sea and the fisheries. Narváez, in 1528, landed in Florida, explored its northwest and sailed through the Texas Coast. Hurricanes, accidents, hardships and cannibals disposed of almost all of the initial six hundred members of his expedition except four: Alvar Núñez Cabeza de Vaca; Esteban de Azamor, nicknamed Estebanico, a black moor (the first black ever to leave a historical imprint in North America); Andrés Dorantes; and Alonso del Castillo. They were separated, except for Cabeza de Vaca and Estebanico, and lived for six years (1528-1534) among the Indians, for the most part as slaves. Cabeza de Vaca progressed from slave to trader to medicine man, discovered new routes and walked, walked, walked. In 1534, starting from Galveston, Texas, he marched west with Estebanico, in the hope of finding land inhabited by Spaniards. In the process he encountered the other two survivors, and together the four crossed on foot Texas, the Río Grande, and hundreds of miles southward until they reached Mexico City in 1536!

The American historian Bolton calls them the real European pioneers of the Great Southwest. Their incredible, astonishing journey (and the book that Cabeza de Vaca wrote recounting it), constitutes one of the most magnificent gests in human history, and besides makes Cabeza de Vaca the first writer, reporter and historian of North America. Estebanico returned later from Mexico under Coronado's leadership. In 1539 he took the lead while crossing the plains of Arizona and was the first one to reach the fabled "Seven Cities" in what is now New Mexico. He named the region Cíbola. There he fell into the hands of Indian warriors who put him to death. His was a poignant and symbolic tribute. The first of all the Black Africans who was to meet a violent death in the New World, a former slave himself, he was at the same time one of the Conquistadores. (There is no monument erected yet, by the way, to Estebanico the Pioneer.)

The famous expedition of Hernando de Soto set out from Cuba in 1539. Starting with Tampa Bay, he explored Florida, Georgia, the Carolinas, Tennessee and Alabama. He spent the winter of 1540 in the area which is now Mississippi. By Spring he had discovered the mighty river (one hundred years before the French). He pursued his exploration through Arkansas, Oklahoma, Missouri, and Kansas, died of malignant fevers in May of 1542, and his body was buried in the majestic waters of the river that he had put on the maps of the world.

While De Soto was doing all this, Coronado was busy exploring Arizona, New Mexico, Colorado, Texas, Oklahoma and Kansas. Nowadays there can be found numerous plaques in all those states, with the terse notation: "Coronado was here". López de Cárdenas, initially one of Coronado's followers, was the first white man ever to contemplate in awe the unique beauty of the Grand Canyon (1541). Almost simultaneously, Alarcón entered the Colorado River at its mouth and traveled it upwards until he reached California, while Lucas Arellano was founding a settlement at Pensacola.

During 1542 and '43, Rodríguez Cabrillo, an able Portuguese navigator sailing under Spanish flags, discovered the coast of California. The first large port he encountered was San Diego. He stopped later at Santa Mónica, and died shortly thereafter at San Miguel Island. His expedition continued northward, though, under the Spanish pilot Ferreló, discovering Capes Mendocino and Fortuna, and the southern coast of Oregon. Before him, Ulloa had sailed around the Gulf of California, proving that Baja California was a peninsula.

The year 1549 saw the founding in Florida of a Dominican Mission. In 1565 Menéndez de Avilés founded the first U.S.A. city: Saint Augustine, in Florida. One year later Pardo and Boyán explored again Georgia, Tennessee and Alabama, while in 1570 the Jesuits opened, bordering Chesapeake Bay, a very active mission: Father Segura's. The years of 1581 and 1582 offered to Chamuscado, Father Rodríguez, and later Espejo, the opportunity to penetrate further into Texas and New Mexico. The century was closed by Oñate colonizing all of New Mexico, and exploring Texas, Oklahoma, Kansas, Missouri, Nebraska and Iowa.

The Spaniards procreated abroad, and those Spaniards born in the New World were called "Criollos" (Creoles). Contrary to popular belief, Creoles are not of mixed ancestry, but persons of the White race born in the New World's regions colonized by Spain, France and Portugal. Generations of Spanish Creoles began to multiply. Creoles born in Mexico, Cuba and Hispaniola took part in successive expeditions, and many of them settled down for good in the new lands. Their names can be read in archives or historical buildings. The "Peninsular Spaniards" from Spain, and the "Creole Spaniards" from the New World who settled in what is now the U.S.A. were, in a sense, the Spanish Pilgrims. Hundreds of thousands of American citizens bear surnames which unequivocally indicate their descent from the Spanish Pilgrims of yesteryear. The first "American" of whom documented proof exists was born in 1566 in St. Augustine. His name: Martín de Argüelles. Also in St. Augustine the marriage of María Viscente with Vicente Solana took place in 1594. Theirs was the first "American family" ever to be registered in the national archives.

Vizcaíno opened the seventeenth century exploring and carefully mapping the Pacific coast to Cape Mendocino. The New Mexico Missions (one in every Indian pueblo) were flourishing by 1630. The Jesuits created a famous center, Loreto (Sonora Valley), in 1650. That center was the place from which all the California Missions were to spring. Terán and Alonso de

León explored Texas in depth from 1686 to 1691. Fort San Carlos at Pensacola was founded in 1698, and San Xavier Mission in Arizona in 1700, thus closing the century.

The next one began more slowly. San Miguel de los Adaes, in Texas, was founded in 1717. A year later San Antonio (a city that today still boasts of an enchanting Spanish colonial atmosphere) was founded in Texas, and within it a famous Mission which later was to have an enormous impact in American history: El Alamo.

Tubac was founded in 1752. Louisiana was incorporated by Spain in 1763. San Diego was founded in 1769. The dissemination of the missions eventually achieved its culmination in that famous chain of California Missions — twenty one, extending from San Diego to San Francisco — which even today marvel the visitors. Fray Junípero Serra and his Franciscan successors erected all of them. A stupendous expedition led by Juan Bautista de Anza arrived in San Francisco Bay in 1776, precisely two weeks before the Declaration of Independence in Philadelphia. The de Anza expedition was a major effort to open a new overland route from Mexico to Upper California. There were 240 settlers, priests and soldiers, and 1,000 head of domestic animals that traveled 1,500 miles from Horcasitas (Sonora) to San Francisco (California). On the way they reinforced San Diego and Monterrey, and joining forces with the mission-building Franciscans, founded San Francisco in honor of their patron saint, St. Francis of Assisi.

The final two decades of the eighteenth century still witnessed the founding of Lake Charles in Louisiana, the recovery of Florida in 1783 by Spain, the path-finding explorations of Vial from San Antonio to Santa Fe, Natchitoches and St. Louis, the occupation by Juan Pérez of Nutka on the Pacific Coast, the foundation of New Madrid, and the carefully prepared expedition of Alejandro Malaspina, who for two years traveled and mapped the northern Pacific coast, making possible what Count Humboldt later wrote: "The considerable number of Spanish names still found in the coast of Vancouver prove that the expeditions ... contributed not a little to our knowledge of a coast which, extending from 45°N. to Cape Douglas east of Cook's entrance, is now more exactly mapped than most of the coasts of Europe". The activities and imposing presence of the Spaniards in the North Pacific Coast is said to have prevented the expansion of the Russian Empire over American shores and lands.

When in 1763 Louisiana, until then French, went under Spanish rule, the Mississippi River divided what is now the continental USA in two enormous zones: one, to the East, English; the other, to the West, Spanish. Later Thomas Jefferson (who spoke Spanish fluently and considered it a most necessary modern language) reflected over that fact and said: "The Spanish and the English covered nearly the whole face of America." Besides, in 1783 Florida was returned to Spain, and once more all the southern land, from Florida to California, was Spanish-ruled. Indeed, the five years from 1783 to 1788 are considered by an author as "the most splendid ones of the Spanish Empire in North America." It was a swan song, though. From then on things took, albeit slowly, a declining course.

Contrary to popular belief, victory, glory and wealth were not often a reward for the Spaniards during their centuries of hegemony over this part of the world "north of the Rio Grande." Almost anything they did was risky, painful, difficult, frequently lethal. There was no gold, silver, or oil for the Spaniards here. Legends and myths, from the Fountain of Youth to Eldorado, were dispelled one by one. What now takes a few lines in a textbook, usually represented then months and years of terrible hardships. Even as late as 1769, when the Spanish government and the Franciscans took over the Jesuit Missions in Lower California and decided to expand northward, tragedy ensued. They began by sending three ships from La Paz and two land divisions from Loreto. It took months for all of the expeditionaries to get together again in San Diego. By the time they did, one ship had disappeared at sea; another had lost to scurvy all of her crew but for one sailor and one cook, as well as many soldiers; the third ship lost eight of her crew to the same disease. After many dangerous incidents, some members of the land forces had perished, too. In general terms, hardships, disease, and death were more the rule than the exception.

On the other hand, the expeditionaries were not just armed conquerors. When Alonso de León went to Texas in 1680, he "deliberately left horses and cows at every river crossing, thus starting the herds of wild cattle that would give rise to a great industry, and the herds of mustangs that would become a western legend". As a matter of fact, the cowboy, the universal American hero, is but the direct heir of the vaquero. Vaquero, translated into English, roughly means "cowman". The cowboy's basic vocabulary is either pure Spanish (rodeo, corral, sombrero, látigo, remuda, tapaderos) or mispronounced Spanish (buckaroo for vaquero, latriat for la reata, lasso for lazo, ranch for rancho, chaps for chaparejos, coosie for cocinero). The long evolution began in Andalusia, Spain, with the "jinete andaluz", and spread to the Americas with the "gaucho", the "llanero", the "vaquero" and eventually the cowboy. The horse, the cattle, the gun, the lasso and the guitar were all provided by Spain, and later by Mexico. Texas' debt to the vaquero is recognized in these words of the Institute of the Texan Cultures, honoring . . . "the men who established ranching as a way of life in Texas, long before the first Anglo-Saxons learned from them everything on which the proud cowboy tradition is based". The Spanish Texans introduced not only ranching, its styles, its techniques and its vocabulary but also, according to the Institute, " . . . the revolutionary ideas of building permanent structures of stone and lumber, of the use of the wheel, of money, of writing, printing, and recording history. They brought advanced concepts of law and government, a new language and a new religion. Eventually they mapped the land, set its bounds, and gave it the name by which it is known today. Two thirds of the recorded history of Texas is Spanish history."

Thus, during the 311 years (1512-1823) of Spanish rule, the expanding and the founding never stopped, with the "presidio", the "misión", the "rancho" and the "pueblo" as the pillars of the system. One hundred Spanish Governors took charge of territory now comprising 24 states. Nevertheless, many crises, setbacks, errors, conflicts and failures slowed down progress considerably. Initially the path of the Spanish Conquistadores, explorers and colonizers, wide and diverse, was traveled with great speed and vigor, but little by little that path got narrow, clogged and troubled.

At the end, Spain was internally wounded, internationally declining, and surrounded by rival powers in Europe, while trying to maintain an impossible Empire in four continents and in the New World, greedily spreading itself too thin throughout all of South, Central and North America. In the meanwhile, almost parallel to this decline, the Thirteen British Colonies, growing with youthful energy, operating within a healthy economy, contiguous and united geographically, politically and culturally, and partially self-governing, were leaning almost inevitably towards independence.

In any case, by the last quarter of the eighteenth century the New World's adolescence was practically over. The whole continent, from the Arctic to the Antarctic, felt that adulthood and independence were in sight. The time of the Conquistadores had faded away. The period of the colonizers had passed, too. The age of the kingdoms was also coming to a close. In contradistinction, the hour of the Liberators and the Republics was dawning... "The Revolution — John Adams wrote for the Thirteen Colonies, but he said it for the whole hemisphere — was effected before the war commenced. The Revolution was in the minds and the hearts of the people...".

Spanish Contribution to the Independence of the United States of America

Because they were rebelling against England, Spain was sympathetic to the struggle of the Thirteen Colonies, and made a substantial contribution to their independence. It has even been said that perhaps the triumph of the Continental Forces was possible because of the decisive intervention of France and its ally, Spain, and that Benjamin Franklin, with his shrewd diplomacy and his European contacts, made possible the military victories as much as Washington did in the battlefields. When in 1778 an official treaty was signed between the representatives of the Thirteen Colonies and the government of France (which presaged the ultimate entrance of Spain, and later Holland, into the conflict) the tide turned heavily against England.

Spain's help, somewhat over-shadowed by France's outstanding participation, was nevertheless much more in quantity, quality and timing than it is customarily credited to her in the traditional history books.

As early as 1776 England was protesting the services rendered by Spanish ports to the "rebel" ships. Juan Miralles, a merchant shipper from Havana, was named observer and personal representative of the Spanish Governor in Havana, with authority to represent Spanish interests before George Washington and the Congress in Philadelphia. Miralles became so enthusiastic about the American cause, that unofficially he was made special advisor concerning the logistics of the extensive maritime front covering the Gulf of Mexico and the borders of the Mississippi. Upon Miralles' recommendation, rebel ships were given safe harbor in Cuban ports and granted the use of the Havana Arsenal facilities (at the time among the best in the continent) for repairing, storing and arming the naval squadron of Commodore Alexander Guillon. Because Guillon lacked funds, a wealthy relative of Miralles, Don Juan Eligio de la Puente, gave his personal guarantee for the operation. Consequently, trade was established between Cuba and the Thirteen Colonies.

The very year of the Declaration of Independence Carlos III of Spain opened ample credit to the Continental forces. The money and the help offered by France and Spain to the independence was chanelled initially through Beaumarchais (the author of the opera "The Barber of Seville") who for years acted as the unsuspected agent of the French government in London. A Spanish firm "Rodríguez, Hortalez and Co." that Beaumarchais headed, functioned as a cover-up. That firm, among other things, paid the trip of the famous Baron Von Steuben, the Prussian officer who did so much to train and discipline in military matters the Continental Army.

The Spanish loans, credits and outright gifts resulted in cannons, mortars, rifles, bayonets, gun carriages, bullets, uniforms, tents, beds, gun powder and quinine in appreciable quantities. The loyalist Governor of Pensacola strongly protested in vain. Carlos III responded indirectly by stating that Spain was not pursuing any territorial gains. England, trying to disuade Spain from entering the war, tantalized her with the possible return of Gibraltar and Florida, fishing rights in Canada, and other advantages.

Spain, a rival of England, an ally of France, a nation with vast interests in the New World and expecting the victory of the rebels in the long run, played the diplomatic game for a while, but nevertheless backed the rebels and eventually ended by fighting directly against Great Britain.

In succession, three Spanish agents were sent to the Continental Congress: Juan Miralles, Francisco Rendón, and Diego de Gardoqui (the last one the first official Ambassador of Spain to the U.S.A.).

The money poured in many denominations: reales de vellón (half-dimes); libras esterlinas (sterling pounds); libras talegas (a sort of Spanish pound); libras tornesas (a kind of French pound) and gold pesos. The value of everything, in material help only, has been estimated by some as perhaps the modern equivalent in purchasing power of 200 million dollars. Aside from the various educated guesses and the probable hyperboles, it can be affirmed that the imponderable, intangible value of the strategic, logistic, political and moral support is simply incalculable.

Two instances, however, deserve a detailed explanation. They were very important, and yet they are little known. Don Bernardo Gálvez, the founder of Galveston (Galveston is a corruption of "Galvez town") in 1777 was appointed Spanish Governor of Louisiana. Patrick Henry, then Governor of Virginia, wrote to him urging increased trade with the southern state. Gálvez answered affirmatively, and helped by granting sanctuary to American ships while denying harbor to British vessels. After 1779, when Spain declared war on England, Gálvez was ready. Texas men, horses and cattle were called in to reinforce his troops. On the orders of the Spanish King, he then entered openly in the fight against the British. Departing from New Orleans, he attacked and conquered the fortresses of Baton Rouge, Manchac and Panmure, the cities of Natchez, Mobile and Pensacola, eastern and western Florida, and eventually the Bahamas Islands. As a result, England was forced to divert its military resources, and lost control of the Mississippi, the Gulf of Mexico, and part of the Eastern seaboard.

Norwin Rush, Director of Libraries and Professor at Florida State University in Tallahasse and a noted member of the Florida Historical Society, wrote a most detailed study about the Battle of Pensacola. He is quoted in the book *Pioneros Cubanos en USA,* by J. Isern, as asserting: "As we contemplate the larger and more comprehensive picture, we begin to see more clearly that the Battle of Pensacola was of large significance in the eventual triumph of the American Revolution in spite of the fact that none of the Thirteen Colonies took part in it. The Battle of Pensacola was one of the most brilliantly executed battles of the war. With the conquest of Pensacola by Spain, England lost a very important military position, its last support position in the Gulf of Mexico".

The Battle of Pensacola (1781) came at a time when the British had already captured Savannah and Charleston in Georgia and South Carolina, and were so well entrenched in Pensacola that Gálvez considered the continued siege of the city useless and hopeless. At that moment Spanish forces (1600 strong), organized in Havana and comprised largely of a "militia" of Cuban Creoles and a "battalion of Negroes and Mulattoes" born in Havana, entered into the picture. They came under the leadership of General Juan Manuel Cagigal-Monserrat, born in Santiago de Cuba. With their reinforcements and at Cagigal-Monserrat's urging, Gálvez, leading 7,000 men and 24 frigates, attacked and decisively won taking 1,200 prisoners. Because Gálvez was from Málaga, the people of the city, then building their cathedral, decided to offer him "a tower of our cathedral" and sent him the money saved for that purpose. Other popular collections in Spain included one-and-one half million of libras tornesas.

The most opportune of those collections, though, came later, at the most decisive battle of the war, when Cornwallis was defeated in Yorktown by Washington, Rochambeau and Lafayette. The historian Stephen Bonsal, in his book *When the French Were Here* describes how the rebel army was about to disband because Washington lacked the means with which to pay his men and had to confiscate from owners the very few provisions left in the country. The monetary chaos was such that barbers papered their shops with revolutionary currency.

The Bicentennial book *200 Years* describes the situation: "An air of crisis hung over patriot headquarters in New England. The war was in its seventh year, and the Continental Army was rapidly shrinking as bone-thin weary men reached the end of their endurance and refused to re-enlist." The Comte of Rochambeau, commander of the French army that had been sent to America in 1780, thus depicted the growing crisis: "These people here are at the end of their resources ... This is the state of affairs and the great crisis at which America finds itself". Some of the troops "were near mutiny ..." says Bonsal. And then he adds: "Washington now sadly revealed his financial situation to Rochambeau ... Rochambeau had his troubles, too. Little money had reached him since his arrival in America ... (presumably) ... captured by alert English cruisers ... Rochambeau sent for his meager war chest ... Of this, he turned half (one hundred thousand ducats) over to Washington, who agreed to return the amount in October".

Cornwallis was entrenched in Yorktown, and the British fleet (nineteen ships) was being brought to the cape of the Chesapeake by Admiral Graves. The French Admiral de Grasse had arrived first, though. He had departed France, in March of 1781, toward the West Indies with orders to cautiously cooperate in the offensive against the British. He was heading a fleet of 23 warships protecting 250 vessels loaded with provisions and equipment valued at 30 million pounds. He arrived in Martinique by the end of April. In Cape Haiti he encountered the frigate Concorde coming from Newport and carrying letters from Washington and Rochambeau informing de Grasse of the bankrupt state of the Thirteen Colonies, and that under the circumstances the Continental Army's provisions and funds would last only until August. The fleet was requested to proceed urgently to Virginia with the provisions, reinforcements and, above all, money. Attempts by de Grasse to raise money in Haiti were unsuccessful (despite the fact that Haiti was then the coffee and sugar capital of the world). The Spanish representative in Haiti suggested negotiations in Havana. De Grasse went there, but found the Spanish treasury empty. It was then that the crisis was resolved by Cuban women. The "ladies of Havana", mainly from the aristocracy but nevertheless very sympathetic to the American Revolution, contributed a donation of one million ducats, offering even their jewels to achieve their goal.

"Washington", says again the Bicentennial book *200 Years,* "was on the road south, near the village of Chester on the Delaware, when a dispatch rider from Baltimore reached him with the thrilling news: Admiral de Grasse had successfully blocked the Chesapeake. Cornwallis was trapped. Washington threw off the dignity of a lifetime and to the astonishment of his staff shouted, whipped his hat into the air, laughed like a boy, and grasped Rochambeau in a bear hug". The Comte Dumas said later that he had never seen a man "moved by greater or sincerer joy".   A few days later the allied troops reached the head of Elk River on the northern tip of the Chesapeake, and the American army was paid at last; money kegs were broken open and silver coins rolled on the ground. That day was the first in which the troops of the United States received one month's pay "in specie". The money "raised the spirits to the required level".

The value of a ducat in modern terms, its actual purchasing power, has been estimated to be in the vicinity of twelve-and-a-half dollars. The Havana donation was roughly equivalent, perhaps, to what now would be twelve-and-a-half million dollars. The Marquis of Saint-Simon, commanding the land forces from West Indies, brought the ducats with him, and put both the men and the money at the disposition of General Washington. The Continental forces encircling Yorktown now swelled to a respectable number. Bonsal specifies: "On September 26 all the troops were concentrated in and around Williamsburg, and they included the Army of Rochambeau from Rhode Island, 4000 men; the Continentals under Washington, 3800; the French contingent from Martinique under the Marquis of Saint-Simon, 3200; the expeditionary force under Lafayette, 2500 veterans of the Virginia campaign; and an uncertain, but daily increasing number of Virginia militia under General Weedon". When the allied armies attacked in October, they were 17500 strong.

The rest is known history. De Grasse's fleet had engaged the English fleet and defeated it early in September. French Admiral de Barras also came to Chesapeake from Rhode Island with siege guns and supplies for Rochambeau. On October 19, 1781, the British gave in, and the defeated troops laid down their arms. Some difficult months remained ahead, yet; but the major battles were over. By 1783 American Independence was officially recognized by the British and by the world.

Bonsal categorically states that the one million Havana ducats, together with the one hundred thousand already given by Rochambeau, "may, in truth, be regarded as the bottom dollars upon which the edifice of American independence was erected".

During all the colonial years and the initial decades of independency Spanish currency was legal. Most surprising, the dollar itself has a Spanish origin. Old silver coins in Germany were called thalers. Spain eventually minted a silver dollar coin with the same value and they were called Spanish thalers. When those coins began to circulate, they were mispronounced and misspelled, and ended first as "dalers", then as "dollars". With independence, the "dollars" acquired the rank of the monetary unit of the new country. Because the Spanish dollars portrayed on the reverse side of the coin the two Pillars of Hercules (two promontories in Gibraltar that were the symbol of the Spanish Empire at the time) those columns, stylized and with the floating ribbon about them, gave rise to the $: the dollar sign.

The Continental Forces made independence possible by soundly defeating the English. Some nations helped them considerably, France and Spain above all. It is impossible to estimate accurately how much their intervention influenced the outcome. At least one American author, Buchanan Parker Thomson, who intensively researched the historical archives of Spain, believes that American independence would have been impossible without the help from Spain.

This opinion could very well be an exaggerated claim and, in any case, is an academic question. Nevertheless, by one of these paradoxes of human history, the fact remains that the USA achieved its independence by fighting against Great Britain, an "Anglo-Saxon" nation, while receiving a decisive help from France and Spain, two "Latin" nations. Beyond any doubt, the Hispanic Prologue, from 1492 to 1783, was an extraordinary prelude to the birth of the United States of America. Spain started it with the discovery, provided the solid foundations, and opportunely assisted in bringing the new country to life. Many forces in turmoil pushed Spain toward that destiny: avid curiosity, daring enterprise, religious zeal, eagerness for glory, wealth and territories, national pride, imperial designs, political ambitions, a civilizing urge ... Of those substances is human history made.

The Hispanic presence in the new nation, then as well as now, is indisputable. From the Atlantic to the Pacific, from geography to history, from the cowboy to the dollar, the imprint is lasting and cannot be ignored. Spanish is the second language of the Union. Today the Americans of Spanish ancestry are the nation's most rapidly growing ethnic minority, and their culture, dormant for so many decades, is awakening with an impressive and far-reaching resurgence.

Suddenly, there is a Hispanic rejuvenation taking place in the United States. It seems as if, after all, Ponce de León and his people have finally found in America the Fountain of Youth, and are avidly drinking of its magical waters.

References

Books

Collier's Encyclopedia Vol. II, The Crowell-Collier Publishing Co., U.S., 1962.

California's Missions, 9th Edition. Herbert A. Lowman, Publisher. Printed by Record Printing Co., 1954.

The Decline of the Californios, Leonard Pitt. University of California Press, 1971.

Naufragios y Comentarios, Alvar Núñez Cabeza de Vaca. Espasa-Calpe, Madrid, 1922.

The Spanish Texans, Institute of Texas Cultures - The University of Texas at San Antonio, 1972.

Spain's Share in the History of the United States of America, Octavio Gil Munilla. Publicaciones Españolas, Madrid, 1952.

Ancient America Series "Great Ages of Man". Time-Life Books, New York, 1967.

200 Years: 1776-1976, U.S. News and World Report, Inc., Washington, D.C., 1973.

The Spanish Pioneers, Charles F. Lummis. A.C. McClung and Co., Chicago (Fifth Edition), 1912.

La Huella de España en América, Rafael Altamira. Madrid, 1924.

The Colonization of North America: 1492-1738, Herbert E. Bolton. The McMillan Co., New York, 1920.

Los Conquistadores Españoles, F.A. Kirkpatrick. Espasa-Calpe, Madrid, 1935.

Spain in America, Charles Gibson. Harper and Row, New York, 1966.

The Spanish Heritage in the U.S.A., Darío Fernández Flores. Publicaciones Españolas, Madrid, 1965.

España Ante La Independencia de Los Estados Unidos, Juan F. Yela Utrillo. Lérida, Spain (2 volumes), 1925.

Bolton and the Spanish Borderlands. Edited by J.F. Bannon, University of Oklahoma Press, Norman, Oklahoma, 1964.

The Cuban Contribution to the American Independence, Eduardo J. Tejera, Ediciones Universal, Miami, 1972.

Pioneros Cubanos en U.S.A. 1575-1898, J. Isern. Cenit Printing, Miami, Florida, 1971.

Centennial, James A. Michener. Fawcett Publications, Inc., Connecticut, 1974.

The Diplomacy of the American Revolution, Samuel Flagg Bennis. Indiana University Press (Seventh Printing), 1967.

The Spanish Borderlands, H.E. Bolton. Yale University Press, Connecticut, 1921.

When the French Were Here, Stephen Bonsal. Kennikat Press, Inc., New York, 1945.

Presencia Española en Los Estados Unidos. C.M. Fernández-Shaw. Ediciones Cultura Hispánica, Madrid, 1972.

Participación de España en la Independencia de Los EE.UU., Francisco Morales Padrón. Publicaciones Españolas, Madrid, 1963.

The Spanish Background of American Literature, Stanley T. Williams. Yale University Press, 1955.

Historia de Cuba en sus Relaciones con Los EE.UU. y España. Herminio Portell Vilá. Mnemosyne Publishing Inc., Miami, Florida, 1969 (4 Volumes).

La Ayuda Española en la Guerra de la Independencia Norteamericana, Buchanan Parker Thomson. Ediciones Cultura Hispánica, Madrid, 1967.

Webster New International Dictionary of the English Language. Published by G. and C. Merriam Co., Springfield, Mass., 1915.

Newspapers
Monthly Editions of *"Bicentennial Times",* organ of the American Revolution Bicentennial Administration.

Articles, Lectures and Personal Communications
"Were you aware that Cuba played a part in the North American War of Independence?", by Gabriel L. Rodríguez, a Cuban-born lawyer and writer. Published in *"Florida Latin News",* April 1975, Vol. 3-No. 1, Miami, Florida.

Erik Martel, Consul of Spain in Houston, Texas. Lectures and talks on occasion of the American Revolution Bicentennial.

Pedro Duelo, Cuban-born lawyer and professor of Spanish, Los Angeles, California.

MISSIONS, PUEBLOS, AND PRESIDIOS:
A NEW LOOK AT SPANISH INSTITUTIONS IN ALTA CALIFORNIA, 1769-1784

Leon G. Campbell, Jr.

To conquer and colonize the province of Alta, or Upper California in 1769, the Spanish Crown utilized three institutions — the mission, the *presidio,* or fortress, and the civil *pueblo,* or town — which had successfully been employed in pushing back the frontiers of New Spain from the sixteenth century onwards. Because the Spanish mission was a distinctive institution, incomparable with devices employed by the French, English, and Anglo-American civilizations also moving westward across North America, it is undoubtedly the best-known of the three historically. Both the presidio and the pueblo had Anglo-American analogues and therefore did not receive the historical attention given to the missions and the mission fathers.

The Franciscan missionaries who founded the Alta California missions and attempted to Christianize the Indians there, notably the redoubtable Father-President Junípero Serra and his successor, Fermín de Lasuén, were strong, literate personalities who left their signatures on early California history. During the Hispanic period, 1769-1821, twenty-one missions were founded, eleven of these during the period of Serra's tenure as president, 1769-1784. It is hardly unusual, therefore, that these first two decades are known as the "mission period" of California history.[1]

Relatively little is known of the civil towns established in Alta-California — San José (1777), Los Angeles (1781), and Branciforte (1797) — although some work on these municipalities has recently been done.[2] In 1975, for example, the California Supreme Court overturned a 1966 trial court decision approving the right of Glendale and Burbank to pump water from the Northern part of the Los Angeles water district. The Supreme Court denied that the pueblo of Los Angeles had been under the control of the missions and presidios and was thus not an independent, self-governing entity under Spanish rule. Rather, the court argued, the pueblo was "the primary instrument for the permanent settlement and development of California," and hence the city of Los Angeles had the right to deny the

This paper is reproduced with permission of the author.

use of its water to areas not having pueblo status in 1781 when the water rights were granted by the Spanish Crown.

The presidio is even more of an unknown quantity than either the mission or pueblo. While the structure and function of the frontier presidios of the old Spanish Southwest have recently been analyzed, no studies exist of the presidios and presidials of Spanish Florida or California. These forts were erected during the latter part of the eighteenth century in coastal locations, unlike those in Texas, New Mexico, Arizona, and the northern Mexican provinces, for the dual purposes of controlling the Indian population and guarding against foreign invasion, and were regulated by different rules than those which controlled the presidios of the Interior Provinces of New Spain.[3]

Indeed, one reading the early histories of the conquest of California might have felt that the Franciscans were, alone, peacefully progressing northwards from Mexico surrounded by adoring natives.[4] The destruction of the Spanish California archives in the 1906 earthquake has helped to perpetuate such a myth by destroying certain presidial records, but ample record groups are available for the studies of the presidios.[5] Historians may well have shied away from presidial studies under the mistaken belief that such efforts were not worth their time and would only yield dreary information about minor battles, pay disputes, and other trivialities. In reality, however, presidial records provide a view of early California history from another perspective than that afforded by the missionaries. In addition, they divulge a considerable amount of information about the government, economy, society, of one of the most remote outposts of Spain in America.

The general texture of life in *este último rincón del mundo,* or "this far corner of the world" as the Spaniards referred to Alta California, was far different from that in Mexico City or Lima, and accordingly, events of imperial significance are seen in a quite different perspective. Social historians are wanting to know more of the varieties of life in Spanish America and from a social historical viewpoint, presidial studies are important. While the soldiery in California lived lonely and dangerous lives, their tasks and concerns reflect those of the larger society. In fact, the social composition and background of the presidials are microcosms of Alta California society generally and tell us much about the first *Californios.* Even more importantly, the soldiers of Alta California often became founders and settlers. Some of the most notable families of the Hispanic period — Argüello, Carrillo, Moraga, Alvarado, Pico, Vallejo, Castro, de la Guerra, Ortega, Peralta, and others — were descended from these soldiers.[6]

This paper has as its purpose the examination of the development of the four Alta California presidios — San Diego (1769), Monterey (1770), San Francisco (1776), and Santa Bárbara (1782) — during the mission period.

During the period 1769-1784 the presidios were inextricably entwined with the eleven missions founded during this same period. Gradually, however, a process of change took place to alter this relationship. First, the pacification of the California Indians and the growing threat of an attack on Alta California by European rivals operating from the Pacific Northwest, led to the presidios becoming defensive agencies whose primary function was less the control of the Indian population and protection of the missions than it was the defense of the province against the threat of a seaborne attack. Secondly, in 1781 the administration of California was defined by a new *Reglamento,* or regulation, promulgated by Governor Felipe de Neve, which replaced one that had been authored by Father Serra in 1773. The Neve Reglamento was designed to reform the province by strengthening the presidios and developing pueblos. With the foundation of San José (1777) and Los Angeles (1781), the presidios were provided with a broader economic base which allowed them to escape somewhat from their perpetual dependence on the missions for foodstuffs and supplies. In addition, the settlers of these towns provided the presidios technical assistance and served as a manpower pool to provide the recruits for the garrisons. Another paper will examine the implications of these changes from 1784 to the coming of independence in 1821.

The romance and importance of the California mission enterprise tends to obscure the fact that under the Spanish Bourbons (1700-1821), the frontier presidio took on a significance in the eighteenth century that it had not even achieved during the conquest of the northern frontiers of New Spain in the seventeenth century. For one thing, France's defeat in the Seven Year's War (1756-1763) and its subsequent withdrawal from North America had strengthened Great Britain's power there. King Charles III strongly desired the development of commerce and mining in Spanish America as part of a larger plan of "defensive modernization" designed to occupy the Pacific Northwest. This policy required that Alta California be occupied as a means of neutralizing the activities of the English and the Russians in the Pacific Northwest. At the same time, Alta California would serve to protect the mines and factories of northern New Spain and the trans-Pacific trade between Mexico and the Phillipines from English attack. The Spanish naval engineer Miguel Costansó, in a report to the viceroy in 1794, expressed his belief that it was for "the preservation of the Sovereign's proprietorship and ownership of these continental coasts... that presidios were established in Upper California."[7] Although the Franciscans saw the California project in entirely different terms, the presidios were key institutions in the foundation and control of the new province, and the presidials were the new missionaries of Charles III who would retain the Pacific Northwest in Spanish hands.

During the conquest and occupation of Baja California, the Society of Jesus had been given unlimited authority in carrying out the missionary enterprise but their independent-mindedness had caused considerable friction with civil and military officials and had resulted in the order's expulsion from Spanish America in 1767. The conversion of Alta California was delegated to the Franciscans two years later, but their activities were limited to the missions and the religious and military were constantly warned of the need to co-operate with one another. In fact there was a basis for accord between the two groups. The prime function of the mission was to transform hostile Indians into willing converts and laborers. The success of the missionary enterprise made it possible for the Crown to militarily occupy Alta California with a small number of troops. As late as 1794, Costansó remarked that Alta Calfornia had a total military force of only 218 men stationed between San Diego and San Francisco, a distance of over 500 miles.[8] On the other hand, the missionaries could not hope to Christianize the Indians without the presidials' support. Located on "the rim of Christendom," far from the capital in Mexico City, Alta California was a tenuous undertaking which depended on the ability of its colonists to work together.

Conflict rather than co-operation, however, best characterizes the relationship between the military and religious during the mission period of California history. To some degree, this conflict was of a personal nature, reflective of the strong personalities of Serra and the military governors of the province.[9] On another level, however, the disputes were really eighteenth-century manifestations of the sixteenth century controversy over the true purpose of the conquest. Serra and the missionaries were the spiritual heirs of Father Las Casas, aware of their crucial role as conversionists and unwilling to accept any conditions imposed by the military authorities which promised to hinder their efforts. The governors and the soldiery, on the other hand were chastened by the fathers' independence and refusal to accept their authority. While they disagreed with the priests' methods of dealing with the opinions of the Indians, the basic disagreement between the two groups was fundamentally over the nature of the mission. The military refused to accept it as the dominant and independent institution which the Franciscans supposed it to be. Rather, they saw the mission as an agency of the Crown, performing an essentially civil function of creating a docile, industrious Indian community instead of Christian enclaves subject only to religious authority. During the mission period these views were never reconciled and accordingly, conflict between the two branches of government never ceased.

As will be explained more fully below, the administrative structure of the Viceroyalty of New Spain, of which Alta California was a distant part, was altered during the period just subsequent to the occupation of California. As a result lines of authority between the military and religious, never clear to begin with, became more complex. With jurisdictional boundaries blurred, the possibility arose for one branch to challenge the authority of another and the archival record stands in testimony of the mutual distrust which existed between the priests and the presidials. This suspicion manifested itself in a ceaseless series of letters between the father-president, the governor, and the authorities in the capital as well as correspondence from these officials to their membership within Alta California. The correspondence fully recounts the rumors, threats, bickering, scandals, and controversies separating the two branches of government.

While scholars have sometimes reported on these, they have often been dismissed as a series of unrelated or superficial squabbles. I propose that these incidents be taken seriously or at least considered more fully than is sometimes the case. When looked at over time, the conflicts between the priests, pueblos, and presidials have a remarkable continuity and reveal both the philosophical differences separating the individuals operating these three important Hispanic institutions on the California frontier as well as their attitudes and primary concerns. As such we can begin to gain an understanding of the social history of this remote part of the far-flung Spanish empire in America.

Presidial Development, 1769-1784

By the end of the mission period in 1784, Alta California possessed eleven missions, four presidios, and two civil towns, all of which were situated along relatively narrow coastal corridor between San Diego and San Francisco. The spiritual conquest of the province is a deservedly well-told story which need not be repeated here. The first five years of the California venture was undeniably a missionary enterprise, yet it was a military one as well. By 1773, there were only nineteen Franciscans at work in five missions, which had an estimated Indian neophyte population of 7000 souls. At the same time, slightly fewer than 150 soldiers garrisoned two presidios and these five missions, and were charged with the responsibility of protecting them against the 135,000 Indians inhabiting the territory.[10]

The occupation of Alta California was part of a larger plan devised by Visitor General José De Gálvez to defend New Spain's northern frontiers from external aggression by creating a vast commandancy-general that included the areas of Sonora, Sinaloa, Chihuahua, and the Californias. A viceroyalty in everything but name, this military district was under the command of a veteran commander headquartered in Arispe. Alta California's "Sacred Expedition" of 1769 was commanded by the Governor of Baja

California, Captain of Dragoons Gaspar de Portolá, assisted by the commandant of the Loreto Presidio Captain Fernando de Rivera y Moncada. These officers were supported by twenty-five soldiers of the veteran Spanish Infantry Company of Catalan Volunteers who had previously served in the campaigns against the rebellious Sonoran Indians. These troops were joined by twenty-seven *soldados de cuera,* or leather-jacketed presidial soldiers from Loreto, all of whom were seasoned Indian fighters. While the Franciscans' presence allowed this venture to be termed a ''Sacred Expedition'' it was structured and executed as a military expedition.[11]

With the return to Mexico of the Catalan Volunteers, California was defended by 146 *soldados de cuera.* As a group they were a tough and hardy breed, well-suited to endure the deprivations of frontier life. Like the settlers of the civil pueblos, the presidials were generally men of *mestizo* or mulatto parentage who had been recruited from among the inhabitants of the ranchos, villages, and presidios of northern New Spain. Few of them were literate — in 1785 only fourteen of the fifty men stationed at Monterey could read or write. As a group they were young, with an average age of about 32, and three-fifths of their number were unmarried. This situation was to change, however, since married men were preferable to bachelors in areas of large Indian populations. By 1790, fully two-thirds of the soldiery were listed as married and living with their wives. Although no complete social profile of these men can be given in such a short space, it is clear that most of the soldiers were men of good character. Even those of questionable background, some of them ex-convicts who had been sent to California to relieve the overcrowded conditions in the Mexican jails, seem to have comported themselves well in California. The picture which emerges of these first *Californios* is on the whole more favorable than that provided by the European-born priests who depicted the presidials as incorrigibles.[12]

This is not to say that the soldiery lived blameless lives. Their robustity and individuality, qualities which so admirably suited them for frontier warfare, also caused them to be disrespectful to the priests of the missions where some of the soldiers were detached and irreligious. Nor could they remain apart from the Indian women. Historians have referred to the conquest of America as a conquest of women and California was no exception to this rule. Some of these women gave their favors freely of course and others eventually married their lovers and raised families, but others were accosted and raped. These illicit relationships brought the priests and presidials into open conflict since they disrupted morale and spread venereal disease within the mission population.[13]

The priesthood responded energetically to stop these violations and see that the guilty men were brought to justice. In fact, their actions were so swift and public that they have tended to color public opinion of the soldiers as rapists and brigands. Yet in certain cases evidence was lacking to prove that rape and seductions were committed. More than this, the relatively small number of cases brought to trial leaves open to some doubt the priests' assertions that the soldiers were of bad character.[14] Given the fact that only a part of the total number of violations of Indian women by soldiers ever reached the trial stage, it can be argued that the maintenance of military discipline required presidial commandants to act on complaints brought before them. Failure to do so would have fostered the insubordination which was perenially a problem in military society, especially in remote areas such as California.

On the other hand, in those cases which were brought to trial, only rarely did the punishment meted out fit the crime. This, of course gives some credence to the fathers' assertions that presidial commandants condoned their soldiers' actions involving Indian women. Certainly the commanders were sensitive to the meddling of their friars in presidial affairs. Also, the fact that each soldier was of unusual importance to the success of the California venture during the mission period at least, perhaps explains the relatively mild sentences handed down. But the charges of coddling largely stem from a sensational case of rape and murder of a young Indian girl by a trio of soldiers from San Diego in 1771, where the defendants were not executed but were only required to remain in California for life as an appropriate punishment. In this instance, however, even the priesthood was not in agreement about the evidence against the men.[15] In general, soldiers regarded Indian women as a benefit of frontier service and cohabited with them freely. Yet cases of violence involving rape and murder seem to have been infrequent enough not to merit a general condemnation of the soldiery as men of bad character and low morals.

When one considers the lives of the frontier soldiery a more realistic picture of their collective deportment emerges. Presidial duty was lonely and frequently dangerous. Pay scales were low and wages were often in arrears. Conditions for the men detached to the missions was sometimes worse than for those in the presidios. Although they were not to be utilized by the priests without the prior approval of the presidial commandant, mission soldiers often were required to chase runaway neophytes, care for mission horses, and perform other menial tasks which they resented, especially when their orders came from priests who sometimes held them openly in contempt. In one case arising at Mission San Luis Obispo, a soldier was denied the right to attend mass because of his disheveled appearance, and mission fathers won the right to send soldiers back to their presidios without being required to state the cause of their displeasure. In response to these slights, commandants might use Indian neophytes as laborers on presidial construction projects instead of the soldiers or use these same persons as auxillaries in warfare. They might even restrict the size of the mission guard below its statutory strength or refuse to release soldiers as escorts or to found additional missions. Only the need to prevent war and the mutually dependent economic relationship between mission and presidio seems to have acted to ameliorate the bitter rivalry between the two groups.

In sum, the California presidials, like those of other frontier areas, seem to have been men taken from the lowest social strata of northern New Spain. It was not difficult to enter the Spanish Army on the frontiers where recruitment was a perennial problem. Catholic males exceeding a height of five feet, two inches possessing no noticeable facial scars were all eligible for duty. Although these soldiers were required by the King to be of good character, this was unenforceable. Yet a relative few seem to have been troublemakers or chronic incorrigibles. They are unfavorably depicted by priests who had good reason to disparage them, and sometimes by presidial commanders themselves, who were often in the process of seeking additional soldiers from the viceroy and hence sought to paint their present group in the worst possible terms. Foreign visitors, however, such as Admiral George Vancouver, were less quick to make judgements about the soldiers and are probably close to the truth in depicting them as more cowboys than true soldiers.[16]

In order to judge the California presidials as soldiers it is necessary to look at the quality of their opposition. Although certain contemporary accounts of the California Indians disparage their fighting abilities, there is no question but that they were capable of becoming formidable opponents who required constant military supervision. Though they possessed few firearms, they were quick to adopt tactics of guerilla warfare — ambush, retreat into impenetrable areas, sniping from cover, and even trench warfare upon occasion. Early attacks made on San Diego Presidio and certain missions brought about a stricter Indian policy after 1770 which resulted in an almost complete cessation of violence after 1784 until the advent of independence. The soldiers employed their horses, organization, and superior equipment to put down insurrections and stop fugitivism. As soldiers, their bravery and military ability helped preserve California in Spanish hands.[17]

Far less is known of the four California presidios from which these soldiers operated than of the missions and civil towns with which they necessarily interacted. What follows is not intended to be a definitive rendition of the foundation and development of these four presidios but rather is designed to give some idea of their relative strengths and their position within the process of California's institutional development during the mission period. My purpose is to bring forth certain data which will perhaps give a better idea of the presidios' working relationship with the missions and civil towns and thereby an understanding of their socioeconomic status in addition to their military value.

The presidio of San Diego was established in 1769 at the foot of what became known as Presidio Hill north of the present city. The area was selected by Captain Rivera because it commanded a view of the bay to the west and was also within view of the Mission San Diego de Alcalá located six miles to the east. The California presidios were initially established on a footing of thirty-two men which raised to seventy-one in 1778. The fort was under the command of a lieutenant, assisted by a sergeant, five corporals, and sixty-two soldiers. Of this number, three corporals and twenty-nine soldiers were detached as mission guards throughout a presidial district which eventually extended from the Tía Juana River in the south to Mission San Fernando Rey de España to the north and included civil town of Nuestra Señora de los Angeles del Río de Porciúncula that had been founded in 1781.[18]

In 1770 Captain Portolá established the Presidio of Monterey on a flat piece of land overlooking the Pacific Ocean. The fort was garrisoned by a sergeant, five corporals, and forty soldiers until 1777 when it was placed under the jurisdiction of the military Governor of California, whose headquarters that year had been transferred from Loreto to Monterrey, symbolizing the fact that Alta California had replaced Baja California in importance. California's lieutenant governor who had formerly commanded in Monterey, being transferred to Loreto. The Monterey Presidio, which initially had five corporals, and forty soldiers, eventually was doubled in size and became the largest of the four California forts after 1777 with primary responsibility for guarding the Missions La Purísima to the north and San Buenaventura to the south along the channel. The Monterey presidial district extended from the Pájaro River to the north to the Santa María River in the south.

The presidios of San Diego and Monterey were established in a period of steadily deteriorating relations between Father-President Serra and the military governors of the province. In July, 1770, following the establishment of the Monterey presidio, Governor Portolá sailed for Mexico, leaving California under the military command of Lieutenant Pedro Fages, a brash young Catalan officer who had commanded the Catalan Volunteers. During the four years of Fages' governorship, 1770-1774, the governor refused Serra's constant petitions for soldiers with whose help several projected missions were to be established. In 1773, Serra's exasperation led him to travel to Mexico where he was able to persuade Viceroy Bucareli to have Fages replaced as governor by Captain Rivera y Moncada who commanded in California from 1774 to 1777.[19]

Historians generally regard Rivera to have been the weakest of California's military governors during the Spanish period.[20] A creole of undistinguished birth unlike his Peninsular predecessors, Rivera had become governor of Baja California fortuitously when the incumbent had died. As governor in California, Rivera was an overly-cautious administrator given to displays of temperament, although he was popular with the soldiers for his steadfast refusal to weaken the existing presidios by granting Serra soldiers with which to colonize new missions. It may have been that Rivera felt threatened by the more experienced Serra, who earlier had sought to have Fages replaced by José Ortega, a sergeant whom the priest had patronized and supported for governor.

Rivera had good cause to fear Serra. By 1773, the intrepid priest had succeeded in having the Crown accept a regulation which he had authored to provisionally govern Alta California. Serra's recommendations were drawn up in a report written by Juan José Echeveste, an officer of the viceregal court in Mexico, who was in charge of supplies sent to Alta California from the port of San Blas in Baja California. Designed to regulate the missions and presidios, the Echeveste Regulation spelled out the means by which the former were to be maintained and designated the military force which it was felt was necessary to support the spiritual conquest and consolidate Spanish control in the territory. As might be expected, the regulation left no doubt that the mission was the dominant Hispanic institution in the province and that the missionaries' interests were paramount to those of the soldiery. The friars were granted complete control over the mission Indians and were permitted to dismiss the mission guards without stated cause. Military were to be paid in goods rather than specie and were otherwise subject to rules they found to be intolerable. In short, the presidio was placed on the defensive and required to serve the mission, on which it already was completely dependent economically. The result was lowered morale in the garrisons and increasing levels of desertion.[21]

In August, 1775, Charles III ordered Viceroy Bucareli to transfer the capital of the Californias from Loreto to Monterey. The order sent Rivera to Loreto and Lieutenant Colonel Felipe de Neve to Alta California. If the Rivera appointment had been unfortunate, Neve's tenure as governor was just the opposite, marking a period of growth and progress for the colony. It also marked a resurgent period for the presidios and for the military.

Although Neve inherited problems with the Indians, who had earlier attacked the San Diego Mission, more critical was the need to extend the Spanish settlement north along the coast to protect it from attack by Spain's European rivals sailing in the waters of the Pacific Northwest.[22] In July, 1776, a primitive barracks and chapel were constructed on a hill overlooking the Golden Gate. Later, the presidio was constructed according to the regulation governing the presidios of northern New Spain. It was the smallest of the four Alta California garrisons, being on an initial footing of thirty-five men, including a lieutenant, a sergeant, four corporals, and twenty-nine soldiers. Part of this group were recruits from the Presidio of Horcasita who had come to California with the Anza expedition the preceding years. The presidio had an adobe wall like the others. The buildings enclosed were nothing more than thatched roof huts with earthen floors and included a church, enlisted and officers' quarters, a storehouse, and a guardhouse. Two corporals and thirteen soldiers were assigned to the San Francisco and Santa Clara Missions located to the south. The presidial district extended from the area near present-day Santa Rosa to the north southwards to the Pájaro River near Santa Cruz.[23]

In 1777, Teodoro de Croix, the newly-appointed commandant of the Interior Provinces of New Spain, under whose jurisdiction Alta California now came, asked Neve to formulate a new regulation to govern Alta California. Croix, more than Bucareli, believed that a strong defense was the key to holding the colony against foreign interlopers. He was aware of the inequities of the Echeveste Regulation and the adverse effect it had had on the California presidials. The Neve Regulation of 1779, which was approved by the Crown in 1781, constitutes a watershed in the early history of Alta California in that it represents a transition from the mission period with its exclusive concern for the conversion of the Indian as set forth in the Echeveste Regulation of 1773 towards a more balanced form of development in which the presidio was to be economically supported by the civil town and was to serve primarily as a bastion against external attack.[24]

Neve recognized that the presidios were weak and isolated and were likely to be of little help unless basic structural reforms were carried out. Already there was a severe lack of commisioned officers to serve as commanders. The necessity of furnishing mail-carriers and mission guards depleted the garrisons substantially; once Monterey was defeated by only twenty men. Since reinforcements could not be sent across the Sonoran Desert or up the coast in the event of an attack, Neve felt that the establishment of civil towns was the only way to assure a sufficient manpower pool to defend the province in an emergency.

Neve also recognized the economic weaknesses of the presidial institution and was determined to correct them. The fact that the forts were located in strategic areas that often lacked sufficient arable land or water to grow crops resulted in their being almost completely dependent on the missions for their food supply.[25] Given the strained relationship between the priests and the soldiers, this situation only bred further animosity as the missions complained that they did not have sufficient grain to feed the soldiers and they latter retorted that they were forced to pay exorbitant prices for their food. To rectify this situation, Neve supervised the foundation of the civil towns of San José (1777) and Los Angeles (1781). The 350 settlers of these towns provided both economic and human support for the presidios thereafter and helped to lessen their dependence on the missions. Although the Franciscans had been among the first to suggest the formation of civil towns, their experience with the presidials soon made it clear that these towns would greatly complicate their missionary labors, representing as they did the secular world. Considering the opposition to the scheme laid down by the fathers it is notable that Croix fully supported Neve's proposals. These were designed to strengthen the presidios yet they would eventually alter California itself by allowing for the development of the civil and military settlements at the expense of the clerical communities.[26]

The Neve Regulation also provided for a series of internal reforms to be made at the presidios. His concern with presidial finance reflected the larger Bourbon solicitude that the Spanish-American colonies be as economically self-sufficient of the mother country as possible in the event of another war with Great Britain which was anticipated. Neve must be credited with recognizing that the presidios constituted economic units and that those placed in charge of these forts were to possess administrative and fiscal skills in addition to military ones. This was crucial since the presidial *situado,* or subsidy from Mexico was often delayed and the California economy was so fragile that a bad winter could result in starvation and suffering. Neve paid special attention to the appointment of soldiers with accounting skills to the post of *guarda almacén,* or storekeeper, and *habilitado*, or paymaster. In addition, he began to pay the troops in specie rather than goods and made presidial commanders responsible for the paymasters' accounts to assure greater fiscal responsibility and prevent cost overruns. All of these measures served to place the California presidios on a sounder economic footing and improved morale within the garrisons.

There are other areas where Neve's military reformism was evident during the period 1777-1784. Better training was provided to the soldiers who had grown ragged and dispirited serving under Rivera, but it is difficult to gauge the effectiveness of this drill. Stricter standards of discipline seem also to have been applied upon occasion. Neve was not above executing a soldier accused of looting following an earthquake which struck Carmel in 1781, nor was he loath to punish guilty soldiers in full view of the offended Indians in order that they could view the Spanish legal system at work. These actions won him the grudging respect of the priests and may have helped to improve relations with the Indian community as well.[27]

The establishment of California's fourth and last presidio at Santa Bárbara in 1782 stemmed from Neve's belief that the important Santa Bárbara

Channel was strategic to the future development of Alta California. Because *El Camino Real,* the land route that connected northern and southern California ran along the coast of the channel and could have easily been closed by the Chumash Indians who inhabited the area, Neve pressed hard to have a fort established in the middle of the channel area. In 1779, Croix had dispatched soldiers to Alta California in response to Neve's petitions for same, but most of this soldier-settler group, under Rivera's command, had been wiped out by the Yuma in the vicinity of the Colorado River in 1781. Fifty-two soldiers and their families had gone ahead and escaped being killed. These men served as supernumeraries in Santa Bárbara, which was established on a footing of a lieutenant, three sergeants, two corporals, and sixty-two cavalrymen, most of whom were drawn from the soldiery at the other presidios. The presidial district ran from the Santa María River to the north southwards to Mission San Fernando Rey. The soldiers of the presidio had primary responsibility for guarding the missions San Buenaventura to the south and Concepción Purísima to the north, each of which was provided with a sergeant and fourteen soldiers. With the formation of this presidial company the defensive structure of Alta California was completed.[28]

Although the Neve Regulation acted to improve the administration of Alta California it also served to drive Neve and Serra further apart. Father Serra had never relinquished his wish to found more missions and he resented the development of the civil towns which seemed to endanger his scheme and threatened to turn California into a purely secular enterprise. The creation of the Provincias Internas of New Spain, which included Nueva Vizcaya, Coahuila, Sinaloa, Sonora, New Mexico, Texas, and the Californias, removed Serra from the jurisdiction of his patron Viceroy Bucareli and placed him under the military command of Croix in Arispe. The lines of authority in California became even more complex after 1777 since Serra's College of San Fernando in Mexico City remained under viceregal control although Serra himself did not. The confusion stemming from the administrative reorganization of 1777 allowed for the possibility of one official challenging the authority of another. This was between the strong-willed Neve and Serra and their relationship, never good, began to worsen after that time.

A review of the correspondence of Neve and Serra leaves little doubt that each distrusted the other and apparently for good reason. Neve's insistence on his right to appoint priests as part of his function as vice-patron rested on the assumption that California was not a mission territory but instead formed part of the Bishopric of Guadalajara and fell under the jurisdiction of the secular clergy. Moreover, Neve had earlier tried to have the mission Indians elect their own local officers who were to report to the governor in order to further undercut Serra's authority.[29] For his part, Neve saw Serra and the priests as secretive and independent-minded men who were using every pretext to defy his authority, and indeed there are examples of this sort of behavior. Father Pablo de Mugártegui, for example, the priest at Mission San Juan Capistrano, wrote Serra in Latin in order to speak more freely about what he termed Neve's scandalous behavior and to frustrate the reading of his letters by the soldiers who carried the mail.[30] Whatever the truth of these assertions, they ended only with the deaths of Neve and Serra, ironically only a week apart, in August, 1784. With the demise of the two men most responsible for the development of Alta California, the mission period there came to an end.

To conclude, it would appear that Alta California's "Mission Period" is somewhat of a misnomer in that it tends to slight the development of other important Hispanic institutions during this time frame. Actually, the first fifteen years of Spanish colonization is marked, not by harmonious mission growth but instead by fierce conflict between the priests and the military governors for control of the province. This struggle was waged in terms of development. With scarce and finite resources, priorities had to be given to the founding of new missions, presidios, and civil towns. The priests, notably Father Serra, worked exhaustively to build eleven missions during the period, to have the mission regarded as the primary institution in the province, and to cause Alta California's government to reflect the priority given to the missionary enterprise. A series of Spanish military governors vigorously opposed Serra's efforts but they were generally unsuccessful. Yet although Governor Neve and his predecessors failed to limit the growth of the missions, Serra and the friars were equally unable to dominate the presidios as they had hoped to do.

Spain's new concern for maintaining the defense of the Pacific Coast, which manifested itself in the creation of the Provincias Internas in 1777, helped to bring about this stalemate. Teodoro de Croix and José de Gálvez were pursuaded that the frontier presidio must necessarily be an economically independent and strengthened institution in order to protect Alta California from external attack. The result of this new policy was the Neve Regulation that the Crown approved in 1781. Fully as concerned with the development of civil towns and presidial reform as Serra's Regulation had been with mission growth, the regulation clearly spelled out the changed function of the presidio from control of the Indian population to defense of the coast based on battlements and artillery companies. Neve's instructions to his successor, Pedro de Fages, written in September, 1782, indicated the extent of this development. He reported that the Monterey presidio alone had in excess of 1000 head of cattle and was developing a series of cottage industries. More than this, the Monterey and San Fran-

cisco presidios had been completely fed that year by the harvest of the
pueblo of San José which had been founded only three years earlier. This
commentary indicates that by 1782 the presidios had begun to break the
cycle of economic domination maintained by the missions and were entering into a more co-operative relationship with them based on a mutuality
of interest and institutional parity.[31]

The importance of the four Alta California presidios to Alta California's
development is also reflected in the non-military activities of the soldiery in
these garrisons. As early as 1775 a soldier, Manuel Butrón, had requested
permission to be released from service in order to be allowed to farm a plot
of land adjacent to Mission San Carlos in Carmel. Although Butrón failed to
develop his land and later moved into San José, other retired soldiers, most
of whom were married to local women, received permission to raise cattle
on lands granted to them by the governor. These poor, mixed-blooded
soldiers did not represent, as some authors contend, a transitory presence
in California. Instead, they initiated a pattern of becoming settlers and *ran-
cheros* that later resulted in the formation of a class of Spanish *Californios*
during the Mexican period.[32]

More research on this group needs to be done before definite conclusions
can be reached, but this paper advances the tentative hypotheses that the
Alta California presidios were important Hispanic institutions and that rapid
social mobility occured within presidial society during the colonial period.
Both the California presidios and the presidials merit the fuller attention
judging from their actions and accomplishments during Alta California's
"Mission Period."

Notes

1. The mission period, 1769-1784, is completely described in John Francis Bannon, *The
Spanish Borderlands Frontier, 1513-1821* (New York 1970), pp. 143-166 cover the founding of
the province. Herbert L. Bolton's seminal article, "The Mission as a Frontier Institution in the
Spanish American Colonies," *American Historical Review*, 23: 1 (October, 1917), 42-61,
remains a key to its understanding.

2. The foremost study of Spanish civil municipalities in California is Florian F. Guest's unpublished doctoral dissertation, "Municipal Institutions in Spanish California, 1769-
1821," University of Southern California, 1961, which is partially summarized in the same
author's "Municipal Government in Spanish California," *California Historical Society Quarterly*, 46: 4 (1967), 301-336. The lawsuit referred to is described in the *Los Angeles Times* of
May 13, 1975, part A, pp. 1, 22.

3. Max L. Moorhead's *The Presidio: Bastion of the Spanish Borderlands* (Norman,
Oklahoma, 1975), is a model study for the institution in the Spanish Southwest but excludes
study of the California and Florida presidios because of the differences involved. My own article, "The First *Californios:* Presidial Society in Spanish California, 1769-1822," *Journal of the
West*, 11 (October, 1972), is an exploratory view of the soldiers who intimated this institution
in California. I have gotten little information from Kibbey M. Horne's, *A History of the Presidio*

of Monterey (Monterey, 1970), George H. Elliot's "The Presidio of San Francisco," *Overland Monthly Magazine,* (1870), or Russel A. Ruiz, "The Santa Barbara Presidio," *Noticias,* 13:1 (1967), 1-13.

The research of Florian Guest, OFM, as yet unpublished, promises to contribute greatly to this relatively unexplored field.

4. As Alberta Johnson Denis, *Spanish Alta California* (New York, 1927), p. 105, notes:
"We have heard much of the peaceful conquest of California by Spain. In fact, there are many, ignorant alike of the regular second phase of Spanish conquest, in which spiritual and military occupation advanced side by side — missions and presidios, the Cross with the Sword behind it, conquest under the flag of Spain, and of the many revolutions of the wheels of state, necessary before the order had been forthcoming "to occupy and fortify San Diego and Monterey," who have no mental vision more definite than of Fray Junípero Serra, staff in hand, alone, perhaps, or with a group of Franciscan friars in attendence, wandering into Alta California from somewhere, converting the Indians, who fall on their knees before them, eager to receive holy baptism, and who with the help of these deeply religious converts, build missions, and, adding to the abundance already on all sides in this new land "flowing with milk and honey," plant vines and fig trees, pomegranates and olives!

Far from being a peaceful progress of gentle friars up through a flower-decked land, surrounded by bands of adoring natives, on every journey they were accompanied by *soldados de cuera* to protect them from the Indians, who, although without firearms, had bows and arrows, and while not so warlike as the Apaches, Seris, and other tribes, were still savages and an ever present danger.

There was illness to be met and the ravages of disease; there was starvation, for they were far distant from a base of supply; and, although undeniably, possession was not secured through supreme sacrifice on the field of battle accompanied by the death song and shell, possession was neither easily gained nor held!"

5. Excellent record groups for the study of the Alta California presidios exist in the Archivo General de las Indias in Seville and the Archivo General de la Nación in Mexico City. The transcriptions of the Spanish Archives of California, made by Hubert Howe Bancroft and his associates, and a variety of other primary data are available in the Bancroft Library at the University of California at Berkeley. Mission and chancery archives are also valuable sources for the study of presidios.

6. The Yuma Massacre of 1781 closed the land route between Mexico and Alta California established earlier by Juan Bautista de Anza and hence, the colony after that date developed on the basis of the population that it had received by that time. For a discussion of soldiers as settlers, see my own "First *Californios,*" and Manuel P. Servín, "California's Hispanic Heritage: A View into the Spanish Myth," *Journal of the San Diego Historical Society,* 19: 1 (Winter, 1973), 7-8. It is simply not true, as alleged by Edwin A. Beilharz, *Felipe de Neve: First Governor of California* (San Francisco, 1971), p. 109, that "the King's officers and soldiers would disappear with their presidios in the turmoil of the colonial revolt against Spain" along with the missions, leaving the civil towns alone to survive and flourish in Mexican California.

7. Manuel P. Servín, ed., "Costansó's 1794 Report on Strengthening New California's Presidios," *California Historical Society Quarterly,* 49: 3 (September, 1970) p. 229. For a more complete survey of the reasons for the founding of Alta California, See María del Carmen Veláquez, *Establecimiento y pérdida del septentrión de Nueva España* (México, 1974) and Bannon, *Spanish Borderlands,* 143-189.

8. Servín, "Constansó," p. 222.

9. The conflict between Serra and the soldiers is fairly explained in Maynard Geiger, *The Life and Times of Fray Junípero Serra,* 2 vols., (Washington, D.C.) The Geiger book is not documented but scholars can easily check the author's sources by referring to the nominal indices of the California Mission Documents and the Serra Collection in the Santa Bárbara

Mission Archives. Also see Antoine Tibesar, ed., *The Writings of Junípero Serra,* 4 vols., (Washington, D.C., 1955-1966).

Donald A. Nuttall's "The Gobernantes of Spanish Upper California: A Profile," *California Historical Society Quarterly,* 51: 3 (Fall, 1972), 253-280, indicates that Serra's protagonists were invariably regular military officers having the rank of lieutenant colonel or higher, who had served an average of twenty-six years in the army prior to assuming command in California. On the whole, they were as qualified to govern the presidios as Serra was the missions, being courageous soldiers and relatively effective administrators.

10. Sherburne F. Cook, *The Conflict Between the California Indian and White Civilization,* 2 vols. (Berkeley and Los Angeles, 1943), I, tables on pp. 4, 12.

11. Biographical information on the commanders is provided in Nuttall, "Gobernantes," 265-271. An excellent study of the social origins and functions of the leather-jackets, so-named for the *cueras,* or cuirasses of deerskin which they wore as protection against Indian arrows, is Max L. Moorhead, *"The Soldado de Cuera:* Stalwart of the Spanish Borderlands," *Journal of the West,* 8: 1 (January, 1969), 38-55. The regulation governing the conquest of California is found in Archivo General de la Nación: Sección Provincias Internas, Legajo 166, 3 (hereafter AGN:PI 166, 3). Viceroy Bucareli to Felipe de Neve, Mexico, September 30, 1774, reprinted in Beilharz, *Felipe de Neve,* 142-152. This makes it clear that the California venture was quite different from the exclusively missionary enterprises carried out earlier in Paraguay and Baja California.

12. This information is drawn from my article, "The First *Californios,"* and Moorhead's *"Soldado de Cuera."* Other information on these men is given in Jack D. Forbes, "Black Pioneers: The Spanish-Speaking Afro-Americans of the Southwest," *Phylon,* 27:3 (Fall, 1966) and Servín, "California's Hispanic Heritage," 1-9. Also helpful is Beilarz' chapter, "The Army," in *Felipe de Neve,* 67-84.

13. The constant tensions between priests and presidials are described at length in the pages of Geiger, Cook, and Beilharz, among others.

14. See Cook, *Conflict,* I, 24-25, 105-106; Beilharz, *Felipe de Neve,* 27-31. A series of military crimes reaching trial covering the period 1773-1779 are located in AGN: Californias, Vol. 2, Part 1, folios 244-293.

15. Geiger's discussion of the 1771 rape and murder at San Gabriel concludes that in this instance conclusive proof of a crime by the defendants was lacking. *Life and Times,* I, 303-308.

16. Vancouver, cited in Beilharz, *Felipe de Neve,* p. 74.

17. Indian warfare in Alta California during the Spanish period is described in Beilharz, *Felipe de Neve,* 66-72, and Cook, *Conflict,* I, 60-63, 65-67, 115-119, 133; II, 32-33. George Harwood Phillips, *Chiefs and Challengers: Indian Resistance and Cooperation in Southern California* (Berkeley, Los Angeles, and London, 1975) explains the relative absence of violence in Spanish California in terms of the fact that it was usually an individual, rather than a collective, response to white intrusion. As Indian civilization regrouped after 1821 violence involving Indians escalated considerably.

18. AGN: Audiencia de México (hereafter AM), Legajo 1281, Felipe de Neve to Teodoro de Croix, Monterey, December 28, 1778.

19. Geiger, *Life and Times,* I, 253, 326-387; Nuttall, "Governantes," p. 260. Serra's writings during the dispute with Fages make it clear that he opposed Fages and his incompetent soldiers but was not anti-military in general. Actually, mission detachments reduced the number of soldiers available at any presidio considerably, as did the departure of those men as mail-carriers and explorers, death and desertion. The San Francisco Presidio provided mission guards at San Francisco and Santa Clara. Monterey furnished guards for Missions San Carlos, San Antonio, and San Luis Obispo. San Diego's presidials guarded the missions in San Diego, San Gabriel, and San Juan Capistrano. When the Santa Bárbara Presidio was founded in 1782 Mission San Gabriel and the channel mission were transferred from San Diego's jurisdiction.

20. Rivera's shortcomings as a soldier and an administrator are outlined in Nuttall, "Governantes," 259-260, and Geiger, *Life and Times*, I, 432-433; II, 36-40, 43-45.

21. The Echeveste Regulation and its impact are described in Beilharz, *Felipe de Neve*, 85-86 and Geiger, *Life and Times*, I, 68-75, 383-385.

22. The revolt against the San Diego Mission is explained in Geiger, *Life and Times*, II, 68-75. For an excellent study of Spanish activity in the Pacific Northwest, see Warren L. Cook, *Flood Tide of Empire: Spain and the Pacific Northwest, 1543-1819* (New Haven and London, 1973).

23. This regulation is translated and reprinted by Sidney B. Brinckerhoff and Odie B. Faulk, eds., *Lancers for the King: A Study of the Frontier Military System of Northern New Spain, with a Translation of the Royal Regulations of 1772* (Phoenix, 1965). For a description of the physical characteristics of a presidio, see Moorhead, *The Presidio*, passim, and Geiger, "A Description of California's Principal Presidio, Monterey, in 1773," *Southern California Quarterly*, 49: 3 (1967), 327-336.

24. The Neve Regulation is translated and republished in the *Annual Publication of the Historical Society of Southern California*, 15: 1 (1931), 156-188, and is fully discussed in Beilharz, *Felipe de Neve*, 34-43, 87-88.

25. Geiger, *Life and Times*, II, 52. Sherburne Cook, *Conflict*, I, 39-40, argues that military rations were adequate but he hardly paints the rosy economic picture for California depicted by Beilharz. Cook feels that the presidios were able to grow as much grain as the missions despite their location, but that this amount was considered insufficient to feed non-Indians.

26. Beilharz, *Felipe de Neve*, 96-109; Guest, "Municipal Institutions," 98-129.

27. Beilharz, *Felipe de Neve*, 74;75, 157; Geiger, *Life and Times*, II, 234.

28. Beilharz, *Felipe de Neve*, 110-120. For the footing of the four Alta California presidios in 1779, see Neve's *Reglamento*, second title.

29. Beilharz, *Felipe de Neve*, 118-120; Geiger, *Life and Times*, II, 152-170, 244-265.

30. Bancroft Library: Bolton Research Materials, Item 97 (hereafter BL: BRM 97) Pablo de Mugártegui to Junípero Serra, San Juan Capistrano, November 28, 1780.

31. Neve's instructions to Pedro Fages are reprinted in Beilharz, *Felipe de Neve*, 156-172. Presidial growth is discussed on 163-164.

32. Servín, "California's Hispanic Heritage," 6-8.

HISPANOAMÉRICA Y ESPAÑA
EN LA INDEPENDENCIA DE LOS ESTADOS UNIDOS

Javier Malagón

Decididamente España es el país que tiene peores relaciones públicas, en contraste con Francia que no sólo ha sabido organizarlas de manera excelente sino también hacer buen uso de ellas. No pretendo con esta afirmación expresar una crítica ni un elogio sinó señalar un hecho de fácil comparación, y la importancia y publicidad de la ayuda de un país y otro a la Independencia de los Estados Unidos de América, simplemente viene a corroborarlo.[1]

Los años en que se gesta, se fomenta, se realiza y culmina la Independencia de las Trece Colonias inglesas son un período de política de aproximación de España a Francia[2] que en el orden internacional se manifiesta en el "Pacto de Familia", o de alianza ofensiva y defensiva para contrarrestar el poderío inglés en Europa y América, que había sido firmado en París (13 de agosto de 1761) por el genovés marqués de Grimaldi en representación de Carlos III y el conde de Chorsul por Luis XV. Grimaldi fue, más tarde, en 1763, Ministro de Estado, cargo en el que continuó hasta 1776, es decir, hasta el nacimiento de los Estados Unidos de América, nombre que surgió del original de "Colonias Unidas de América", en vez del de "Columbia" que se le quiso dar a propuesta de Philip Frenan, en Boston en 1795, con el respaldo de Franklin y Jefferson, en homenaje al descubridor del Nuevo Mundo.[3]

La participación de España en la ayuda a la independencia de los Estados Unidos es ignorada o a lo sumo se la presenta como mínima y sin importancia, o bien como forzada por acontecimientos ajenos a la posición de los colonos y respondiendo sólo a los intereses de España, concretamente a la recuperación de Mahón y Gilbraltar ocupadas por la Gran Bretaña.

Woodrow Wilson dice que "España y Francia se aprovecharon de la revolución de los Colonias para atacar una vez más a Inglaterra y no por simpatía hacia América ni hacia el ideal de la libertad que representaba, contando con obtener beneficios de un desastre seguro".[4]

Efectivamente, Wilson tiene razón, pero su afirmación puede aplicarse no sólo al caso concreto de la Independencia de las antiguas colonias de Inglaterra, sinó en general a cualquier situación internacional semejante, por ejemplo, en nuestros días la participación de Estados Unidos en Vietnam o el apoyo dado a Yugoeslavia (país comunista) frente a Rusia.

Si Francia, que mantuvo guerras continuas en el siglo XVIII con Inglaterra apoyó a las Colonias no lo hizo por razones ideológicas, sinó por su posición antibritánica como consecuencia de la guerra de los siete años (1756-63) y de la Paz de París (1763) por la que, entre otras cosas, Francia perdía el Canadá, islas de Cabo Bretón y todas las islas y costas del río San Lorenzo y, sobre todo, la obligación de desarmar el puerto de Dunkerque y autorizar la instalación de un comisario británico. "La Providencia ha señalado esta época para la humillación de una potencia orgullosa y voraz..." escribía un Ministro francés al Gobierno español, justificando la necesidad de ayuda a las colonias rebeldes de América frente a Inglaterra. Ello además tendría las siguientes ventajas para Francia:

a) Limitaría el poderío de Inglaterra,

b) Disminuiría el comercio inglés y

c) Francia recuperaría algunas de sus colonias que habían pasado a poder de Inglaterra.

El apoyo de Francia era claramente oportunista: destruir el iniciado auge político-militar de la Corona inglesa.

La situación de España no era, en principio, distinta a la de Francia, pero con una excepción esencial: mientras Francia no sentía el menor interés por América, al extremo de que cuando hubo de ceder Canadá, se cuenta que uno de los Minitros de Luis XV dijo "que se había contentado a Inglaterra con unas cuantas leguas de tierra nevada..."5 y a España, a su vez, le entregó la Luisiana que era aproximadamente la cuarta parte del territorio actual de Estados Unidos con gran descontento de los colonos franceses que la habitaban. España, por el contrario, tenía lo que se ha llamado "vocación americana". La expansión de su imperio se concentraba principalmente en América, desde el Norte al extremo Sur. Era vecina inmediata de las Colonias que buscaban la Independencia, y esas mismas se habían engrandecido bajo la bandera inglesa con territorios que pertenecían a España.

Así, pues, a las razones puramente de rivalidad que España, como Francia, tenía contra Inglaterra se unía su presencia en América, y la mayoría de sus hombres de gobierno no favorecían el apoyo a las colonias:

1. Era un antecedente peligroso para la conservación de los reinos españoles en América, pues la Corona se vería obligada a conceder ciertas libertades a los Españoles americanos y quienes al no obtenerlas habrían de luchar por independizarse de la metrópoli.

2. La vecindad de las colonias inglesas convertidas en nación independiente iba a originar conflictos con la Corona española, ya que la nueva nación trataría de seguir una política expansionista a costa de los territorios españoles fronterizos, como efectivamente ocurrió apenas

firmado el Tratado de 1783.[6]

3. La creación de un Estado en el Nuevo Mundo suponía un cambio total en la política internacional, especialmente de España la cual en el futuro no estaría basada en la amistad o rivalidad de los reyes absolutos que regían Europa, sinó que debería tener en cuenta a la nueva nación, cuyo régimen político democrático representaba los intereses del pueblo y no los del jefe del Estado.

4. La creación de la nueva nación plantearía una serie de problemas religiosos, culturales, económicos, emigratorios, sociales, etc., que necesariamente debían repercutir en los territorios españoles en América.

5. A más de estas razones en el período de la guerra de Independencia de Estados Unidos hubo una serie de rebeliones en las provincias españolas de América (Paraguay, Bolivia, Colombia, Perú y Venezuela) que aunque no tuvieron conexión visible con los revolucionarios anglo-sajones, sí mostraron ya la existencia de un espíritu de autodeterminación.

Por añadidura, la guerra de Independencia de las Colonias no suponía para Europa simplemente una actitud separatista, sinó que llevaba implícita una revolución política, no diferente en cierto aspecto de la que se produciría pocos años más tarde en Francia o de las del siglo XX. Era un cambio total en los principios de gobierno y en la dirección política del Estado. Por un lado se trataba de un grupo de súbditos del monarca inglés que se levantaba contra él ignorando su autoridad, pero que al mismo tiempo creaba una forma de gobierno republicano.

Para las monarquías europeas de las grandes potencias, y entre ellas España, de tipo absolutista y en las que el jefe del Estado basaba su poder en el derecho divino, era difícil, sinó imposible, simpatizar y por lo tanto prestar ayuda a la independencia de las Colonias y más cuando una proporción importante de los dos millones de europeos que las poblaban no eran partidarios de la revolución independentista, muchos de los cuales emigraron al Canadá.

Sin embargo consiguieron esa ayuda de Francia y España, por toda una serie de motivos muy complejos, sin lo cual no hubieran logrado en aquel momento la Independencia;[7] y en lo que a España se refiere con la participacion de hombres, barcos y dinero de sus territorios de América.

El auxilio que recibió fue, lógicamente, de los territorios cercanos a las Colonias, empezando por los que hoy forman parte de los Estados Unidos, como la Luisiana, que abarcaba todo el valle del Mississippi y las llanuras del centro del país, Florida, más las islas del Caribe, las Antillas mayores de Cuba, Santo Domingo y Puerto Rico y la Nueva España. De todos ellos salieron fuerzas que, unidas a las especialmente enviadas de la Península, contribuyeron a una serie de operaciones militares, que facilitaron la victoria, no sin derrotas, de los ejércitos de Washington y sus colaboradores.

La participación de España y la América española en lo que a hombres se refiere ha de ir forzosamente encabezada por Bernardo Gálvez, Gobernador de Luisiana y más tarde Virrey de la Nueva España, Luís de Unzaga, Gobernador de Luisiana y posteriormente de Caracas; Francisco de Miranda, el Precursor por autonomasia de la Independencia de Hispanoamérica, que como comandante del regimiento de Aragón tomó parte en la conquista de Pensacola, el Coronel José Ezpeleta, el capitán Riano, el teniente Gobernador de St. Louis, Missouri, Fernando de Leyba, y el Almirante José Solano, jefe de la escuadra que desde España y de Cuba transportó las tropas que pusieron fin al dominio inglés en Florida y colaboró con sus barcos en la lucha, etc. Sin contar a personajes de la Corte como el Conde de Aranda, Floridablanca, Muzquis y el propio monarca Carlos III entre otros que con sus decisiones políticas contribuyeron a la ayuda que España dió a la consecución de la independencia por los Estados Unidos de América.

Individualmente, de manera análoga a la de Lafayette, intervinieron personajes como el menorquino Jorge Ferragut, y los agentes oficiosos en Filadelfia Juan de Miralles y Francisco Rendón y en cuanto a las fuerzas que lucharon en el Sur no hay que olvidar que si bien en la mayoría de los casos los oficiales de las tropas regulares eran peninsulares, gran número de soldados y los oficiales de milicia procedían de Santo Domingo, Cuba, Puerto Rico y Mexico, a partir de los contingentes de la propia Luisiana formados por criollos, negros y los indios que voluntariamente se unieron a ellos.

En todas las operaciones participaron también angloamericanos lo que confirma que éstos las consideraban no como de interés exclusivo de España sinó también como una manera de colaborar en la independencia de la nueva nación. La coordinación y colaboración de hispanos y angloamericanos fué mayor en casi todos los casos que la hispanofrancesa y en muchos que la angloamericana-francesa.

El Congreso y las autoridades de los nacientes Estados Unidos estuvieron conscientes de la ayuda de España realizándose operaciones militares por sugerencia de aquellos.

La participación de Gálvez, aunque sabida, no ha sido valorada ni reconocida por los Estados Unidos de América. Sus hazañas no se limitan a la conquista de una serie de fuertes como Fort Monchac, Fort Panmure, y de las plazas de Baton Rouge, Mobile y Pensacola, sinó que logra el control del Mississippi permitiendo la libre navegación de los barcos españoles y angloamericanos; desbarata los planes de los ingleses de conquistar la cuenca de ese rio para cercar los ejércitos de Washington por el Oeste; sabe atraerse a las tribus indias; ayuda eficazmente a George R. Clark, John Montgomery,

Olivier Pollock, el irlandés agente de los independentistas, y sobre todo, como ha dicho el historiador Thomson, dió la más importante "ayuda a las Colonias americanas en su lucha por la independencia...al ofrecer la seguridad de las fronteras del Sudeste y Oeste".[9]

Gálvez ere el típico militar ilustrado, muy semejante en este aspecto a Francisco Miranda, con un gran conocimiento de América a la que había llegado a los 19 años de edad acompañando a su tío José Gálvez visitador de la Nueva España y más tarde Ministro de Indias. Como capitán fue destinado a la frontera distinguiéndose en la campaña contra los apaches. Permaneció en México hasta 1776, tras haber estudiado en Francia por tres años, y participado en la campaña de Argel. Era hombre que reunía las condiciones para gobernar una provincia española recién recuperada de Francia y habitada en gran parte por ciudadanos franceses; su experiencia en la lucha con los apaches era de gran utilidad para conseguir la colaboración de los pueblos indios que vivían en el territorio de su gobernación; y a ello hay que añadir que no fue un militar de "escritorio" o de "valor se le supone" sinó que era hombre que había luchado en los campos de batalla del Nuevo Mundo y de África, siendo herido en Argel, y de esta experiencia de militar de acción y acostumbrado al mando, dió pruebas en sus campañas en Florida y Luisiana. No debemos olvidar que además fue un eficaz administrador y político de visión, cualidades que debió adquirir en sus puestos anteriores, sin duda alguna aconsejado por su tío José Gálvez, uno de los mejores colaboradores de Carlos III.[10]

Otro de los personajes hispánicos, olvidado por el relieve que alcanzó su hijo, ya nacido en Estados Unidos, David, primer almirante de la armada de este país,[11] fue Jorge Ferragut, natural de Cuidadela en la Isla de Menorca (1755). En 1772 pasó a Luisiana y como capitán de un pequeño barco comerciaba con La Habana y Veracruz. Iniciado el levantamiento de las Trece Colonias decide poner su fortuna y vida al servicio de la independencia, por su animadversión contra los ingleses a los que había tenido que sufrir durante la ocupación de su isla natal. Fue primero corsario y más tarde teniente de navío de una galera al servicio de Carolina de Sur y luchó contra el ejército británico en la defensa de Savannah. Hecho prisionero en Charleston fue canjeado más tarde. Transferido al ejército de tierra llegó a comandante de artillería tomando parte en las batallas de Cowpens y Wilmington. Se unió como capitán de caballería, y después como comandante, a las fuerzas de Carolina del Norte, siendo herido en unas de las batallas. Terminada la guerra volvió a la marina mercante. A él se le atribuye el dicho: "la paz ha dado a mi país de adopción libertad e independencia, pero a mi me ha dejado sin un centavo". Mas tarde en 1812 luchó nuevamente en el ejercito de Estados Unidos contra los ingleses.

El caraqueño Francisco de Miranda,[12] el Precursor de la independencia de Hispanoamérica, toma también parte en la lucha de España contra Inglaterra y, como comandante del regimiento Aragón, participa en la toma de Pensacola. Grafómano, lleva un diario meticuloso sobre todos los aspectos de la compaña desde la partida de las tropas de La Habana hasta la rendición de la plaza, ataques, bajas, desertores, armamento utilizado, incluso el número de cañonazos intercambiados entre los sitiadores y sitiados, fuerzas inglesas que guarnecían la plaza, etc.[13] Era un oficial español que incorporado al ejército en la Península, a la que llegó en 1771, toma parte en la defensa de Melilla y en 1780 regresa al Nuevo Mundo con las fuerzas enviadas por Carlos III al intervenir en la guerra de independencia de los Estados Unidos de América. Su conducta en la conquista de Pensacola debió ser ejemplar pues asciende a teniente coronel. Participa, a las órdenes de Cagigal con quien le unía una vieja amistad desde España, en la expedición contra las Bahamas. Miranda actúa también como negociador y diplomático y es él quien trata con un almirante francés, en aguas de Cuba, sobre las provisiones y auxilios que debían llevarse a los colonos rebeldes de la bahía de Chesapeake.

Más tarde en 1783 renuncia al ejército y viaja a Estados Unidos donde visita gran parte del nuevo país, interesándose en la vida política y, como militar, en los antiguos campos de batalla.

Una figura anónima, pero a la que no debemos olvidar, es la del negro esclavo Santiago, a quien el Gobernador Gálvez felicita el primero de julio de 1781 por su actuación en el sitio de Pensacola por "haber cumplido sus obligaciones con gran celo y puntualidad mostrando en la expedición, ataques y defensa, un decidido interés en el servicio al rey..." No tengo conocimiento de que exista información sobre la conducta de este esclavo que mereció, frente a tantos otros que participaron en la batalla por Pensacola, blancos, indios o negros, libres o esclavos, criollos o peninsulares, miembros del ejército o voluntarios, soldados u oficiales, esta citación especial del jefe del ejército y gobernador de Luisiana.[14]

Sabemos, como hemos señalado, cuales fueron las fuerzas que, procedentes de las provincias españolas del Caribe unidas a las peninsulares, participaron en la lucha que contribuyó a conseguir y consolidar la Independencia de los Estados Unidos de América, pero no conocemos su actuación o, si se quiere, es una tema no trabajado. Son ocho o diez los hombres más destacados sin contar las bajas por muerte en combate de oficiales y de soldados, como el teniente de milicias Pedro Baurelle, muerto en el sitio de Mobile, el coronel del regimiento del Rey, Luis Rebollo, muerto al frente de la columna que manda en Pensacola, el subteniente del regimiento de España Manuel de Córdoba en Mobile,[15] a los que se podría añadir una larga lista, ya que las bajas no fueron pocas teniendo en cuenta las fuerzas que intervinieron en la campaña.

Se ha destacado la participación de Francia y de individuos de diversas nacionalidades que jugaron un papel en la lucha contra Inglaterra y se ha ignorado la de la corona española-de sus provincias americanas y peninsulares-o por lo menos en los escritos sobre ella, no en los contemporáneos, se le ha restado importancia.

Los dirigentes de la Independencia de los Estados Unidos de América comprendieron la posición de Espana y agradecieron su ayuda. Así nos lo prueban una serie de hechos de menor o mayor importancia.

George Washington presidió el entierro con honores militares del primer representante oficioso de España Juan Miralles, fallecido en Morristown el 28 de abril de 1780.[16]

—Washington, esposa e hijos se alojaron durante el invierno de 1781 en la casa del agente español, Francisco Rendón, en Filadelfia;[17]

—Francisco Miranda recibió una serie de atenciones cuando acompañado por Rendón visitó a Washington a su paso por Filadelfia en diciembre de 1783, entregándole "una carta que traía de recomendación del General Cagigal ("Gobernador y Capitán General de Cuba") y continúa narrando Miranda "debíle en consecuencia bastante agasajo y tuve el gusto de comer en su compañía todo el tiempo que estuvo esta ocasión en Filadelfia..."[18]

—Se reconoce a España la ayuda que presta a las tropas del General Rochambeau, cuando a mediados de 1781 se dirigía al Sur con el fin de preparar el golpe final contra los ingleses, donde se encontró con los campos esquilmados y sin recursos económicos. Ante la necesad de fondos para proseguir la lucha y evitar que los colonos apoyaran a los ingleses trató por intermedio del almirante Grasse obtenerlos de Saint Domingue, cosa que no consiguió; y gracias a las autoridades españolas la ciudad de la Habana aportó un millón y medio de libras tornesas lo que permitió a Rochambeau la continuación de la campaña y la victoria en Yorktown el 17 de octubre de 1781, en la que de hecho se dió por terminada la guerra de Independencia;

—En el orden diplomático la actitud de la Corona española fue igualmente clara, y así lo reconoció el Congreso de la Unión, pues se desenvolvió en términos tales, "que haciendo honor a la alianza irregular pero cierta que le ligaba con los rebeldes se adelantaba a todas las peticiones de paz con que Inglaterra le brindaba, advertiendo que no trataría nada sin la previa declaración de independencia de las Colonias."[19]

España actuó consciente de las consecuencias que acarrearía su apoyo a los revolucionarios americanos y no obstante tomó una serie de medidas, por ejemplo:

—Prestar ayuda económica desde el primer momento, y en efecto ya en el ano 1776 (7 de junio) entregó un millon de libras tornesas, igual cantidad que la aportada por Francia. En diversos momentos adelantó otras sumas ya no por intermedio del Gobierno francés, sino por conducto del comerciante bilbaino Diego Gardoqui, aparte de otras procedentes de las cajas de América que en total se elevaron a unos 8.744.326 reales de vellón con 16 maravedís.[20]

A ello habría que añadir el valor del costo de las operaciones militares realizadas como consecuencia de la propia guerra, para las que se desplazaron fuerzas regulares de la Península, ya que España no tuvo nunca un ejército de ocupación en sus provincias americanas y por lo tanto el estado militar en éstas era débil en cuanto a efectivos y material.

—El 20 de enero de 1780 José Gálvez ordenó, desde El Pardo, que la Casa de la Moneda de México acuñara monedas de plata para entregarlas a los indios sometidos por el Gobernador de Luisiana, como premio a su fidelidad.

—El Gobierno Español permitió embarcar a Lafayette y a oficiales franceses en Pasajes, en la nave *Victoria*, quienes casi furtivamente se dirigieron a las Colonias bajo la mirada airada de Luix XVI. Después de regresar a Francia Lafayette volvió al Nuevo Mundo con el beneplácito y simpatías de su monarca en marzo de 1780, quien le dió instrucciones precisas, copia de las cuales se facilitó a Floridablanca.[21]

—España tuvo, desde 1777 (diciembre), un agente oficioso o comisionado en Filadelfia, D. Juan Miralles Tryllon, vecino de La Habana. Por su parte los Estados Unidos, enviaron un comisionado a España quien fijó su residencia en la corte en 1779.

—Los gobernadores de Luisiana, Luis de Ungaza y Ameraga y su sucesor Bernardo de Gálvez, desde 1776 suministraron alimentos, vestuario, armas, medicinas y, sobre todo, protección militar.

—El hecho de que las autoridades de la frontera tanto del Oeste como del Sureste simpatizaran con la causa de las Colonias, les permitió a éstas concentrar sus esfuerzos militares en los lugares y frentes convenientes sin temor a sorpresas.

—Gracias a la libertad de corso concedida a los mercantes de Hispanoamérica, las Colonias pudieron comerciar con las provincias españolas en América.

No cabe la menor duda de que la ayuda de España y sus provincias americanas fue de importancia primordial en la creación de la nueva y primera nación en el Nuevo Mundo y lo prueba el interés y empeño que pusieron los revolucionarios en conseguir ese apoyo; tal vez en cierto aspecto de mayor valor que el de Francia.

Había para ello varias razones, aunque algunas parezcan contradictorias. Ante todo, España figuraba todavía en el mundo como una primera potencia y con un gran poderío naval, tal vez el único que en cierto sentido podía enfrentarse con la armada inglesa. En segundo lugar, la presencia de España en América con sus provincias fronterizas de las Colonias permitió, lógicamente, como se probó, un auxilio más fácil en hombres y pertrechos (por ejemplo, los primeros aportes de pólvora a las fuerzas de Washington procedían de las fábricas de México). En tercer lugar, era conveniente por encima de todo tener no sólo una frontera amiga sinó aliada. Inglaterra lo entendió así y trató de que España se uniera a ella frente a las Colonias separatistas.

La participación de España en la guerra no fue con fuerzas en el campo de batalla de las trece Colonias, como en cierto momento lo hizo Francia, sinó en la periferia, en territorios en conflicto entre Inglaterra y España, lo que contribuyó a que aquella tuviera que desplegar parte de su ejército de tierra y mar en dichos lugares, en vez de reforzar a los que combatían contra los rebeldes.[22]

Francia que favoreció, como consecuencia del Pacto de Familia, la participación de España en la guerra, mostró cierto recelo por el papel que jugaba ésta en el conflicto armado, y según nos cuenta Francisco de Miranda, (Filadelfia, enero de 1784):

"el Ministro de Francia (Chevalier de la Luzerne) y sobre todo el baladuque Marbois (Consul General)...se alarmaron de tal modo viendo de que sus tramas y enredos políticos no me eran ocultos y que asimismo los falsos dogmas que tenían imbuídos en la generalidad de las gentes relativamente... (al) *vergonzoso proceder de la España en todas las operaciones de la última guerra* (esta y su doctrina favorita y la máxima que con mayor ardor procuran inculcar en el espíritu de los americanos...)"[23]

Este Cónsul General y Ministro actuarían por cuenta propia, pero no cabe la menor duda de que responderían, si se quiere con exceso, a la posición de la Corte de París. Miranda por su parte se sentía insultado y dolido como persona que había actuado en las fuerzas que se menospreciaban y como súbdito español.

Otras causas contribuyeron a desconocer y ocultar esa participación de las provincias peninsulares y americanas en la guerra de independencia de los Estados Unidos de América como son la rivalidad que el nuevo país, desde su creación y a través de todo el siglo XIX, tuvo con la propia España y con los pueblos que al constituirse en naciones la heredaron, como México, Cuba y Santo Domingo, en la política expansionista de la gran nación del Norte.

Los Estados Unidos han sido herederos en el Nuevo Mundo de la enemistad de Inglaterra con España que se ha mantenido frente a las naciones de origen hispánico, en todos los campos de la cultura, religion y política[25]. Por eso estaban espiritualmente mal dispuestos a reconocer la ayuda, que si en un momento la necesitaron y buscaron, más tarde la quisieron olvidar.

Ha llegado, pues, el momento en que de la misma manera que Hispanoamérica reconoce el papel que el primer pueblo en el Nuevo Mundo constituído en nación jugó en su independencia e influyó en la constitución y organización de las nuevas nacionalidades, se reconozca y estudie sin prejuicio alguno la realidad de la partipación de Hispanoamérica y de la Corona española en la lucha de las Colonias Inglesas por independizarse y crear la gran nación que es hoy Estados Unidos de América.[26]

Notas

1. Los escritos sobre la participación de España en la Independencia de Estados Unidos son muy pocos y la mayoría de principios del siglo actual: Manuel CONROTTE, *La intervención de España en la Independencia de los Estados Unidos,* Madrid, 1920 y Juan F. YELA UTRILLA, *España ante la Independencia de los Estados Unidos* (2 tomos), Lérida 1925. De fechas más recientes son las de Francisco MORALES PADRON, *Participación de España en la Independencia de Estados Unidos,* Madrid 1952 (Es un folleto de divulgación). Manuel FRAGA IRIBARNE, *Spain's contribution to the birth development and independence of the United States* (a lecture by...) Washington, D.C., 1961; y Octavio GIL MUNILLA *Participación de España en la génesis histórica de los Estados Unidos,* Madrid, 1952; (Es un folleto de 46 páginas sin aportar nueva información). Hay toda una serie de obras como la de Emilio CARRIGUES, *Los Españoles en la Otra América,* Madrid, 1965; Carlos M FERNANDEZ-SHAW. *Presencia española en los Estados Unidos.* Madrid, 1972; y Darío FERNANDEZ FLORES, *The Spanish Heritage in the United States.* Madrid, 1965, que dedica una parte de ella al papel jugado por España e Hispanoamérica en la Independencia de Estados Unidos. Falta en realidad un estudio completo y debidamente documentado sobre el tema.

EL CIECC en su VI Reunión (México, enero de 1975) acordó que la OEA convocara un concurso sobre el tema "Participación de Latino América en la Independencia de EUA". Es de esperar que el trabajo que resulte premiado sea una aportación definitiva sobre este aspecto de la historia común de Estados Unidos de América e Hispanoamérica.

2. De la bibliografía relitiva a Francia cabe señalar; H. DONIOL *Histoire de la participation de la France à l'établissement des Etats Unis* (cinco tomos) París, 1884-1889. Francis RENANT *Le Pacte de Famille et l'Amérique.* La Politique colonial Franco-Espagnole de 1760 a 1792. Paris, 1922; E. CORNWILL, *French policy and the American Alliance of 1778.* Princeton, N.J., 1916.

3. FERNANDEZ-SHAW, *op. cit.* p. 77-78

4. CAROTTE, *op. cit.* p. 215-216

5. *Id. id. p. 18*

6. El Conde de Aranda, Embajador en París, partidario de la ayuda a los independentistas americanos en su comunicación a la corte de Carlos III decía en 1782: "El primer paso de esta potencia (E.U.) será apoderarse de las Floridas a fin de dominar el Golfo de México. Después de molestarnos así y nuestras relaciones con la Nueva España aspirará a la conquista de este vasto imperio..." Fué profético.

7. MORALES PADRON, *op. cit.* p. 6-9

8. Los historiadores americanos han trabajado la presencia de España en esta región de los hoy E.U. En abril de 1970 se celebró una mesa redonda, patrocinada por la Southern Illinois University, sobre "The Spanish in the Mississippi Valley" en la que se presentaron 16 trabajos más tarde recogidos en un volumen con el titulo *"The Spanish in the Mississippi Valley 1762-1804* (Urbana, University of Illinois Press, 1974) editado por John Francis McDERMONT. De ellos conviene destacar como información sobre los estudios realizados y fuentes archivísticas

para futuras investigaciones: Charles E. O'NEILL, S.J., "The State of Studies on Spanish Colonial Luisiana"; A.O. HEBERT, Jr. "Resources in Louisiana for the Study of Spanish Activities in Louisiana"; y C.H. GARDINER "The Mexican Archives and the Historiography of the Mississippi Valley in the Spanish Period"

9. BUCHANAN P. THOMSON. *La ayuda española en la guerra de la Independencia de Norteamérica*. Madrid, 1967, p. 193.

10. Sobre Gálvez véase John W. CAUGNEY *Bernardo de Gálvez in Louisiana*. Berkeley, California, 1934, y Buchanan P. THOMSON *Falcon over the River* (hay traducción española con el título de *La Ayuda española en la guerra de Independencia Norteamericana*. Madrid, 1967).

11. David G. FARRAGUT nació en Stony Point, Tennessee en 1801. Muy joven ingresó en la marina llegando al rango de almirante, que fué creado para premiar sus servicios. Charles L. LEWIS *David G. FARRAGUT admiral in the making*. Annapolis, 1941,. Manuel CENCILIO DE PINEDA, *David G. Farragut*, Madrid 1950.

12. La bibliografía sobre Francisco de Miranda es muy numerosa pero de los últimos estudios debe verse Mariano PICON SALAS, *Miranda*. Buenos Aires, 1946 (hay reimpresión en Caracas. 1966).

13. "Diario de Penzacola...de lo más particular ocurrido desde el dia de nuestra salida de La Habana" y "Diario de lo ocurrido en la escuadra y tropas, que al mando del Jefe de Escuadra don Josef Solano, y del Mariscal de Campo, Don Juan Manuel Cagigal, salieron de La Havana de 9 el abril de 1781, para socorrer al ejército español, que atacaba la plaza de Penzacola...sitio de dicha plaza...su rendición, etc." *Archivo Miranda, Vol. I.* Caracas, 1929, p. 141-178.

14. *Annual Report of the American Historical Association for the year 1945*. Vol. II "Spain in the Mississippi Valley, 1765-1794 & The Revolutionary Period 1765-1781" edit. by Lawrence Kinnaird, Washington, D.C. 1949, p. 428-429.

15. CONROTTE, *op. cit.* p. 90

16. CONROTTE, *op. cit.* p. 125-126

17 YELA UTRILLA, op. cit. p. 395-396.

18. *Archivo Miranda*, Vol. I. p. 232. Igual presentación, del Gobernador y Capitán General de Cuba llevaba para el Gobernador de South Carolina, Benjamin Guerard, "y en consecuencia-narra Miranda-me ha colmado de honras y agasajos durante todo el tiempo de mi residencia en esta Capital" (Charlestown, junio-octubre 1783) y continúa "los principales sujetos del país y oficiales del ejército del Sur (a quienes fui introducido por el Gobernador en un gran convite que me dió cuatro días después de mi arribo) que a la sazón se hallaban aquí estuvieron a visitarme..." *Op. cit.* Vol. I p. 205-6.

19. CONROTTE, *op. cit.* p. 218. Inglaterra llegó a proponer a España la entrega de Gibraltar "...si se obtiene que no se ligue con las Colonias..."

20. CONROTTE, *op. cit.* p. 213

21. CONROTTE, *op. cit.* p. 92.

22. GARRIGUES, *op. cit.* p. 157-158.

23. *Archivo Miranda*, Vol. I., p. 238-239.

24. Miranda en su "Diario" (noviembre de 1783) presenta a Marbois como al hombre que dirigía los intereses franceses en Filadelfia y no lo describió diciendo: "sus talentos ni su habilidad creo que son remarcables en ninguna especie y mucho menos en política; bien que su presunción y osadía e ignorancia le persuade todo lo contrario...cuando la paz última se rumoreaba escribió una carta al Ministro de Francia persuadiéndole sería muy conveniente *el que la pesca de Terranova no se acordara a los americanos y que la guerra continuase algún tiempo más, para que bien azotados estos se recordasen mejor del beneficio que debían a Francia*...la carta fue interceptada y leída públicamente en el Congreso (bien que bajo el juramento de que ninguno de los miembros mencionase fuera el asunto por dos años).... La intriga es su pasión dominante y el conducto por el que pretende manejar todas sus transacciones políticias y

privadas; empleando a veces bajísimas medidas para el logro de sus fines...''. *Archivo Miranda*, Vol. I, p. 226.

25. Ver Philip W. POWELL. *Tree of Hate. Propaganda and Prejudice Affecting U.S. Relations with Spanish World.* New York, 1971.

26. El tema de la independencia de Estados Unidos e Hispanoamérica, ha empezado a interesar a los americanos. Un pionero en este campo es el Embajador de Estados Unidos en México, John Jova, quien a más de dar una conferencia en México sobre el tema, ha pedido a su gobierno alguna forma de reconocimiento de la participación del mundo hispánico en la creación e independencia de Estados Unidos. A ello hay que anadir la labor de ''proselitismo'' que está haciendo entre los historiadores de EU y de México, para que trabajen sobre este aspecto poco estudiado de los orígenes de la nación Norteamericana.

SPANISH LEGACY IN AMERICAN LAW

A. D. Azios

The United States of America is one of the largest nations in land area in the world. In its infancy and during its growing pains era, the young, expanding republic had to attract and invite people from all over the world to colonize it and to protect it from foreign invaders and also from, ironically, original settlers, namely, the American Indians.

While North America is inhabited by peoples from every nation in the world, only three legal systems have contributed to its present laws, namely, English common law, Spanish law and French law.

Spanish law contributions to the United States have been mostly in three fields: water law, Homestead, and Community property. In Texas, Spanish land measurements are still used:[1]

Vara	= 33 1/3 inches
Square Vara	= 7.7 square feet, 0.86 square yards or 0.00018 acres
Caballeria	= 108 acres
Labor	= 1,000,000 square varas or 177.1 acres
League	= 5,000 varas
Square league	= 25,000,000 square varas, 25 labores or 4,428.4 acres
Sitio	= Square league
Sitio de ganado mayor	= Square league
Sitio de ganado menor	= 11,111,111 square varas or 1,968.18 acres

The Moors, Visigoths, Romans and Egyptians never set foot in the United States, but they sent their ancient waters laws to the western and southwest part of the United States via the Spanish Conquistadores.

In the United States, there are three principal systems of water law: riparian, prior appropriation and administrative.

Under the riparian system, the owner of the bank of the stream (*ripa* in Latin) is entitled to the use of the waters of the stream as an appurtenance to his land.

The system of prior appropriation holds that the person who first puts the water to a beneficial use, whether he owns the land along the stream or wherever he may use the water acquires a right to the continued use of the water. "First in time is first in right."

The administrative system provides for the issuing of permits for the use of water by some state agency.[2]

In Europe, national boundaries historically have changed according to the fortunes of war or the might of the conqueror, but in the United States, we are still trying to decide water rights in our courts, not in the battlefield, although, as history reflects, the early settlers in the west did shed blood for access to water.

In the preface to The Spanish Element in Texas Water Law, Betty Eakle Dobkins states the following:

The question of the Spanish elements in Texas water law is now being considered in the courts of the state. The outcome is a matter of moment to many landholders whose livelihood is dependent upon securing water for irrigation, and to many communities, especially in the Rio Grande Valley, concerned about water supply. The reason for this concern is that the titles to some 26,280,000 acres of Texas' 170,000,000 acres originated in grants made by the Crown of Spain or the Republic of Mexico. The water rights which go with these lands are, under our state laws, determined by the terms of the original grants. For these 26,280,000 acres, the prevailing law, even in 1958, is the Hispanic-American Civil law. The question of determining just what water rights were granted by the Crown of Spain in disposing of lands in Texas is more than a matter of historical interest; it is a subject of great practical importance in Texas today.

The Spanish law background enters directly in the case of these lands, but its influence is by no means confined to them. The water laws and institutions of Texas trace their roots not to the English common law, nor to the Western doctrine of prior appropriation, both of which were in time incorporated in Texas law, but primarily to the Spanish law. It is possible that a clearer recognition of this background might have saved the state much of its present confusion and chaos in water law.[3]

"Most of the Spaniards who settled in Mexico and in the present southwestern part of the United States came from the arid part of Spain. This part of Spain is an extremely dry country which is able to support its population only when the utmost care is exercised in the conservation and use of the scanty rainfall."[4]

One may wonder how the Spaniards were so successful in the dry part of the New World to implement life-saving, ingenious irrigation projects, some of which are still in existence. The answer lies, partly, in the preceding paragraph and because irrigation has been a way of life in arid Spain'for centuries. Betty E. Dobkins states in her The Spanish Element in Texas Water Law, page 65:

Irrigation has a long history in Spain. The Roman invaders built several irrigation works in Spain, some of which are still in existence.

When the Moors invaded Spain from the dry part of Africa, they brought an extensive knowledge of irrigation. They built new and elaborate works.

As the Moors constructed the irrigation works, they also developed laws and customs for their administration. Moslem law, closely related to religion, took its central concepts from the Koran. Since law was regarded as derived from the will of God, obedience to it was a religious as well as a social duty. True followers of Mohammed constituted a community, among whose members mutual help in time of need was a legal duty. This concept of community and mutual help is reflected in Moslem water law.

According to Moslem tradition, to deny surplus water to one in need was to risk eternal punishment. "No one can refuse surplus water without sinning against Allah and against man." Moslem water law was based on the concept of beneficial use but not abuse.

It is interesting to note that many Spanish irrigation words are of Arabic sources, i.e., "acequia" meaning "canal"; "noria" meaning "chain pump" and "acena" meaning "water well" are some of the words.

Another addition to Spanish water law in the new world was a system of irrigation the native Indians of central Mexico had when the Spaniards arrived.

The native Indians of central Mexico had developed a system of irrigation by terracing and irrigating their lands on which they produced corn, beans, potatoes, squash, cotton and other crops. Their system was so well developed that a Spanish law of 1536 provided that the Indians' method of dividing and apportioning water for irrigation should be retained.[5]

As the Spaniards discovered more and more land, they realized that they were discovering a lot of ground but very little water. So in order to conquer the new world for their queen, they had to capture and distribute water to as many people as possible.

Being the products of a people experienced in the needs of an arid and semiarid land and of a society that stressed the place of the Crown, the community and the Church, they passed laws consistent with that background. Both influences — the emphasis on the group and the necessities of an arid environment — shaped Spanish American water institutions. The Spanish-American system was in some ways more rigid than the individualistic method of acquiring land and water which prevailed in Anglo-America.

The Spanish developed the public acequias system. Modern New Mexico has an acequia system.

F.C. Barker, who had lived in Spain several years and later settled in the Mesilla Valley of New Mexico, comments on the striking similarities between the irrigation practices of the Mexicans in this valley and those he had observed in what used to be Moorish Spain.[6]

Original Spanish grants always stated what water rights went with the land; so those rights still attach to the land. In dry West Texas and Southwest Texas, these water rights are the life-blood of the land and the people affected by them.

For all lands granted in Texas before January 20, 1840, the Spanish Civil law determined what rights went with the land. However, said civil laws were modified by the Anglo-Americans to suit their circumstances. After Mexico obtained its independence from Spain, the water rights remained the same, as Mexican law was based on Spanish law.

Notwithstanding the change in sovereignty from Spanish to Mexican, then Mexican to Republic of Texas, then to State of Texas, all land grants granted by those governments were binding, and the right in effect at the time the rights were issued were controlling; so when Texas adopted the English Common Law, Water Rights were in the main left undisturbed. There have been many statutory changes in Texas; in 1917, Texas adopted a new Water Code. Many efforts have been made to recodify Texas laws relating to surface waters, but they have been unsuccessful.[7]

The revolution against Mexican rule meant that the influence of the Spanish law in Texas steadily waned, while the English common law became ascendant.

In the early years of the Republic of Texas, the lawyers and judges were willing to experiment, to borrow from both the Spanish Civil law and the English common law. Of this, Dean McCormick has written:

"The mingling of the common law which the settlers had brought with them and the civil law which they were required to accept in the colonial period, and the need for making a practical compromise between the two when independence came promoted the feeling that there was nothing sacred and unchangeable in either system. They borrowed many things from both."[8]

This borrowing from both systems has led to a myriad of litigations and to confusion. The changes in the system have been many, the court rulings too voluminous and contradictory to attempt to recite them in this paper. The courts of New Mexico and Arizona have generally reached different conclusions from those of Texas. Whatever the differences, the strong undercurrent of our water laws in the southwestern part of the United States remains Spanish water laws.

The Spanish system had among its chief characteristics:
(1) It was to a great extent a system of communal waters.
(2) It was an administered system rather than one centered around vested rights. Once a right was established, however, it was generally protected so long as the water was put to beneficial use.
(3) It was actively concerned with the administration of waters and the development of water resources. It did not take water use for granted, nor did it allow water policy to develop simply as a by-product of land law.[9]

Now that Texas is growing tremendously and is becoming an industrial state with unquenchable need for water, Texas is looking for means of bringing water from the Mississippi River. This involves interstate law. Many wells have been dug in the Gulf Coast area, partially around Baytown. Due to constant and enormous draining of underground water, there is a chaotic subsidence causing houses, factories, buildings, highways and farmland to become flooded with the slightest high tide or rain. Subsidence Districts have been created by state law to control the draining of underground water, but the subsidence continues. The writer wonders whether this draining should be legislated as "water law" or "land law", for if it is "water law", the Spanish water law will surely enter into the picture. If it is "land law", the English common law admittedly would be more instrumental.

Community Property

While the water laws of Spain have been changed in Texas and in some of the other southwestern states, the law of Community Property which we inherited from Spain is still with us as a great legacy.

The community property system is an institution peculiar to civil law. Its exact origin has never been conclusively determined. There is evidence of earlier community property systems in ancient Egypt, Greece and Babylonia.

The predominant universal cause of a community property was the natural desire to provide for the wife's support and to curb the husband's despotic power. The marital community is an association consisting of husband and wife, and community property is the property belonging to this association. By investing the wife with an interest in such property the law affords her security. The earliest community property systems could be explained as the efforts of different cultures to achieve the same goal, the protection of the weaker spouse.[10]

Although most of the Louisiana Civil Code is derived from the Code Napoleon, the basic structure of our community property system is derived from the Spanish law. Spanish law viewed marriage as a partnership in which the spouses devoted their talents, energies and resources to the common good. Thus it followed that all acquisitions and gains attributable to such expenditure of labor and resources should be shared by the partnership. This basic concept was the premise underlaying classification of property in the Spanish community. Mode and time of acquisition were important factors in application of the basic principle. Thus, the property acquired before marriage remained the separate property of the owner. Fruits produced from property, even separate property, inured to the partnership because the labor of the spouses was employed in its production. However, if property was acquired during marriage by gratuitous title (donation or inheritance), it was not considered the result of the labor of either spouse; hence it belonged to the spouse acquiring it.

The Louisiana Civil Code of 1825 reproduced the three basic features of the Spanish community of acquests and gains. First, all the property owned by either spouse prior to the marriage remained the separate property of the spouse. Second, acquests after the marriage were classified as separate or community according to the time and mode of acquisition regardless of which spouse acquired the property. This followed the Spanish law. Third, the fruits of all property, community and separate, inured to the community.[11]

The community property laws of Texas, Louisiana, California, New Mexico, Arizona and other southwestern states are very similar. Their central purpose and effect are the same, namely, to protect the wife's interest and to define what interest each spouse has in the property acquired during their marriage.

Homestead And Other Exemptions

Another Spanish law which we inherited is the Homestead and Exemption of Other Property from the forced application to the payment of debts.

The exemption of certain property from the payment of certain debts is in furtherance of a humane and generous public policy. Such laws are as much for the general benefit of society as they are for the individuals or classes protected. The reserving to the improvident or unfortunate debtor, as against the demands of his creditors, of certain articles of property, is intended for the purpose of enabling him by the use thereof to earn a livelihood and to maintain himself and those dependent upon him, to the end dependents may become useful members of society instead of charges or burdens thereon.

The exemption of property from the forced application to the payment of debts was unknown to the Common law. Under the Spanish Law in force in Texas, prior to its independence from Mexico and for a short time thereafter, certain property was exempted from forced sale for the payment of debts. Among the things thus exempted were beasts of burden, implements of husbandry, bread of bakers, tools of artificers, books of advocates and students, wearing apparel and of other things in daily use. In the days of the Republic of Texas, it became the policy of the Government to establish liberal exemption laws; and this policy has been extended and enlarged by constitutional provisions and legislative enactments, and by judicial interpretations. Texas is in the forefront of all of the states of the Union.

The Constitution of the Republic contains no provisions with reference to exemptions. The first constitution of Texas has this provision:

"The Legislature shall have power to protect by law from forced sale, a certain portion of the property of all heads of families. The homestead of a family not to exceed two hundred acres of land, (not included in a town or city,) or any town or city lot or lots, in value not to exceed two thousand dollars, shall not be subject to forced sale, for any debts hereafter contracted, nor shall the owner, if a married man, be at liberty to alienate the same, unless by the consent of the wife, in such manner as the Legislature may hereafter point out."

The Constitution of 1861 followed that of 1845 and carried forward the same provisions in the same language.[11]

So as we celebrate our Bicentennial, those of Hispanic origin should celebrate with pride, for Spanish law will forever be part of the United States of America, because America loves justice, and Spanish laws handed down to us are very just.

References

1. *The Spanish Element in Texas Water Law*, Betty Eakle Dobkins (University of Texas, Austin, 1959) Preface.

2. Dobkins, *op. cit.*, p. 16.

3. Dobkins, *op. cit.*, Preface.

4. Dobkins, *op. cit.*, p. 65.

5. Dobkins, *op. cit.*, p. 92.

6. Dobkins, *op. cit.*, pp. 99; 70.

7. *Ibid*, p. 27.

8. *Ibid*, p. 133.

9. *Ibid*, p. 156.

10. Howard W. L'Enfant, Jr., Origin & Historical Development of The Community Property System. Louisiana Law Review, XXV (1964) pp. 78, 79.

11. *Ibid*, pp. 96, 97.

MEXICAN INFLUENCE ON U.S. ART
1930-1936

Jacinto Quirarte

Historians of art are accustomed to thinking in terms of influences, their origins, extent, and nature when studying works of art. Works of art are thus considered to have predecessor as well as successor status. Each, while building on its past, is in the process of becoming part of a tradition. Each in turn is known by its own characteristics or style.

In charting the development and duration of a particular style of art, the art historian tries to retrace on a selective basis the presumed steps taken by artists during specific periods of time. Usually only a few generations of artists are considered. Sometimes the search is expanded to encompass centuries and even several millennia. Ultimately, the number of artists and works included in books of general as well as specialized scope are determined by the temporal and spatial confines established by the historian.

The art historian then is concerned with pulling together the various strands which can be designated as having been used as sources and inspiration by artists. Such concerns manifested in studies of ancient and modern art are familiar to everyone. The Egyptian influence on early Greek art is well known as is the influence of later Greek art on Roman art. The reemergence of an interest in Greek and Roman art by Italian artists of the fifteenth and sixteenth centuries is also well known. There are numerous other examples of this process throughout the history of art. The point is that part of any effort to understand fully a body of work must take into account the study of sources and influences.

I intend to discuss such a topic in an area that has received little attention from historians of art — the influence of Mexican art on American art of the 1930's. Although a Mexican influence on American art is generally conceded, the extent and nature of this influence has not been fully assessed. I will discuss one portion of the process in this paper — the manner in which these influences took place. The other questions require far greater exposition than is possible in this essay.

Specifically, I will discuss the actual contacts American artists had with the Mexican muralists — José Clemente Orozco, Diego Rivera, and David Alfaro Siqueiros — and their works during the early thirties *and their reactions to both.* This will help us again a little better understanding of American art of this period.

There is a number of ways in which influences normally take place: 1) the primary vehicle is, of course, the work of art itself with 2) the presence of the artist and his pronouncements performing an equally important role. The process involves interaction between artists and exposure to works of art. Specifically, artists can travel to see and study works of art in foreign countries, or they can study them secondhand through copies or reproductions. Roman copies of Greek sculptures served this purpose as did woodcuts of major European works which were distributed throughout Europe and the Americas during the sixteenth and seventeenth centuries. More recently, this type of indirect influence has been and continues to be achieved by the widespread use of black and white and color reproductions in art magazines and books.

The influence exerted by the Mexican muralists on American artists during the early and mid-thirties followed the familiar pattern described above. First of all, American artists were keenly aware of the developments in mural painting in Mexico during the late twenties through the publication of books and articles on this material.[1] *Their* awareness and subsequent contact with the artists and their work in the U.S. were to greatly alter the work of American artists during this period. Interestingly enough, there was never a steady stream of American artists going to Mexico during this period to study the murals being done there.[2] Instead, the Mexican muralists traveled to various parts of the U.S. during the early years of the thirties to paint murals, thus altering slightly the traditional way in which influences were affected.

Actual influences will be discussed in the following manner: I) The influence of an artist or artists whose works, presence, and pronouncements constitute and represent a recognizable movement which affects other artists outside the generating center. The latter will usually create similar works. II) The influence of *one or more* artists' work on that of younger artists who are affected momentarily or later develop individual styles after a formative period in which one or more influences are felt.

I

Mexican influences were very directly felt along a broad front during the thirties but later submerged by subsequent developments in American art postdating World War II. In spite of the fact that the Mexican influence did not have an apparent lasting impact, the influence was very real during the depression years in various parts of the U.S.[3]

The impact on American artists was felt at different levels. The most immediate revolved around the use of the fresco technique which attracted many of the American artists even though many were to eventually paint murals with modern materials and non-fresco techniques. The thematic content of these works was also of great interest to American artists. These dealt with general themes such as history, technology, industry, manufacture, agriculture and transportation. It was not unusual to see works in which vast panoramic views of process and events such as mining and manufacture and the history of a people were depicted respectively. Reference could be made to a specific industry and place such as auto manufacturing in Detroit by Diego Rivera[4], or to the history of man in The Americas by José Clemente Orozco. Other murals dealt with historical figures or man in general.

Even the ideological underpinnings of the selected themes found a receptive audience among American artists. The Mexican muralists' views on economic, social, and political matters were accepted as appropriate approaches to the creation of works of art by American artists for they shared the same concerns. The economic conditions in the U.S. made such views seem timely and appropriate. Specifically, the artistic import of an object was based as much on its assigned function and purpose as it did on its aesthetic content. The mural, available to all the people, was considered the ideal vehicle for these matters and served the needs of the community.

By the time the Mexican muralists arrived in this country, they had developed what were to become the standard arrangements of single and massed figures used to tell a story. Differences in size and placement of figures became recognizable characteristics of their work.

Thus, the formal, thematic and ideological aspects of the Mexican muralists' works were of great interest to American artists during the thirties. Their full impact, however, has yet to be assessed fully by historians of art. The numerous murals and other works painted under the various federal art projects will have to be studied and analyzed before American art of the last thirty years can be more fully understood.

Artists, Murals, and Pronouncements:

The interest in the Mexican muralists developed as a result of a number of economic and political factors as well as a desire on the part of most Americans to free themselves of European entanglements and influences. The Great Depression and most Americans' desire to search for an American identity by looking inward led to the enthusiastic embrace extended to the Mexican muralists at that time.

Requests to have Mexican artists carry out commissions in the U.S. had been made as early as 1926. In that year, William Gerstle, President of the

San Francisco Arts Commission, invited Diego Rivera to paint a mural at the California School of Fine Arts.[5] Three years later Rivera received another request from the Architect of the San Francisco Stock Exchange. The artist finally carried out both commissions and others in 1930.

Three of the best known Mexican muralists were to paint murals in this country from 1930 to 1935. It was during this period that American artists became almost universally aware of the Mexican muralist movement.[6] José Clemente Orozco painted murals in Claremont, California (1930), New York City (1930-31), and Dartmouth, New Hampshire (1932-34). Diego Rivera painted murals in San Francisco (1930-31 and 1940), Detroit (1932-33), and New York City (1933-34). David Alfaro Siqueiros painted murals in Los Angleles (1932) and operated an experimental workshop in New York (1936).[7]

The influences exerted by the Mexican muralists were affected as much by the works themselves as by the presence of the artists in American cities. The ambiance created by the artists, the interest in their work, the furor created by it on occasion, and all of the other features related to their activities as muralists in various parts of the country had a lasting impact on the then budding American muralists.

The impact of the Mexican muralists' presence was so strong that it dominated a good portion of all discussions dealing with art during this period in the specialized as well as general press. When Diego Rivera first arrived in San Francisco in late 1930 with his wife Frida Kahlo, there was an outcry from artists as well as the local newspapers on political and economic grounds.[8] The same concerns were to be expressed by similar groups in Hanover, New Hampshire in 1932 when Orozco was asked to work on the murals in Baker Library in Dartmouth College. All of these were, of course, nothing compared to the furor generated by Diego Rivera's mural in Rockefeller Center which prompted a number of editorials in the New York Times as well as the development of a number of camps around which artists in New York allied themselves.[9] The strong ideological battle was waged when Rivera included the portrait of Lenin in the mural entitled "Man at the Crossroads". This caused such a storm that Rivera was barred from completing the mural. It was finally destroyed in early 1934.[10]

Added to the works as well as the presence of the Mexican muralists were their pronouncements as direct influences on the American artists of the thirties. Examples are the lectures given by Diego Rivera and the experimental art demonstrations presented by Siqueiros.[11] In addition to these was the artists' involvement with the first American Artists Congress held in New York on February 14, 1936. Among the ten delegates from three Latin American nations were the Mexican artists, Orozco, Siqueiros, and Rufino Tamayo. The "papers presented by Orozco and Siqueiros were printed in a small pamphlet which also contained the catalogue of an exhibition of the A.C.A. Gallery of work by thirteen Mexican painters... Forty of the papers delivered were published later in a 112 page booklet that sold for fifty cents.[12]

II

American Artists and the Federal Government

The involvement of the federal government as a patron for American artists proved to be the most influential factor in the entire process. It all started when George Biddle, an American artist and close friend of President Roosevelt, became interested in setting up a government sponsored project based on the Mexican experiment of the early twenties. He wrote to the President outlining his plan.[13] In that letter, he referred to the success of the Mexican experience and suggested that it be used as a model for the establishment in this country of a similar program of mural painting.[14]

The federal government sponsored four art programs from 1933 to 1943.[15] The first of these, the *Public Works of Art Project* (PWAP), lasted from December 1933 to June 1934. The second program dealing with painting and sculpture and called the *Section of Fine Arts* was in operation from October 1934 to 1943. The third program, the *Treasury Relief Art Project* (TRAP), lasted from July 1935 to about June 1939. The fourth program under which most of the murals were funded was the *Works Progress Administration's Federal Art Project* (WPA/FAP) which lasted from August 1935 to June 1943. More than 2,500 murals were sponsored under this program throughout the nation.

A short-lived art project (June 1934 to August 1934) based in New York City and funded by the *Temporary Emergency Relief Administration* (TERA), was run by the *College Art Association* (CAA). Earlier, the College Art Association had sponsored a mural project with private funds from December 1932 to June 1934.

Among the young artists affected by the presence of the Mexican artists and their works as well by the federal funded art projects were Edward Laning and Jackson Pollock. Laning, who worked on a number of mural projects during those years, recently wrote down his memoirs as a muralist while working for the New Deal Mural Projects.[16] He recalls that he and friends would often visit Diego Rivera and Frida Kahlo, his wife, in their apartment in 1933 when Rivera was working on the Rockefeller Center mural. The young artists would then accompany Rivera on his trips to the Center where he would work every evening from around four or five in the afternoon to one or two in the morning. Laning would watch him night after night as he worked on the mural. After Rivera was barred from working further on the Rockefeller Center mural he went on to work on a series of panels at the New Workers School. Laning recalls that he "... followed him there and learned a lot more about fresco at close quarters than (he) had been able to gather in the vast spaces of the RCA Building.[17]

By the time Rivera had been ousted from the Rockefeller Center project and begun work on the New Workers School murals in 1933, another young artist, Jackson Pollock, was in New York studying art. During that summer he watched Rivera paint murals at the New School.[18]

Pollock had expressed an interest in Rivera's work as early as 1929. In a letter to his brothers, Charles and Frank, dated October 22, 1929, Pollock mentions seeing one of Rivera's paintings in a Los Angeles museum and an article by Rivera. "I found the Creative Art January 1929 article on Rivera. I certainly admire his work."[19]

It is difficult to assess the influences of the Mexican muralists upon the American artists since the work of the artists involved have to be analyzed in great detail in order to trace such influences in a concrete manner. The influenced artist may be impressed by the other artist's approach to the creation of a work of art, or by the work itself — its size, content and expression. Jackson Pollock's admiration of Diego Rivera's work has already been noted.

Another instance difficult to evaluate is the often quoted interest by Jackson Pollock's in the work of the mature Mexican artist, José Clemente Orozco, during the mid-thirties.[20] It is generally reported that the expressive qualities of Orozco's work deeply impressed Jackson Pollock. How the two Mexican artists' influences are to be assessed along with the other influences Jackson Pollock experienced during these years before emerging as a mature artist himself is difficult to do within the confines of this essay. Further, it is difficult to point to specific constituents as being derivative of a specific source since a truly creative artist does not slavishly emulate the "master".

Perhaps easier to document is the specific reference to Jackson Pollock's contact with David Alfaro Siqueiros' experimental work being done in New York in the mid-thirties and the possible influence this may have had on his later development as an artist.

Joseph Solman, one of the other early muralists of that period, recounts a story told by Axel Horn, a member of the Works Progress Administration/Fine Arts Program and an early friend of Jackson Pollock, concerning the impact that contact with David Alfaro Siqueiros had on this one artist. Siqueiros was then conducting experiments in his workshop on 14th Street in New York.

According to Joseph Solman, "Axel brought Pollock up to the Mexican workshop to view work in progress. Pollock was witness to one of the experimental techniques Siqueiros was using, namely, a spray gun full of multiple colors being siphoned onto a canvas panel quite larger in size. When the first layers of accidental tones and colors appeared, the artist would then reshape the colors while still in flux into the revolutionary subjects he already had in mind. Axel says that Pollock was so excited about this initial procedure that he begged his friend to take him back for another visit. Axel claims this was the determining factor in the development of the famous drip style."[21]

No firmer document of the Mexican influence along a broader front is afforded than the response given by most former New Deal artists who received questionnaires from Frances V. O'Connor several years ago. Audrey McMahon, Director of the College Art Association and regional director for one of the early New Deal mural projects, "... was amazed to read in the questionnaire that many artists were enormously influenced by the Mexicans. They felt that art in Mexico had made so much progress that art in America should do likewise. They speak of the Mexicans as 'giants' and feel themselves 'pygmies' in comparison. All this comes through as rather naive. Yet it is true that all the major Mexicans — Orozco, Rivera, Siqueiros — painted murals here during the early 1930's."[22]

In more concrete terms, the Mexican muralists' impact can best be illustrated by referring to one of the murals painted in San Francisco in the Coit Tower by Victor Arnautoff in 1934 under the Public Works of Art Project, a forerunner of the WPA Federal Art Project. The mural entitled "City Life" is amazingly close stylistically to the work of Rivera and Orozco.[23] The panoramic mural shows a number of street scenes. On the left side of the horizontal panel men are shown at work with motorized traffic moving from left to right, people milling around and shown as a backdrop for a mailman recovering mail from a mailbox, a man in an overcoat being held up by a man holding a gun to his side while another picks his pocket; a pedestrian and auto accident is shown in the middle ground; others get off the cable car; well known landmarks of San Francisco are included in the background, among them City Hall, the Museum of the Legion of Honor, and others.

The articulation and definition of figures is surprisingly close to the work of Rivera. The emphasis on the anecdotal aspects of city life is close to some of the approaches used by Orozco in some of his early murals that were closer to caricature than narrative muralism. Examples are his Preparatoria murals in Mexico City.

Summary

The Mexican muralists' works as well as their presence in various parts of this country during the early thirties made a strong impact on American artists and citizens. The themes, arrangements, and points of view expressed by the Mexican artists were echoed in numerous murals painted by Americans throughout the U.S.

The work of Orozco and Siqueiros influenced the young Jackson Pollock during his formative years in the mid-thirties. His work later became synonomous with American art during the late forties and early fifties.

More recently — although space prohibits the discussion — the works of the Mexican muralists, particularly that of Siqueiros, has been of great interest to the Chicano muralists of the Southwest and the Chicago area.[24]

Notes

1. A few of the published materials in English available before 1930 will illustrate this point. Brenner, Anita, "A Mexican Renascence," *Arts.* New York, Vol. 8, No. 3 Sept. 1925. Brenner, Anita, *Idols Behind Altars,* Payson & Clarke, Ltd., New York, 1929. Evans, Ernestine, *The Frescoes of Diego Rivera,* Harcourt, Brace, New York, 1929. Rivera, Diego, "The Revolution in Painting." *Creative Art.* New York, Vol. 4, No. 1, Jan. 1929. Tablada, José Juan, "José Clemente Orozco, The Mexican Goya," *International Studio.* New York, Vol. 78, No. 322, March 1924. Tablada, José Juan, "Mexican Painting of Today," *International Studio,* New York, Vol. 76, No. 308, Jan. 1923. Tablada, José Juan, "The Arts in Modern Mexico," *Parnassus,* New York, Vol. 1, No. III, March 1929.

2. Marion Greenwood was one of the few American artists who studied with the Mexican muralists in Mexico in 1932 (Orozco and Rivera) and later painted murals in that country and the U.S. For details and a discussion of her work see Francis V. O'Connor, "New Deal Murals in New York," *Art Forum.* Vol. VII, No. 3, November 1968. pp. 46-47 and note 21.

3. For an interesting glimpse into the period, the events, and the activities of a number of New Deal muralists see *The New Deal Art Projects, An Anthology of Memoirs* edited by Francis V. O'Connor, Smithsonian Institution Press, Washington, D.C., 1972.

4. See Appendix 1 for a list of this and other murals in the U.S. painted by Mexican artists. See also Virginia and Jaime Plenn, *A Guide to Modern Mexican Murals,* Ediciones Tolteca S.A., Mexico. 1963. pp. 137-149.

5. Myers, Bernard, *Mexican Painting in Our Time.* Oxford University Press, New York, 1956. p. 80.

6. For a discussion of the Mexican muralists in this country see my *Mexican American Artists,* University of Texas Press, Austin and London, 1973. pp. 31-38.

7. Siqueiros established an "Experimental Workshop" at 5 West 14th Street in the spring of 1936.

8. Myers, *Mexican Painting.* p. 80.

9. Artists boycotted an exhibition that was being organized for the official opening of

Rockefeller Center. See Edward Laning's memoir for a discussion of this protest and Rivera's talk at the rally in *The New Deal Projects,* pp. 82-83.

10. The barring of Rivera from completing the mural and its destruction created a storm of protest. The New York Times ran six editorials in 1933 (Feb. 18, p. 3; May 10, p. 1; May 11, p. 1; May 14, pp. 1-2, 27; May 15, p. 4; and May 18, p. 4) and one in 1934 (Feb. 19). The destruction of the mural was reported on February 13, 1934, p. 21 and on p. 3 of the same issue the following article appeared, "Does A Work of Art Possess an Intangible Value."

The following are some of the articles which appeared in art magazines during that period:

"The Rivera Affair," *The Art Digest,* VII (April 1, 1933).

"Rivera Again," *The Art Digest,* II (May 15, 1933). pp. 41-42.

"Rockefeller Dissento," *Architectural Forum* LIX (June, 1933).

"Walls and Ethics," *The Art Digest,* III (March 1, 1934). pp. 3-4.

"Murder of Art," *Architectural Forum,* XL: sup. (March, 1934).

11. Among the young American artists working there was Jackson Pollock. See *Jackson Pollock,* p. 21 and note 9 above.

12. *The New Deal Art Programs.* p. 210.

13. Biddle, George, *An American Artist's Story.* Boston, 1939. p. 268.

14. Laning, a young American muralist, also remembers this event very well. He relates that he and Reginald Marsh went over to Biddle's house soon after Roosevelt's election in 1932 where they were joined by other artists invited by Biddle "... to discuss his plans for organizing a group of artists along the lines of the Mexican 'syndicate' — Rivera, Orozco, Siqueiros, Charlot, et al — to paint murals in the Justice Department and Post Office Buildings in Washington, D.C." Others involved in this project were Maurice Sterne, Henry Varnum Poor, Bardman Robinson, and Thomas Hart Benton. See *The New Deal Art Projects.* p. 86.

15. For a detailed discussion of these programs see *The New Deal Art Programs,* pp. 11-49 and Francis V. O'Connor, "New Deal Murals in New York," *Art Forum,* Vol. VII, No. 3, November 1968, pp. 41-49.

16. *The New Deal Arts Projects.* pp. 78-113.

17. *Ibid.* p. 82.

18. O'Connor, Francis V., *Jackson Pollock,* The Museum of Modern Art, New York, 1967, p. 18.

19. *Jackson Pollock,* p. 14. See also note 1 for Diego Rivera's article mentioned by Pollock.

20. The following are two of the books in which references to this influence are noted:

Hunter, Sam, *Modern American Painting and Sculpture.* Dell Publishing Co. Inc., New York, 4th Edition, 1963. p. 139.

Rose, Barbara, *American Art Since 1900.* A Critical History, Praeger, New York, 2nd Edition, 1968. p. 153.

21. *The New Deal. p. 128.*

22. *Ibid.* pp. 318-319.

23. For a foldout reproduction of the Coit Tower mural see *American Heritage.* "A Sampler of New Deal Murals," Vol. XXI, No. 6, October 1970. pp. 51-54.

24. Quirarte, Jacinto, "The Murals of El Barrio," *Exxon U.S.A.,* Vol. XIII, No. 4, Fourth Quarter, 1974. pp. 2-9.

Appendix 1

A. Murals by José Clemente Orozco in the U.S.

   1. Title: *Prometheus*   Date: 1930

Location: Frary Hall, Pomona College
Claremont, California
Theme: Prometheus supports the vault; on either side are the conflicting forces, *Chaos and the Monsters* and *Chaos and the Gods.*

2. Title: No specific title   Date 1930-31
Location: New School for Social Research
New York City
Themes: *Table of Brotherhood, Struggle in the Orient, Struggle in the Occident, The Universal Family, Science, Labor, and Art,* and *The Strike.*

3. Title: *History of America*   Date: 1932-34
Location: Baker Library, Dartmouth College
Hanover, New Hampshire
Themes: West Wing/General: The Story of Quetzalcoatl
The Migration, Ancient Human Sacrifice, Aztec Warriors, The Coming of Quetzalcoatl, the *Golden Age* (Pre-Columbian), *Departure of Quetzalcoatl The Prophesy.*
East Wing/General: The Return of Quetzalcoatl
Cortez and the Cross, The Machine, Anglo-America, Hispano America, Gods of the Modern World, Modern Human Sacrifice, Christ Destroying His Cross.

B. Murals by Diego Rivera in the U.S.
1. Title: No specific title   Date: 1931
Location: Luncheon Club Staircase
San Francisco Stock Exchange
Theme: Allegory of California
Deals with the various natural and industrial resources of the state.
2. Title: No specific title   Date 1931
Location: California School of Fine Arts
San Francisco
Theme: Glory of Modern Industry
Deals with building construction — workers, mechanics, engineers, and architects — a rear view of the artist working on a scaffold dominates the central part of the mural.

3. Title: *Abundance and Health*   Date: 1931
Location Home of Mrs. Stern
Fresno, California
Theme: Agriculture, Tractors, etc.

4. Title: *Portrait of Detroit*   Date: 1932-34
Location: Detroit Institute of Fine Arts
Theme: Evolution of industry to its basic components: lime, coal, iron, and sand which are symbolized by the four races: White, Black, Red, and Yellow. Automobile Manufacture, Steam, Electric Power, and Aviation, Agricultural Symbols.

5. Title: *Man at the Crossroads*   Date: 1933 (unfinished)
Destroyed: 1934
Location: Rockefeller Center

Theme: The worker holds a lever which gives him a choice between the world of socialism at his left or the world of capitalism at his right. Lenin appears in the central part of the right side of the mural. The comparable space on the left is balanced by a night club scene.

C. Murals by David Alfaro Siqueiros in the U.S.
   1. Title: *Street Scene*   Date: 1932
     Location: Chouinard Art School
              Los Angeles
     Theme: Self-explanatory

   2. Title: *Portrait of Mexico*   Date: 1932
     Location: Dudley Murphy Residence Patio
              Santa Monica

     Theme: The Betrayal of the Mexican Revolution by Calles (an ex-president of Mexico in 1932)

   3. Title: *Tropical America*   Date: 1932
     Location: Plaza Art Center
              Los Angeles
     Theme: A crucified peon, a United States eagle perched at the top of the cross and a group of Mexicans standing below.

EL BICENTENARIO Y LOS ESTUDIOS GRADUADOS EN LAS LITERATURAS Y LENGUAS HISPÁNICAS EN LOS ESTADOS UNIDOS

Enrique Ruiz-Fornells

En este año de 1976 es casi obligado referirse a la independencia de los Estados Unidos ocurrida precisamente hace dos siglos. Casi ya terminado el año pueden apreciarse todas las actividades que han tenido lugar con este motivo. En Madrid se formó la Comisión Española del Bicentenario de la Independencia de los Estados Unidos[1] con un comité especial, dependiente de esa Comisión, compuesto por diversas personalidades de California, Texas, Nueva York, Alabama y otras partes del país. La Asociación Americana de profesores de Español y Portugués celebrará en Atlanta la reunión anual el próximo mes de diciembre bajo el tema "Hispanic Contributions to America, Then and Now." En Miami el profesor Román Campora al conmemorarse el décimo aniversario de la fundación de la Cámara de Comercio Latina en los Estados Unidos pronunció una conferencia sobre "El aporte hispano a los Estados Unidos de América." En los primeros días del mes de junio el rey Juan Carlos I y la reina Sofía de España visitaron al presidente Ford y otros diversos lugares y personalidades para resaltar la contribución española a la Guerra de la Independencia. Es decir, todo estaba dispuesto para una gran celebración del Bicentenario, y al celebrar este hecho no podía eludirse la referencia a lo hispánico como elemento básico de la misma.

Leyendo unas páginas de la historia de España y de los Estados Unidos, se averigua con facilidad que España estuvo presente en lo que hoy es el territorio continental de esta gran nación durante 309 años (1513-1822), mientras que Inglaterra lo hizo sólo durante 197 años (1586-1776), Francia 91 años (1672-1763), y Méjico en California y Nuevo Méjico 27 años (1821-1848).

Sería largo y repetitivo mencionar todos los acontecimientos históricos que ocurrieron a través de esos 309 años de la presencia española, pero sí conviene mencionar algunos de ellos que fácilmente pueden encontrarse en cualquier enciclopedia y que dan la medida de la presencia de España.[2] Juan Ponce de León llegó a Florida en 1513, Lucas Vázquez de Ayllón a Carolina del Sur en 1526, Pánfilo de Narváez a Tampa en 1528, Hernando de

Soto estuvo por estos lugares en 1540, también en el mismo año Francisco Vázquez de Coronado llegó a Nuevo Méjico, Oklahoma y Nebraska, Tristán de Luna estuvo en Pensacola en 1559, Juan Pardo y Hernando Boyano en 1566 y 1567 respectivamente en Georgia, Alabama y las Carolinas. En 1570 los jesuitas fundaron misiones en Florida y Georgia, en 1581 el Hermano Agustín Rodríguez y Francisco Sánchez Chamuscado estuvieron en Texas y Nuevo Méjico y Juan de Oñate estuvo en Nuevo Méjico en 1598. Se fundó Santa Fe en 1610 y no olvidemos a Fray Junípero Serra y las misiones de California en 1769. En fin así podríamos seguir mencionando nombres de ríos, exploración de costas, cartas cartográficas, creación de misiones, fundación de ciudades etc., etc.

España estuvo asimismo presente en 1776 cuando se consiguió la independencia de Inglaterra. Materialmente su colaboración fue decisiva en varios momentos como han demostrado historiadores de la categoría de José A. Sobrino, F. Morales Padrón, Octavio Gil Munilla, Buchanan Parker Thompson, Darío Fernández Florez y Emilio Garrigues.[3] Las operaciones del gobernador de la Luisiana, Bernardo Gálvez, fueron de gran utilidad al convertir a Nueva Orleans en una base para corsarios y al apoderarse de los puertos militares británicos en la Florida occidental. Diplomáticamente la ayuda española tuvo proporciones extensas. La Habana, señala el profesor Román Campora, fue asimismo centro desde el que España canalizó una ayuda diplomática, económica, y militar eficaz. Añadiendo que ya después de la independencia el dólar español fue declarado de curso legal por el Congreso en 1793, que la primera moneda conmemorativa apareció en 1892 teniendo en el anverso la efigie de Cristobal Colón y en el reverso la carabela Santa María. Casi al mismo tiempo se fabricaron monedas de veinticinco centavos con la efigie de Isabel de Castilla. En 1935 se acuñaron a su vez otras de cincuenta centavos y al no encontrar el retrato de Cabeza de Vaca, se puso una cabeza de vaca como indica su apellido.

Cincuenta y tres gobernadores representaron a España en la Florida, trienta y siete en Tejas, sensenta en Nuevo Méjico, y diez en California. El primer blanco que nació en el territorio de los Estados Unidos fue Martín de Argüelles en 1566 en San Agustín. El primer libro escrito en español fue el del Hermano Domingo Agustín. Baez en 1569, jesuita de las misiones de Georgia. La primera representación teatral en español fue la celebrada en El Paso, con motivo de la toma de posesión de Juan de Oxate de Reino de Nuevo Méjico el 30 de abril de 1598. Y pasando a tiempos recientes el director cinematográfico Walt Disney fue hijo de José Zamora, y nació en Almería el 5 de diciembre de 1901. Tanto él como su hermano al quedar huérfanos fueron adoptados por Elias Disney, y aunque en este país se le conoció por Walt Disney, su real nombre fue José Luis Zamora. Thomas Jefferson hablaba correctamente el español, y durante el período presiden-

cial de Nixon se proclamó la Semana Nacional de la Herencia Española que
tiene lugar cada mes de septiembre en reconocimiento de la Hispanidad.[4]

Estos factores han presionado por la fuerza de su importancia en los
medios académicos y en todo el sistema educativo, a establecer cursos de
lengua española en las universidades e institutos de enseñanza media, de
manera que junto a otros idiomas puede también estudiarse el español, con-
vertido, sólo por el número de personas que lo hablan, en el segundo
idioma de los Estados Unidos.

Desde época temprana después de la independencia las universidades y
centros de enseñanza superior y media han mantenido actividades en
relación con las civilizaciones, la lengua, y las literaturas hispánicas que
suponen un caudal de trabajo que aventaja al realizado en otras lenguas
nacionales. Entre estas actividades, aparte de cursos y programas no
graduados, sobresale la abundancia de tesis doctorales terminadas, muchas
ya publicadas, que se han escrito en literatura hispánica desde que se defendió la primera por Lucius Henry Buckingham bajo el título "That the
Romance Languages, in Deriving from the Latin, Followed Tendencies to
Change, Which the Latin Already Exhibited, Is Illustrated by the Study of
Romance Verbal Formations," en la Universidad de Harvard en 1876.

A partir de ese año la investigación a nivel doctoral ha sido creciente,
abarcando todo el amplio espectro de las literaturas y de las lenguas iberoamericanas. En este sentido se han publicado una serie de artículos y libros
que recogen ampliamente esta información. En el último, aparecido en
1970 y publicado por la Universidad de Kentucky, se observa que de las
1640 - 1783 si incluimos el portugués-tesis doctorales escritas entre 1876 y
1966, las especialidades que se han investigado son bastante numerosas. En
1927 encontramos ya trabajos bibliográficos notables sobre este tema, como
el que publicó R. M. Merrill, *American Doctoral Dissertations in the
Romance Field, 1876-1926.* En años posteriores merece citarse el del profesor James R. Chatham que se publicó con mi colaboración, *Dissertations
in Hispanic Languages and Literatures, 1876-1966.*[5] En forma de artículos
o pequeñas bibliografías recordamos el de Frank Sedwick "Theses on
Miguel de Unamuno at North American Universities," aparecido en *Kentucky Foreign Languages Quarterly* en 1956; el del profesor Lomas L.
Barrett, "Theses Dealing with Hispano-American Language and Literature," que empezó a publicar periódicamente en 1945 en *Hispania,* órgano
oficial de la Asociación Americana de Profesores de Español y Portugués, y
que más tarde continuó el profesor Claude L. Hulet; el del profesor
Homero Castillo, "La literatura hispanoamericana en las tesis doctorales de
los Estados Unidos," impreso en *Anales de la Universidad de Chile* en
1961; además de otros en la *Revista de Filología Española, Modern
Language Journal, Hispanófila, Luso-Brazilian Review,* etc.

Tomando como base 1966, en que terminan las estadísticas oficiales, apreciamos que se han escrito en universidades norteamericanas, incluyendo las canadienses, 1295 tesis doctorales, sobre temas de literatura española y portuguesa, 1640 sumando todas las concernientes al castellano. Un examen detenido de los centros de enseñanza superior donde este elevado número de tesis ha sido defendido nos pone en disposición de observar cuales son las instituciones que destacan por su quehacer hispánico. Sin dificultad puede observarse que de las 71 universidades con programas de doctorado sobresalen algunas que se han distinguido por su labor en favor de la investigación de la lengua y literaturas hispánicas a ese nivel. Por ejemplo, en la Universidad de Columbia, siempre hasta 1966 como ya se ha mencionado, se han escrito, defendido y aprobado 134. En la de Wisconsin 121 y en la de Harvard 102. Con menos del centenar figura a la cabeza California en Berkeley con 92 a la que siguen Illinois con 80, Michigan con 72, Texas con 67, Pennsylvania con 63, Yale con 60 y Stanford con 57. El resto varía en esta clasificación numérica y oscila desde una hasta el medio centenar. Con una o dos tesis aprobadas aparecen Alabama con una, Cincinnati con 2, Connecticut también con 2, Emory con una, Oklahoma con dos, Massachusetts Institute of Technology con una, etc. Claro está, que se trata de lo que podríamos llamar casos tardíos, y no quiere decir que entre 1966 y 1976 no hayan aumentado el número de sus doctores. De todas formas, lo que es interesante no es considerar los casos aislados sino todo el trabajo realizado en su conjunto con objeto de poder apreciar el volumen de la obra alcanzada.

De las 1783 tesis escritas hasta 1966, 1152 corresponden a la literatura española, 143 a Brasil y Portugal, y 488 a la literatura hispanoamericana. En el primer grupo encontramos 26 dedicadas a Alfonso X, que es el autor más estudiado entre los de la Edad Media. A continuación, en el Siglo de Oro, Lope de Vega es el escritor que recibe mayor atención con 74 tesis, siguiéndole Pedro Calderón de la Barca con 26. El teatro en general de esta época acapara la atención de los hispanistas norteamericanos con 44 trabajos. El siglo XIX es también objeto de investigación especial, y en él sobresale Benito Pérez Galdós, sobre cuya obra se han redactado 54 tesis. A Pérez Galdós le siguen Emilia Pardo Bazán con 11, José María de Pereda con 6, Juan Valera con 8, Clarín también con 8, Gustavo Adolfo Bécquer y Rosalía de Castro con 5 cada uno, continuando la lista otros nombres conocidos aunque en menor número. En cuanto al teatro de este período existen con carácter general 13 tesis, 14 sobre diversos aspectos de la época, al neoclasicismo le corresponden 10 y al romanticismo 13. En el siglo XX Miguel de Unamuno tiene un lugar destacado con 23 tesis, y sus compañeros de generación Pío Baroja y Azorín 14 y 9 respectivamente. José Ortega y Gasset tiene 10, Ramón María del Valle Inclán 9. Entre los poetas

Federico García Lorca, Antonio Machado, y Juan Ramón Jiménez figuran
los tres con 9 tesis cada uno, y entre los dramaturgos sobresale Jacinto
Benavente, también con 9. Otros autores en estas mismas especialidades y
otras están representados con una cantidad más reducida. Sin embargo,
nadie ha sido olvidado y no existe autor o tendencia que se ignore.

La literatura hispanoamericana es un sector en que la investigación se ha
iniciado en años recientes pues la primera tesis, "The Life and Dramatic
Works of Gertrudis Gómez de Avellaneda," fue defendida por Edwin
Bucher Williams en la Universidad de Pennsylvania en 1924. Más tarde
esta especialidad se ha ido ampliando al compás del crecimiento de los
distintos departamentos de lenguas de las universidadades, hasta llegar a la
actualidad en que constituye una parte importante de las disciplinas de los
programas de estudio.

Por países, como razonablemente podía esperarse por motivos de
proximidad y vecindad, la nación que figura con el mayor número de tesis
es Méjico, que aparece con 41, seguida por la Argentina con 15 y Chile con
12. Después continúan el Perú con 8, Ecuador con 6, Cuba y Guatemala
con 5, Colombia, Bolivia, Costa Rica y Venezuela con 3 cada una, y
Panamá, Paraguay y Puerto Rico con una. Entre los autores que han
despertado mayor curiosidad pueden destacarse, entre otros, a Rubén
Darío con 7, José Enrique Rodó con 6, Alfonso Reyes con 5, Carlos Reyles
y Ricardo Palma con 5 también, Jorge Luis Borges con 4, Rómulo Gallegos
con el mismo número, y a Manuel González Prada, Ricardo Güiraldes,
Nicolás Guillén y Eduardo Mallea con tres. En cuanto a conceptos e ideas
literarias notamos en primer término una sección general con 25 tesis que
fluctuan desde el significado de la Hispanidad hasta el estudio de los Estados
Unidos en la prensa de esas naciones pasando por la influencia alemana en
la filología hispanoamericana y tocando temas, por ejemplo, como la
literatura picaresca en Hispanoamérica, Unamuno en Hispanoamérica, la
evolución de la literatura gauchesca, apreciaciones de los Estados Unidos,
etc. Al modernismo se le han dedicado 12, a la novela, incluyendo la
histórica, 10, a la literatura indianista-indigenista 10, al costumbrismo 8, al
romanticismo 8, al teatro 5, al folklore 5, a la literatura gauchesca 5, y al
realismo 2. En total 155 escritores han sido objeto de estudio en estas tesis,
correspondiendo a los movimientos literarios, y otros aspectos, en general,
33. Los estudios realizados cubren una amplia extension en el tiempo, ya
que abarcan desde Sor Juana Inés de la Cruz hasta Vargas Llosa o García
Márquez que han merecido, estos últimos, una buena atención entre las
tesis contemporáneas.

Respecto a Portugal y Brasil encontramos que el mismo criterio de
clasificación que se ha mencionado para la literatura escrita en español
puede aplicarse a la escrita en portugués. Hasta el año 1966 se habían ter-

minado dos tesis sobre bibliografía, una sobre el adjetivo, 3 sobre dialectos, 8 sobre lexicografía, 6 sobre análisis lingüísticos, una sobre sufijos, 2 sobre sintaxis y 2 sobre el verbo. En literatura figuraban aprobadas, en dicho año, 55, teniendo la fecha de 1917 la primera que se defendió en esta especialidad en la Universidad de Pennsylvania acerca de "The German Element in Brazil, Colonies and Dialect," escrita por Benjamin Franklin Schapelle. El autor que tiene en su haber más estudios es Luis Camões con 5, y después aparecen otros con cantidades diversas como Eugenio de Castro, José Maria Eça de Queiroz, Jorge Ferreira de Vasconcellos, Jeronymo Lobo, Francisco Machado, Gil Vicente, y António Vieira. Respecto al Brasil el total es de 45. Entre ellas, aparte de una que versa sobre bibliografía, hay investigaciones dedicadas a José Alençar, Jorge Amado, Luis Delfino dos Santos, Alfredo Escragnolle Taunay, Bernardo Guimarães, Jorge de Lima, José Lins de Rego, Henriqueta Lisboa, Joaquim Maria Machado de Assis, José Bento Monteiro Lobato, Rachel de Queiroz, Graciliano Ramos, Joao Guimarães Rosa, y Franklin Távora.[6]

Las tesis en portugués, aunque con menor volumen, indican asimismo el interés que existe en los medios académicos de Norteamérica por este idioma.

La aportación de los Estados Unidos a la especialidad de las lenguas y literaturas iberoamericanas que en estas líneas se ha tratado de reflejar brevemente, ha sido importante durante los dos siglos que existe como nación independiente. Esto no es de extrañar por el interés que ha existido siempre en los centros de estudio pero también, sin duda, por el hecho de que dentro de sus fronteras viven cerca de veinte millones de hispanoparlantes que hacen de esa lengua la segunda del país después del inglés.

Notas

1. El propósito inicial de esta Comisión fue el de coordinar todas las actividades españolas en 1976. El Director Ejecutivo fue Manuel García Miranda al que reemplazó después Fernando Sartorious.

2. Uno de los libros recientes y mejor documentados en estos temas es el de Carlos Fernández-Shaw *Presencia de España en los Estados Unidos,* Ediciones Cultura Hispánica, Madrid, 1971, 932 págs.

3. Desde 1963 el Instituto de Cultura Hispánica de Madrid ha publicado una serie de libros que sirven para observar el punto de vista español sobre las relaciones históricas con los Estados Unidos y, en especial, la ayuda de España a la guerra de la independencia. Pueden citarse entre otros el ya mencionado de Carlos Fernández-Shaw, *Presencia de España en los Estados Unidos* (1971); Emilio Garrigues, *Los españoles en la otra orilla* (1965); Octavio Gil Munilla, *Participación de España en la génesis histórica de la independencia de los E.E.U.U.* (1963); Francisco Morales Padrón, *Participación de España en la independencia política de los E.E.U.U.* (1963); Buchanan Parker Thomson, *La ayuda española en la guerra de la independencia nor-*

teamericana (1966). Publicaciones Españolas presentó a su vez en 1968 el libro de Darío Fernández-Flórez, *The Spanish Heritage in the United States.*

4. Todos estos datos junto a un relato detallado sobre ellos pueden encontrarse en el libro de Carlos Fernández-Shaw ya aludido.

5. James R. Chatham y Enrique Ruiz-Fornells con la colaboración de Sara Mathews Scales, *Dissertations in Hispanic Languages and Literatures, 1876-1966.* The University of Kentucky Press, Lexington (Kentucky), 1970, 120 págs.

6. Se refleja aquí parte de mi ponencia "La literatura hispanoamericana y su investigación crítica en las tesis doctorales de los Estados Unidos," presentada al Congreso del Instituto Internacional de Literatura Iberoamericana celebrado en Madrid en marzo de 1975.

GEORGE SANTAYANA: A SPANISH GLORY
IN AMERICAN PHILOSOPHY AND LETTERS

Carlos H. Monsanto
and
Harold Durham

George Santayana (1863-1952) must be included among the many Spanish and Spanish-American figures who have contributed substantially to every aspect of the American way of life in its first two hundred years of existence. Having never relinquished his Spanish citizenship, he lived many years of his life in the United States and became an eminent philosopher, poet, critic, essayist, novelist, humorist and prose stylist. It behooves us first to review briefly the most significant highlights of his life, with particular emphasis on his contributions to American thought and letters, and then we shall analyze with some detail his transcendental importance in philosophy.

George Santayana, christened as a Catholic with the name Jorge Agustín Nicolás de Santayana, was born in Madrid, Spain, December 16, 1863. His mother, Da. Josefa Borrás, was the daughter of a liberal Spanish republican who migrated to Virginia, and then settled in the Philippines. Her first marriage was to a young Boston merchant named Sturgis with whom she had five children. Some time after her first husband's death, while in Madrid, she married Agustín Ruiz de Santayana, who had been a friend of the Sturgises in the Philippines, and who was an extreme liberal thinker. He also is remembered for having translated into Spanish verse Seneca's tragedies.

George Santayana spent the first nine years of his life in Spain, mostly in the legendary city of Avila. Undoubtedly, this early life experience left a deep spiritual impression on him. Of Avila he has said that he was nearly seventy years old when it ceased to be the center of his life.[1] It was in this city, and later on in Boston, through the efforts of his life-long confidant, his half-sister Susana Sturgis, that he was taught his catechism and Catholic prayers. He never became a devout believer in Catholicism, however. His relationship to that religion was "a matter of sympathy and traditional allegiance not of philosophy."[2] He soon agreed with his father in regarding all religions as works of human imagination.

81

The Hispanic elements in Santayana's personality and philosophical and literary works are still being probed by his biographers and critics, and not without some controversies or polemics among them. We know that he spoke English without a trace of an accent, and he never wrote a book in his native tongue, Spanish; and, furthermore, until the completion of his novel *Person and Places* (1944) he seldom mentioned Spain in his works. Despite these facts, important critics such as J.M. Alonso Gamo, have devoted many hours to define Santayana's HISPANISM (españolismo). We are reminded, for example, that during Santayana's stay at Harvard University, he was known as a "young Spanish poet, mysteriously exotic."[3]

When William Lyon Phelps stated in his Little Essays (1920) that George Santayana's mother was an American, the author of *Persons and Places* was quick to rectify that statement as follows: "The only fact that is wrong is your saying that my mother was an American, she was Spanish — we never spoke English together — but had been first married (in Manila) to one of the Boston Sturgises, so that my half-sisters and half-brothers there belonged to that once prosperous and always agreeable tribe; and it was in consequence of this connection, and money matters concerned in it, that we went to live in America."[4]

Santayana had such a Spanish temperament that he felt a foreigner in Boston: "Being a foreigner and coming from a rather different intellectual and moral milieu, I have a lighter and less-conscience-striken way of taking things, which produces the impression of idleness and frivolity in the absence of scholar proof that after all I do as much work as other people."[5]

William James described Santayana as a "half-Spaniard, half-Yankee, and a genuine philosophic intelligence if ever there was one. He has the real dialectic zest, of playing with distinctions for the mere sweet fun of the thing, but is withal of a most serious turn—a Catholic in fact."[6] But there is no doubt in many scholars' minds that he was more truthfully Spaniard than Yankee, an unrooted Spaniard taken from Spain not to be given but to be loaned to North-america. By keeping this in mind, we can understand why his many famous essays could not have been "written by a pure anglosaxon; they are the products of a mentality which was essentially Latin, catholically educated, and saturated with medieval scholastic philosophy."[7]

Santayana's poetry was even more Spanish in essence than his philosophical works. H. Gregoric and M. Zaturenska, in their *History of American Poetry* recognize that Santayana's muse was not of English origin and that, while it would be difficult to show the mere evidence of Roman Catholic tradition, the only and complex truth of the matter is that Santayana had identified himself with Spain.[8] The contemporary critic Concha Zardoya, corroborates Gregoric and Zaturenska's poetic hispanism stating that "Castilla has taught Santayana with absolute certainty, his love for the essential and lasting, his disdain for what is banal and adventitious."[9]

To find other eloquent testimonies of Santayana's close ties with his native Spain, we must read many of his letters. We learn, for example, that the fact that he retained his legal Spanish nationality was not an accident or an affectation: it was a symbol of the truth. Until the death of his sisters, who had returned to Avila, he went there every year. In one of his poems he tells us that he wants to "die among the hills of Spain/and o'er the treeless melancholy plain/await the coming of the final gloom."[11]

George Santayana did not die in Spain because political and personal reasons kept him from doing so. He certainly did not want to die in Boston. We insist that he never felt at home there, even though it was the cradle of his fame. Let us review how he achieved this fame there.

At age nine Santayana was sent to Boston to join his mother, who had promised her first husband to bring up their children there. Santayana's father, incidentally, felt that his son had more opportunities for a good future in Boston than in Spain. At any rate, once in that great city, after attending the Brimmer Public Grammar School, he was admitted to the Boston Latin School, honored as the oldest of American public institutions of learning. His progress in English was so remarkable that it was while enrolled at this institution that he published his first work, *Lines on Leaving the Bedford Street Schoolhouse.* At this time he also became one of the original board of editors of the *Boston Latin Register.*

In 1882, at age nineteen, he registered at Harvard College, where he did outstanding work in philosophy and English composition. He was an introspective student, unlike his typical New England peers, but by no means a recluse. For several years he drew several compositions for the *Lampoon,* helped to found the *Harvard Monthly,* and helped to keep alive the Art Club, the Chess Club, the O K Society, Phi Beta Kappa, the Philosophical Club, and many other worthwhile organizations.

In June, 1886 he received his B.A. and a Fellowship, which he used to travel to Germany to study at the University of Berlin. He returned later to Harvard for an additional year of study and in 1889 he became probably the first Spaniard to receive from this institution the combined degrees of Master of Arts and Doctor of Philosophy. Later, in 1912, he was granted a Lit. D. Degree from the University of Wisconsin.

As to his career as a noted educator, it also began with a position at the Harvard Department of Philosophy. There he became the colleague of such notables as William James, Josiah Royce, and George H. Palmer. It must be kept in mind, however, that to become an educator was not an easy decision for Santayana. The young philosopher then made several trips to visit his father in Spain, and with him tried unsuccessfully to secure a position in the Spanish army or the Spanish diplomatic service. When all efforts failed, the "prospect of a quiet academic existence seemed the least of evils."[12] Little did he know then that he was to become the inspiring teacher of such remarkable thinkers as T.S. Eliot, Conrad Aiken, Walter Lippmann, Felix Frankfurter and Robert Benchley. At Radcliff he also was Gertrude Steins's favorite instructor.

As we already know, it was in Boston that he began his literary career. His first poems, *Sonnets and Other verses* were published in 1894. To this first collection there followed *Lucifer: A Theological Tragedy* (1899) and *The Hermit of Carmel* (9101). Admired for their mystery of form, they were poorly received by some critics who felt that his verses were cold, "aspiring to a classical severity, but succeeding often in being only austere."

To Santayana, a poet had to live in the continual presence of all experience to respect it; and he had to have a delicate sense for the ideal echoes on one's own passions, and for all the colors of one's possible happiness. "The poet's task is to reconstitute the shattered picture of the world, and the philosopher's to reconstitute the shattered picture of existence itself."[14]

To determine how does the philosopher reconstitute the shattered picture of existence itself, it behooves us now to look more carefully at Santayana the philosopher. Let us remember that while at Harvard, he studied under Josiah Royce and William James. Royce was an idealist who believed reality was subordinate to thought and there exists an Absolute truth. He was the best known exponent of this position in the United States. William James was a pragmatic empiricist believing that reality was not subordinate to thought but is primary and independent of our minds. For the pragmatist truth was determined by what works. James was one of the founders of pragmatism which is said to be the first truly American philosophy. Santayana attributes little influence to these men "I accordingly heard James and Royce with more wonder than serious agreement: my scholastic logic would have wished to reduce James at once to a materialist and Royce to a solipsist, and it seemed strangely irrational in them to resist such simplification."[15] Santayana mentions scholastic logic which Richard Butler points out must be taken loosely to mean a logic developed through his interest in theology. Butler in discussing the influence of the various philosophers on Santayana's work says, "The main streams of philosophical thought which flowed into his own system were those that watered the budding philosophy already in him when he entered Harvard and began his formal studies."[16]

Among the many philosophers whose philosophy reinforced his own were the early Greeks. A special importance was also found in the writings

of the Latin poet Lucretius. He had first come in contact with Lucretius
through his father who used to quote from him. He later wrote that he
always carried a copy with him and knew long passages by heart. From
Lucretius, Santayana learned the primary importance of matter and the
ongoing relations of matter (nature). He said of his work, *De Rerum
Natura,* "Even the physical and biological theories seemed instructive, not
as scientific finalities, if science could be final, but as serving to dispel the
notion that anything is not natural or miraculous. If the theory suggested
were false, another no less naturalistic would be true: and this presumption
recommended itself to me and has become one of my first principles not
that a particular philosophy called naturalism must be true a priori but that
nature sets the standard on naturalness."[17] Another source of Santayana's
philosophy was the historical spirit of the nineteenth century. "There was
one lesson, which I was readier to learn...from the general temper of that
age well represented for me by the Revue des Deux Mondes (which I
habitually read from cover to cover) and by the works of Paine and of Mat-
thew Arnold — I refer to the historical spirit of the nineteenth century, and
to that splendid panorama of nations and religions, literatures and arts,
which it unrolled before the imagination. These picturesque vistas into the
past came to fill in circumstantially that geographical and moral vastness to
which my imagination was already accustomed."[18]

Santayana's own philosophy may be related to these expressed interests.
His belief in nature determining what is natural, along with the importance
of nature is at the base of his aesthetic and moral theories. His first book,
The Sense of Beauty argues in part that the beauty of material found in nature is the foundation of all higher beauty and only through the imagination
is higher beauty possible. The recognition of the vastness of human imagination was primary for Santayana throughout his philosophy. His work
The Life of Reason (in his own words),"...was intended to be a summary
history of the human imagination, expressly distinguishing those phases of
it which showed what Herbert Spencer called an adjustment of inner to
outer relations; in other words, an adaption of fancy and habit to material
facts and opportunities."[19] In his later philosophy he turned to epist-
emological and ontological questions which are raised by recognizing that,
(for him) all human knowledge, being arrived at through the imagination,
is based on symbolic representation of objects in the material world. This
being due to the fact that symbols are the "raw material" of the imagination.

Santayana said of his work, "My philosophy is not an academic opinion
adopted because tendencies seemed at any moment to favor it...I ask myself only what are the fundamental presuppositions that I cannot live
without making. And I find they are summed up in the word

materialism.''[20] Santayana at times calls his philosophy materialism, at others, naturalism. What he means by these terms is that he believes that matter is the only substance, power, or agency in the universe. His belief in materialism was not in exclusion of a belief in spiritual values. As he said, ''The recognition of the material world and of the conditions of existence in it merely enlightens the spirit concerning the source of its troubles and the means to its happiness or deliverance...[21]

Santayana's philosophy attempts to explore what he calls the ''life of reason'' and how it might lead to happiness or deliverance. Bertrand Russell noted this aspect of Santayana's work, ''Santayana's philosophy is at once ethical and naturalistic. He views man as an animal plunged into a given environment and endowed with a variety of tastes and impulses. 'Reason' consists in taking account of our whole nature and also of our environment as revealed by science and endeavoring to produce the greatest attainable harmony both inwardly and outwardly.''[22] To extend somewhat Russell's view, man is an animal who is in a flux of experience. From the various sense organs, he receives a constant flow of data. The data is interpreted and given meaning by reason which acts to produce the greatest possible accord between the variety of desires and impulses in man. Reason combines the insights of past experience and knowledge of the conditions of existence in the material world with the creativity of the imagination to produce harmony and accord in the life and institutions of man. The five volumes which constitute *The Life of Reason* indicate the areas in which Santayana saw reason at work - in common sense, in society, in religion, in art, and in science.

In the book, *Scepticism and Animal Faith,* he outlines his epistemology. He believed that the existence of objects in the exterior world could never be proved arguing that we do not have any knowledge of the substance of the exterior world even if it does exist. It must be understood that he means knowledge based on an argument leading to a conclusion which we are said to know. All at best we have is knowledge of our mental constructions which we place upon the information which arrives in our brain. This is a radical sceptism in which at the same time is realized that to continue living we must believe in and have knowledge of the exterior world. This belief he argues is not based on any deductive reasoning but rather on animal faith. Santayana points out, ''My dogmatism asserts that, in an observable biological sense, knowledge is possible, and on the same biological grounds, that knowledge is relative.''[23] My scepticism remains merely the confession that faith is faith without any rebellion against the physical necessity of believing.''[24] His scepticism and faith are complementary. At first, this may seem to conflict with his naturalism but in fact it does not. Santayana is discussing what can be known, not his particular beliefs about the world.

The "mental constructions" made reference to above were called essences by Santayana. Essences are that which our minds glean from the exterior world through the mediating senses and other parts of the nervous system. That which we think about, reflect upon..., is not part of the material world, though thought itself is a product of material organization. Essences are the objects of thought, symbolically representing that if anything to which they refer. Santayana said of them, "It (the totality of essences) is simply the unwritten catalogue, prosaic and infinite of all the characters possessed by such things as happen to exist, together with the characters which all different things would possess if they existed. It is the sum of mentionable objects, of terms about which something might be said."[25]

The book, *Scepticism and Animal Faith* was followed by a four volume work *The Realms of Being*. The latter completed Santayana's system of philosophy. The four volumes are *The Realm of Essence, The Realm of Matter, The Realm of Truth* and *The Realm of Spirit*. H.E. Van Wesep had said of this work, "In the *Realms* we get a well sketched out ontology, or Science of Being, a real addition to what went before in all of American philosophy and a real addition also to Santayana's own *Life of Reason*." In these books Santayana distinguishes the different types of reality that he encounters. There is no hierachy in the various realms, each is as real as the others.

The influence of Santayana's work on American philosophy has been limited. His work is discussed in all of the major histories of American philosophy and noted as being extremely important but his works are not that widely read. Bertand Russell wrote over fifty years ago, "Mr. Santayana is a philosopher whose importance has not been adequately recognized. Professors pass him by because he does not flatter the prejudices of our age."[26] Whether or not this will change is a speculative question, though his work definitely merits study.

As early as 1922 Santayana had tried his fortunes as a prose writer, with the publications of his *Soliloquies in England*. He did have to wait until he was seventy two years old to become famous as a novelist, with the publication of his only novel, *The Last Puritan*. This work became a book-of-the-month selection and a bestseller. Its author call it "a memoir in the form of a novel." To a certain extent it is a discussion of United States manners customs, as well as an application of Santayana's philosophy. Its hero is struggling with a terrible problem, trying to save his soul. To him puritanism did not mean priggishness or assertion. He plays football, tries to develop a love relationship, fights in a war although he ignores what he is fighting for. Perhaps the overall message of the novel is that puritanism does not have anything to do with purity. It is neither timidity, nor fanaticism, nor calculated hardness. It is a deep and speculative thing, "hatred of all shame, scorn of all mummeries, a bitter merciless pleasure in the hard facts."[27]

Some critics feel that *The Last Puritan* is "a book worth attacking, worth defending, worth digesting."[28] Others feel that the novel has no plot, characters, dialogue, nor climax, and, it is, therefore, not a true novel. Ellen Glasgow recommends it to all those who prefer to think while they read, who relish a deep inward irony, who are interested more in the drama of ideas than in the play of conditional reflexes."[29]

George Santayana spent the last twenty nine years of his life in Rome. By that time all his closest friends and relatives had died. Although he loved to show, specially to young people, the sights of Rome, he lived a lonely, isolated life full of war-time hardships, such as lacking warmth and meat during entire winters. Yet, this remarkable man maintained an excellent health until the fifties, when he became progressively feeble, and, eventually totally blind.

He loved Spain until the very end. Curiously enough, he was returning from renewing his Spanish passport when he fell ill with the malady that was to kill him. His fame as a philosopher and literary figure, as well as that of an inspiring teacher of great minds still lingers on. Few persons of Hispanic origin have done so much for American philosophy and letters as this genuine son of Spain, and thus, he fully deserves the place he occupies in the annals of American history.

Notes

1."Santayana (George) *Current Biography. Who's News and Why* (New York: H. W. Wilson Co., 1944) p. 590.

2. Ibid.

3. J.M. Alonso Gamo, *Un español en el mundo Santayana* (Madrid: Ediciones Cultura Hispanica, 1966) p. 53.

4. *The Letters of George Santayana*, edited by Daniel Cory (New York: Charles Scriber's Sons, 1955) pp. 186-187.

5. Ibid., p. 32.

6. Ralph Barton Perry, *The Thought and Character of William James* (Boston; Little, Brown, and Company, 1935) pp. 640-641.

7. *Un español en el mundo*, p. 39.

8. Ibid., p. 41.

9. Ibid., p. 42.

10. *The Letters of George Santayana*, pp. 292-293.

11. *Un español en el mundo*, p. 325.

12. *Current Biography*, p. 591.

13. Ibid., 591.

14. Ibid.

15. George Santayana, "A General Confession" in Paul A. Schilpple *The Philosophy of George Santayana* (New York: Tudor Publishing Company, 1951) p. 8.

16. Richard Butler, *The Mind of Santayana* (Chicago: Henry Regnery Co., 1955) p. 39.

17. George Santayana, *Persons and Places* (New York: Charles Scriber's Sons, 1944) p. 239.

18. "A General Confession." loc. cit., p. 9.

19. George Santayana "A Brief History of My Opinions" in *The Philosophy of Santayana*, edited by Irwin Edman (New York: Charles Scriber's Sons, 1953) p. 12.

20. *The Philosophy of George Santayana*, loc. cit., p. 505.

21. "A General Confession" loc. cit., p. 11.

22. Bertrand Russell, "A Synthetic Mind", in *Dial* v. 74, 1923, p. 617.

23. *The Philosophy of George Santayana*, loc. cit., p. 515.

24. Ibid, p. 516.

25. George Santayana, *Scepticism and Animal Faith* (New York: Charles Scriber's Sons, 1923) p. 77.

26. "A Synthetic Mind", loc. cit., p. 615.

27. *Current Biography*, loc. cit., p. 593.

28. Ibid.

29. Ibid.

SPAIN — UNITED STATES
HISTORICAL PARALLELISM AND MUTUAL INFLUENCE
Juan García

On this bicentennial celebration I have chosen, as my subject, the history of two great nations that shaped the world in completely different ways. And this is understandable since they reflect two different cultures and civilizations and two different peoples.

At a time when the United States did not exist, Spain was such a big empire that the sun never set on its territory.

Today when Spain has become no bigger than Texas, the United States is the strongest military power on earth and the biggest economic empire of the non-communist world.

Suffice it to say that the United States produce twice as much as Europe, and this figure is about one third of the production of the whole world. Yet the United States' surface is only 7% of the world and it has only 6% of the world's population.

What were the aims and ideals behind these two imperialistic conceptions?

The discovery of America by Spain was the greatest event of the XV and XVI centuries. Its implications and repercussions were tremendous. It opened up new problems of geography, unknown peoples, religions, politics, and fed the imagination of Europeans with dreams of adventure.

This impact on European thinking was, nevertheless, surpassed by the impact on the natives of America who had never seen a gun or the combination horse-man-gun irresistible in battle.

Even though the Spaniards' sense of Catholic mission seemed to justify everything, the Indians always saw them as people who came to shatter their past and their religion as well as their life and customs.

In spite of the resistance, the conquest was surprisingly fast and easy. And the influence of Spanish colonization on South America was so strong that still today, in spite of the great effort in the search for national identity, people find themselves prisoners of the Spanish tradition: its structure, society, language, religion and, worst of all, the military cast with its "pronunciamientos".

Although the first English settlers in North America are considered to be the 102 Presbyterian Pilgrims brought from England by the "Mayflower" in 1620, the first English settlement was established May 24th, 1607 in S.E. Virginia by the London Company. The name given to this settlement was Jamestown, in honor of the reigning English monarch, James I. This, in spite of the fact that the Colonists were dissidents escaping his tyranny.

Before landing, the "Mayflower" pilgrims reached an agreement on the temporary government of the colony, called the "Mayflower Compact". This document was designed to enable the settlers to work together. The covenant set up the "Mayflower" pilgrims into a "...civil Body Politick which would frame just and equal laws and provide for the general good of the colony".

All later governments of the colony contributed to develop the "Compact".

One century earlier, in 1513, Juan Ponce de León landed a little north of what it is today Saint Augustine, Florida, which is the oldest city in the United States.

One of the first things Ponce de León tried to secure was the governorship of Florida. He went back to Spain where the King commissioned him to conquer and colonize the "Isle of Florida". At that time Ponce thought it was an island. Thus he returned with soldiers and missionaries and claimed Florida for Spain, but, to his surprise, the Indians assaulted his camp, killed nearly all his soldiers and he, with a bad arrow wound, fled to Cuba where shortly afterwards died.

Despite Ponce de León's failure, Francisco de Garay tried twice without success to establish new settlements. And so did Lucas Vázquez de Ayllon, Pánfilo Narvaez and Hernando de Soto whose death led to the abandonment of Florida.

Finally, in 1565, Pedro Mendoza de Avilés landed with 500 soldiers, artillery, a few friars and some settlers, and solemnly took possession of Florida in the King's name.

There is no doubt that the Spanish enterprise was colossal. The motives for it were many: geographical discovery and conquest; the vision of extending the confines of the earth; the propagation of the Catholic faith and the evangelization of the natives; the gold and silver "stocked" in ever-elusive Eldorado and "Seven Cities of Gold". And above all, the glory which great men always dream.

But Florida, California, New Mexico, Arizona and Texas were not Peru, and the Spanish dreams became a never ending hardship. Yet what remained of that epic adventure was the faith and the spirit of Christianization and civilization sown by the Jesuits and Franciscans. Thus, still today, traveling from San Francisco to San Diego is like reciting a litany of the Saints. It could be said that the King's Highway (El Camino Real) was paved with the names of the Saints.

Obviously the "Conquistadores" were adventurous and strong minded men born for action. They were soldiers and as such they were accused of being cruel in spite of the fact that they were always accompanied by friars. One of them, the Dominican Father Bartolomé de las Casas, wrote a book "Brevísma relación de la destrucción de las Indias" in which many inhuman atrocities are mentioned.

Since the Spaniards came to Texas, the general understanding is that Texas is a Spanish name. It actually came from the Assinai Indians who said in their language that they were "texia", that is to say "friends". Perhaps we could venture to say that this is also the origin of the characteristic Texans' friendliness.

While the first goal of the Spaniards was to establish forts and missions conquering the land and the souls by the sword and the cross, the British founded trading posts, mainly in Virginia, and two companies were floated to colonize the Atlantic coast of North America. One was set up in London and the other in Plymouth.

The "Mayflower" settlement of 102 puritan refugees grew rapidly. Ten years later it had 12,000 colonizers.

The pilgrims spread their influence by founding Boston in 1630. There John Winthrop established the main colony of the "Massachusetts Bay Company". The colony of Connecticut was founded in 1639, and Maine and New Hampshire in 1650.

From the start, Boston was a center of American Puritanism contributing to a vigorous intellectual life. The Boston Public Latin School opened in 1635. Harvard University was founded in 1636 (only six years after the foundation of Boston and 16 years after arrival of the "Mayflower"). A public library was founded in 1653.

Thus, enlightenment, as well as freedom, justice and well-being were the goals.

By the Treaty of Paris, in 1763, Spain obtained part of French Louisiana, with New Orleans, but lost Florida which went to Britain. But twenty years later, in 1783, Spain recovered it again by the Treaty of Versailles. At this time, which was the peak of Spanish domination, North America was divided into two almost equal areas, the Spanish and the British, separated by the Mississippi.

From the time when Ponce de León discovered Florida to the moment when Spain recovered it from the British, 270 years had passed.

Finally, in 1819, Florida was sold to the United States for $5 million. The official U.S. occupation took place in 1821, and in 1845, Florida was admitted as the 27th state of the Union.

Texas declared its independence March 2, 1836, and became the 28th state of the Union in 1845.

California was admitted as the 31st state of the Union in 1850. And New Mexico and Arizona as the 47th and 48th states in 1912.

We mention these states because of the Spanish influence on them.

Today little of the Spanish conquest is remembered, yet many things speak of Spain: The names of the cities, the rivers, the mountains, the churches and the family and Christian names of the people. The impact of Spanish civilization always remains.

As for intellectual life, Dr. Scholes declares: "In reality the friars were the only men of erudition in the community where, equally in daily conversation or in the pulpit, the people heard the highest standard of speech." But this, important as it was at that moment, left no trace or influence in the field of higher education, while the Puritans had founded Harvard University which became one of the great universities of the world.

Because of the time limitations, it is not my intention to talk extensively about the American Revolution, yet some considerations are pertinent in the present context.

Even though the French revolution exercised a greater influence upon subsequent political and social changes, the American revolution was as important, if not more so, as an experiment in affecting miscellaneous people, tongues and beliefs through the melting-pot of new institutions. The two and a half million people who achieved their independence in the eighteenth century became, in such a short time, the richest and the most powerful country in the world. This is the best proof of the tremendous success of their experiment, not only because they established a new nation, but because they made inherent in that nation a new conception of republican-democratic institutions with far reaching repercussions in a world dominated by imperialistic kings.

Much has been written about the reasons for revolt against England. Generally the main reason given is "the repeated injuries and usurpations all having in direct object, the establishment of an absolute tyranny over these States". But the research of the last 50 years leads to the conclusion that the real reasons were rather of an economic nature and a clash of interests, as the "Boston tea party" shows. This led in time to the five laws called by the patriots the "intolerable acts", such as the "Stamp Act" which was a harsh denial of economic freedom. All this resulted in the incompatibility of political principles and practices.

At the bottom of the problem lay two basic reasons for resentment and revolt: Britain established the Colonies in order to benefit from them; but the English colonists, who went out to settle in a new land, carried with them their rights of citizenship and they refused to be placed in a position of inferiority. Besides, the ideals of these first settlers were conflictive in

England, so they came to America to create their own system.

This mental attitude worked, consciously or unconsciously, toward their own independence. Thus the revolution was the culminating point of an evolution leading inevitably to self-government.

The first shots of the revolution, which is also called American War of Independence, were exchanged on the morning of April 19, 1775, and the war lasted till 1783.

The point of no return was reached on July 2, 1776, when the Congress adopted the resolution that "These United Colonies are, and, of right, ought to be free and independent States" and "They are absolved from all allegiances to the British Crown".

This was the Declaration of Independence which took place on July 2, not on July 4.

The purpose of the "Declaration" adopted July 4 was to proclaim to the world the reasons for the "Resolution" and seek its support by supplying a legal justification for the revolution. Among these justifications were that "all men are endowed by their Creator with certain unalienable Rights" including "Life, liberty and the pursuit of happiness". And "whenever a form of government becomes destructive of these ends, it is the right of the people to alter or abolish it..."

This "Declaration" established two revolutionist principles:
1) That revolution can be a just cause.
2) That the overthrow of a tyranny, by an oppressed people, is a legal and noble right.

The "Declaration of Independence" was drafted by Jefferson. Modifications came, mainly, from the more conservative John Adams. The rest of the members, nominated by the Congress, were Benjamin Franklin, Roger Sherman and Robert R. Livingston.

Even though the "Declaration" was the work of these men, their ideas went back to the first settlers. In December 1641, the Massachusets Colony adopted "The Body of Liberties" which contained the main principles which we enjoy today, as we can see by the following:

— Freedom of speech and publication at any town meeting
— Freedom to leave the colony at any time
— Right of the people to elect those who will govern them
— Equal justice under the law for citizens and foreigners
— No punishment except by an express law
— Right to trial by jury
— Prohibition of use of torture and the hated inquisitional oath forcing an accused or any other person testify to things that might incriminate him.

The impact of the "Declaration" on the whole world was so great that its ideals were adopted in almost all declarations of principles and constitutions thereafter.

Even the draft of the famous "Declaration des droits de l'homme" of the French revolution, was submitted to Jefferson (then American ambassador in France) for correction and advice. And doubtless, many of the principles, which became universal, were inspired by the American "Declaration".

But this does not mean that everything was wonderful in the New America. A black spot was disturbing time and again the liberal mind. It was, and still is, the racial problem, which began with slavery.

In 1774, before the war of independence, Jefferson wrote that "the abolition of slavery was the great object of desire in the Colonies" and that "the King was wrong in encouraging the slave trade". The King was wrong, but the Colonies were equally at fault because, when two years later Jefferson included the abolition of slavery in the first draft of the "Delcaration of Independence", that paragraph was stricken.

The elimination of slavery was long and difficult. Dred Scott, a negro, asked the Supreme Court for his freedom. The Court in March 6, 1857, denied his freedom because, first: "Negros, by reason of their inferior status when the Constitution was adopted, could not be citizens of the United States". Second: "Because the Missouri Act — in which Scott based his claim — was unconstitutional, since Congress had no power to exclude slavery from the Territories".

On January 1, 1863, during the civil war, Abraham Lincoln issued the "Emancipation Proclamation" by which almost 3,500,000 slaves were freed.

And, two years later, the Thirteenth Amendment to the Constitution, outlawed the Scott judicial decision with this provision: "Neither slavery nor unvoluntary servitude, except as a punishment for crimes whereof the party shall have been duly convicted, shall exist within the United States, or any place subject to their jurisdiction".

On July 28, 1868, the Fourteenth Amendment was added to the Constitution with these reforms:

1) "All persons born or naturalized in the United States are citizens of the U. S. wherein they reside. Thus the sons and daughters of the immigrants, as well as the Negro slaves born here, become citizens".

2) "The States are forbidden from:
   - Abridging the privileges or immunities of citizens of the United States.
   - Depriving any person of life, liberty or property without due process of law.
   - Denying any person equal protection of the laws.

On March 30, 1870, the Fifteenth Amendment completed the basic rights with this declaration: "The right of citizens of the United States to vote shall not be denied or abridged by the United States or any other State on account of race, color, or previous condition of servitude".

But even though the 14th Amendment provided that "All persons born in the United States were citizens" the Supreme Court in 1894 held that American Indians were not included. It took an Act of Congress in 1924 to make them citizens.

Since some difficulties persisted, in 1952, the McCarran-Walter Act provided: "The right of a person to become a naturalized citizen of the United States shall not be denied or abridged because of race".

It is interesting to note that although the Spanish colonies in South America had less liberty, inferior economic conditions and much less self-rule, it took them three centuries to revolt, while it took half that time for the British colonies to do so.

Although Spain gave some assistance to the patriots and entered the war against England in June 1779 (one year later than France), Spanish help was not of great importance to the United States, while French supplies, money and men were a decisive contribution. Besides, Spain entered the war against Great Britain because such was the agreement with France by the Treaty of Aranjuez of April 1779. But Spain neither became the ally of the United States — as France did — nor agreed to recognize them. In fact Spain offered such a recognition only at the end of the war.

After the Revolution, the Civil War, in 1861-1865, between Northern and Southern States was the most important factor leading to the greatness of this country.

Since all wars are evil, a peaceful solution of the differences perhaps would have been better; but then the right solution would not have been possible without agreeing to the perpetuation of slavery, which was intolerable, or the split of the Union, which was unacceptable, because of the weakening of the whole nation and the destruction of the Union.

Thus, however great the loss of life, property and social organization which had taken two centuries to build, the issues for which the war was fought were settled: "Indissolubility of the Union, Government of the people, by the people, for the people and the abolition of slavery".

Even though the war began with the shelling of Fort Sumter by the Confederates, the Civil War had really begun some years before, when as a result of the Industrial Revolution, manufacturing developed in the North. The South was limited to an agricultural society which, without a protectionist policy from the North and the acceptance of slavery on which its economic structure was based, would have collapsed, or, at least, such was the fear.

The reasons for revolt were not only economic, but also of an idealistic character. The South deviated from the principles on which the Union was based in order to perpetuate slavery (which had no room in the Northern States) at the price of secession and the setting up of a nation of its own.

From an economic point of view, the demand for cotton and cotton production made the slave great value because of the belief that "without slavery there could be no cotton". Thus, the South was convinced that a general emancipation would totally destroy the cotton industry, because the negroes would not work. As Reed (a Southener) put it: "The Slaves, regarded as property, were the most desirable investment open to the generality of people that has ever been known ... Their labor was richly remunerative, their market value was constantly rising. They were everywhere more easily convertible into money than the best securities".

All this and the divergence of constitutional views based on self-interest, influenced the political situation leading to secession and war.

The South did not realize that a great moral change had taken place not only in the North, but also in the rest of the world where a feeling of brotherhood totally rejected slavery. The only reason the South gave for slavery was that "a superior race had a right to enslave an inferior one". To this way of thinking, Jefferson answered with a letter to Henri Gregoire (a negro) in 1809: "Whatever be the blacks' degree of talent, it is no measure of their rights. Because Sir Issac Newton was superior to others in understanding, he was not therefore lord of the person or property of others".

The South was also wrong in its fears that the emancipation would destroy the cotton industry. In less than 40 years, from the beginning of the Civil War, the cotton crop was more than doubled under free labor.

Never before, or after, has a war been fought with more chivalry, charity and generosity.

Almost in no way can this war be compared with the last Spanish Civil War, particularly in the way it ended. In America the winners were the liberators of slavery, the defenders of freedom, democracy and equal rights. The victory of the Union saved its integrity and "The government of the people, by the people, for the people".

What a magnanimous and political foresight was that of Abraham Lincoln. This great man said to the Cabinet, close to the end of the war: "I hope there will be no persecution, no bloody work after the war is over ... We must extinguish our resentment if we expect peace".

Perhaps nothing reflects the generosity of Americans more than the end of the war. On January 31, 1865, under the cover of a flag of truce, three Confederate peace commissioners, headed by Vice President Alexander H. Stephens, passed through the Federal lines to confer with President Lincoln on board of a warship in Hampton Roads. Lincoln told them they could write their own terms, provided they agreed to rejoining an indissoluble Union and abolish slavery. The conference ended without agreement and the war went on.

But on April 9, after Lee had lost 6,266 men, killed or wounded, 13,769 prisoners, and thousands more had deserted, Lee capitulated to Ulysses S. Grant at Appomattox.

Even at the moment of capitulation, the personality and character of the two dignataries summed up in themselves, the North and the South in their character and ideals, in their democracy and aristocracy, in their lords and their people, in their future and their past.

"At the interview between the two leaders (we quote from J.K. Hosmer) Lee appeared in a new and handsome uniform, complete to the elegant sword at his side. No finer type of manly grace and dignity can be imagined than the Confederate leader as he stepped down that day from his eminent position. Grant, on the other hand, not anticipating the meeting, was in the blouse of a private soldier, dusty from riding. His face was haggard from illness which he had suffered during the preceding night. The two men met courteously, exchanging reminiscences of experiences which they had shared in the old army. At last Grant wrote out his terms — arms to be surrendered, the Army of Northern Virginia to be paroled until exchanged, the officers to retain their side-arms and private horses; after a pause, the "horse clause" was extended to include each private soldier claiming to own a horse or a mule, Grant conceiving that as "small farmers", which most of them were, the animals would be needed "to put in the crop". This concession Lee believed "would have a happy effect".

This generosity was appreciated by the Southern Army as we can see by Forrest's farewell circular to his men: "The terms upon which you were surrendered manifest a spirit of magnanimity and liberality on the part of the Federal authorities which should be met on our part by a faithful compliance with all the stipulations and conditions therein ..."

Thus, the war ended on a note of national reconciliation and reunification, displaying the mutual respect of the soldiers on both sides, and one of the finest gestures of a victorious army.

But the real glory of this magnanimous ending goes to the greatest American who ever lived; Abraham Lincoln who, with patience, devotion, judgment and resolution, avoided the split of the country and preserved the Union which has become the great country it is today.

Following the historical parallelism, or rather deviation, let us see the differences between the American and the Spanish Civil War of 1936-1939.

The reasons given for the Spanish revolt were: political turmoil, strikes, burning of churches and the killing of 269 persons during the five years of republican regime.

In order to evaluate these reasons let us see how Americans, reacted before similar events.

It is true that some churches were burned in Spain, but it is also true that, mainly in the South, churches were bombed and burned. In Los Angeles, Detroit, Washington and other cities entire neighborhoods were burned. But not a single American thought that a civil war could be the solution to these extreme reactions.

The majority of the 269 killings in Spain were the result of police action in order to repress revolutionist strikes. A very few were political assasinations like the one, by the fascists, of lieutenant Castillo which provoked the revenge of his fellow police officers who killed Calvo Sotelo, a leader of the political right. But here, in America, President John Kennedy, his brother Robert Kennedy, Martin Luther King and many civil rights leaders were also assasinated, without crossing the mind of any American to engage in civil war.

Political turmoil and strikes were other reasons given, but Americans know something about that also, (political unrest during the war in Vietnam, reaction to the Martin Luther King assasination). Yet nobody thought that revolt against the Government was the way to stop these wrongs.

So how can one justify in Spain what is injustifiable in the United States?

Moreover, on the 10th of August 1932, the same military forces under the leadership of general Sanjurjo (Franco became the leader when Sansurjo died) revolted, without the reasons mentioned above, but its uprising failed, among other things because Hitler's Germany and Mussolini's Italy did not intervene in that occasion.

I believe that the real reason both in 1932 and in 1936 was that when the Republic was proclaimed in 1931, the Army had 16 incomplete divisions which required only 80 generals and colonels, and yet the Army had on its payroll 800 generals and 26,000 officers. Since Spain did not need such an Army, the Republic reduced it to 8 divisions with 7,600 officers, including generals.

The Government gave an alternative to the remaining 19,200 officers: either to enter the reserve or to retire, receiving in both cases, full payment for the rest of their lives. But the Army never bought this.

The Catholic Church, which called the revolt a "Crusade", resented the Republican regime because, with the Monarchy, it enjoyed the privilege of being the State religion and receiving a subvention, while the Republic cut the subvention and separated the Church from the State, as is the case in the United States.

As for the aristocracy and the landlords, they were also against the Republic because the latter initiated a rather conservative agrarian reform.

Thus, the conspiracy against the Republic never ceased because the Army, the Church and the Aristocracy, the main forces in Spain, could not accept "the Government of the people, by the people, for the people".

Besides, the Army never accepted a government unless it was of its liking. Suffice it to say that during the reign of Isabella the Second, there had been no less than 18 "Pronunciamientos" (coups d' état). An average of one every 23 months. So in 35 years the Army saved the country (as they used to say) 18 times from ... the army.

The civil war, as all wars are, was hell, but the worst part of it did not take place at the front lines, but in the rear, in the cities where in the middle of the night men and women were pulled from their beds and shot in the street; others were killed by firing squads or condemned to 20 or 30 years in jail. Why? Because they were reds or blues, democrats or fascists, catholics or freemasons. Often, simply because they voted for the right or for the left.

I know that this must be shocking to Americans who, as I said before during the civil war did not shoot, persecute or jail any single civilian.

But, alas!, this was not the only way it happened in Spain. Worst still, it continued after the end of the war.

Count Ciano, Mussolini's son-in-law, visiting Spain four months after the end of the war reported 200,000 persons in prison, with "trials going on every day at a speed which I would almost call summary . . . There is still a great number of shootings. In Madrid alone, between 200 and 250 *a day*. In Barcelona 150. In Seville 80."

Hugh Thomas, a British historian considered the best expert on this subject, gives 241,000 people in jail three years after the end of the war. More than one million went to prison or concentration camps. Half a million fled the country.

Gabriel Jackson, of the University of California, who has written a few books on this subject, says that 200,000 death sentences were handed down by the Nationalists and as many people assasinated or executed during the heat of the war.

The figure agreed upon by almost all historians is that the number of persons killed behind the lines was, at least, double the number of people killed in the front, which is calculated over 600,000.

Now it will be better understood why I praised so highly Lincoln's magnanimity and compassion, since not a single person was shot or put in jail.

As a Spaniard I realize better than Americans, how much suffering, misery and hate was spared to your fellow countrymen who so gallantly fought in that civil war and who, once it was over, went back to their homes, their families, their fields and their farms to rebuild the country and to heal the wounds.

Thus 40 years later, under the presidence of Theodore Roosevelt, the United States became a great power with great influence in all America and in Europe.

Forty years after the Spanish civil war, the forces which revolted against democracy are busy demolishing everything they fought for and kept by force and repression, in order to go back to democracy. The transformation which is taking place today in Spain is not coming from the left, which has no power at all, but from the right, from Franco's ministers, ambassadors and high officials.

So, if Spain is going back to the point of departure in 1936 what good did the civil war do? What is the meaning of the thousands and thousands of killings?

Perhaps the best answer is another question: What would one say of the frightening crimes of the Spanish Inquisition — perpetrated in the name of God — if right and freedom prevailed?

I guess this is the way liberty has to be won in Spain while Americans take it for granted because 200 years ago their country was born free and they have kept it that way.

UNITED STATES — LATIN AMERICAN ECONOMIC RELATIONS: A BICENTENNIAL OVERVIEW

Louis J. Rodríguez

It is fitting that in this year of the United States Bicentennial attention should be directed to Latin American-United States economic relations. There is a long history of cooperation as well as conflict in the economic exchange between these two regions. The objective of this paper is to present an overall view of economic affairs between these two areas. Specifically, the procedure will be to: (1) look at the past, (2) examine recent United States-Latin American economic relations, (3) analyze Latin America's economic dilemma, and (4) consider possible future developments. This effort is primarily intended as an overview for those who have a general interest in United States-Latin American economic relations.

Historical Evolution

Restrictive policies on the part of Spain and Portugal resulted in the economic stagnation of the colonial domains of these two nations. When Napoleon occupied the Iberian Peninsula in the early part of the 19th century, colonial ties with the two European nations were weakened and subsequently severed. England, because of her lead in the industrial revolution, took the initiative in instituting a system of free trade. The Latin nations' economic activities were complimentary to her own and America as a whole functioned under this system until the end of the First World War. Latin American nations were expected to participate as exporters of raw materials and importers of manufactured goods and capital both physical and financial in nature.

Rapid economic growth took place in several Latin American nations based on export activity. By the end of the eighteen hundreds Latin America's portion of world trade was close to that of the United States and in 1890 Latin America's share of world exports reached eight percent. Foreign investments during 1875-1913 permitted a big increase in Latin America's trade and in general assisted the maintaining of a favorable balance of trade. Foreign exchange resources needed to repay the dividends on foreign investments were provided by export earnings generated by the investment itself. Economic contacts between Latin America and Europe led to considerable immigration from European nations to Latin America, particularly emanating from Spain, Portugal, and Italy. By the end of 1913 the peak of Latin American economic relations with Europe had been reached. Of the Region's export trade 65 percent was directed toward Europe and three-fourths of all investments in Latin America at the start of World War I were of European origin. The year 1914 marked the beginning of Latin America's economic shift from economic dependence on Europe to dependence on the United States.[2]

With the conclusion of World War I Latin America's economic relations with the United States became more important than those with Europe. The United States had been a developing nation during most of the 19th century, and thus was a net importer of capital. At the end of World War I the position of the United States in this respect changed. The rapidly expanding industrial empire of the United States showed increasing interest in foreign markets and external sources on mineral and tropical food products. United States investments in Latin America increased from $300 million in 1897 to $2.4 billion in 1929. The latter figure accounted for 40 percent of all external investment sources in Latin America.[3] The Great Depression played havoc with foreign investments. A significant number of German interests were expropriated and Latin America nationalized many of the English and French investments, paticularly in railroad and public service firms.

Europe and Japan were left in economic shambles at the conclusion of World War II and the United States loomed as the only major exporter of capital in the Western World. World War II weakened Latin America's trade with Europe. In 1938 imports from the United States accounted for 40 percent of all Latin American exports, and by the end of World War II the United States was responsible for over half of all Latin America's foreign trade.[4] Part of the increased economic exchange between the United States and Latin America was the result of President Franklin D. Roosevelt's Good Neighbor Policy. Trade agreements were signed and various Latin nations were provided credits through the Export-Import Bank. The inter-American system was further strengthened in 1948 with the drawing up of the Charter of the Organization of American States. President Harry Truman's "Point Four" program provided technical and financial assistance. In 1958, in response to Latin-American requests, the United States established the Inter-American Development Bank to support economic and social development projects in Latin America.

Since 1950 there has been a constant decline in Latin America's share of world trade. Immediately before and after World War II, Latin America's share of world export trade was about 10 percent. This percentage declined continuously and in 1972 exports from Latin America represented less than five percent of world exports. Thus, in 1972, Latin America was exporting

$16 billion dollars worth of services whereas if the 1950 ratio had been maintained, it would have been $30 billion.

The increase in international trade in the post World War II period was predominately in manufactured goods. Europe and Japan initiated industries in which the United States had low productivity. These were the results of both Europe and Japan being in better positions to bring about efficiencies in labor intensive economic activities. It became apparent that internationally, economies were being realigned on the basis of industrial productivity abilities results rather than on natural resources. Generally, Latin America continued primarily to export commodities and this resulted in a reduction in its share of international trade. The decline has been worldwide for Latin America. However, there have been changes in the direction of Latin American exports. At the beginning of the 1950s the United States was responsible for approximately 60 percent of the value of Latin American exports to industrialized nations. By 1970, while the United States was still the area's biggest customer, its share had declined to 42 percent. The Cuban development explains part of this, but by no means the major portion. *The point is that these previously enumerated changes were not the result of any intended plan for a special trade policy on the part of Latin America, but the result of the post World War II changes in the pattern of trade.*

Similar patterns to those that were occuring in trade were taking place in the area of financial exchange. In 1970 the United States was still Latin America's largest source of foreign private investments, accounting for approximately 60 percent of the total. However, European and Japanese investments were moving into Latin America at a faster rate than those from the United States. As a result of the United States' protection of industry, in 1950 approximately 40 percent of all total investment in Latin America was in the manufacturing sector compared with seven percent in 1914. Starting in 1955 private foreign investments in Latin America were supplemented by private and public external loans and credits. This enabled Latin America to purchase larger volumes of capital goods and industrial items than would have been possible if funds had to be obtained soley from export revenues. During 1961 many of these bilateral public sector financial flows from the United States were channeled through the Alliance for Progress.

Contrary to some popular beliefs, the extent of external investments in Latin America since 1914 has not been particularly impressive. In 1914 there were $8.5 billion of investments. If this figure had been reconverted into 1970 values, it would have equaled approximately $25 billion. The actual foreign contributions to Latin America by 1970 were $40 billion. On a per capita basis foreign capital investment in 1914 was twice as large as in

1969.[5] However, while capital flows into Latin America since 1950 have not been particularly large, they have been a major service burden to the Region. Exports have not grown sufficiently to finance the servicing of these investments as well as imports. This has placed a burden on Latin America's limited foreign exchange and has resulted in a substantial debt burden.

Medium and long term public official guaranteed external indebtedness rose from $7 billion in 1960 to $20 billion in 1972 and the yearly servicing of interest and amortization amounted to $2.5 billion. The servicing plus the remittance of profits on these foreign investments and other private sector obligations required approximately 30 percent of Latin American earnings from exports of goods and services yearly. *While some of this burden can be assigned to reverse credit conditions, the amount of grants, and at times excessive profits on investments, the major and inescapable cause is the inability of Latin American exports to compete on the world market.* A larger volume of exports would have provided needed foreign exchange to service these debts. Additionally, if manufactured goods had accounted for a larger share of Latin American exports this would have put the Region in a better trade position.

At the turn of this decade more than 90 percent of Latin America's exports were primary products. The old familiar problems of external market trends, import restrictions in the industrialized world, relatively inelastic demand for many of the food items which have persisted over the years in the trade of primary commodities were and are still operative. The Region is a victim of wide fluctuations in the price of tropical agricultural products such as sugar and coffee because of wide changes in supply conditions. Demand for grains, vegetables, and meats vary because foreign importers purchase quantities to supplement their domestic production which is a variable factor. In the area of minerals some of the markets are controlled by a small number of buyers who are able to influence prices. The business cycle activities in the industrialized areas further introduce some uncertainty and variation in the export picture for Latin America. The demand and prices for Latin American exports are at times affected by internal tax structures in the importing nations. In an effort to break down these external controls and fluctuations exporting nations are beginning to combine in order to bring about greater bargaining strengths. An example of this type of activity is the member nations of the Organization of Petroleum Exporting Countries (OPEC).

Latin America in order to reduce its reliance on primary exports will have to increase the export of manufactured items. In the early 1970s the proportion of manufactured goods in total Latin American exports was less than 10 percent which compared with 20 percent for the developing countries.[6]

Recently, the export of manufactured commodities among the Latin American nations has increased. Brazil has made the greatest advance in the export of manufactured items. However, overall export levels remain low, totaling $269 million in 1960 exports and $1.1 billion in 1969.

The Great Depression taught Latin Americans the need to attempt at all costs to reduce dependence on external markets. In Mexico during 1928-1932 production in constant prices fell by 16 percent and export revenues by 42 percent. Chilean exports declined to a very small percentage of their former level. Imports to Santos, the port serving Sao Paulo, declined from 1.5 million contos in 1928 to 440,000 in 1932. Argentina's exports decreased by 55 percent between 1928 and 1932. These setbacks led to efforts to increase public outlays by issuing money and reducing imports by means of exchange controls, as well as tariffs which provided greater protection for industry and stimulated the production of manufactured goods. This "import substitution" emphasis was further aided by the inability to obtain manufactured goods from traditional sources. These attempts at protection lasted until approximately 1950 when the world markets once again began to have some semblance of normal supply conditions. Industrial gains further supported the idea of import substitution. This approach resulted in attacks upon economists in the developed nations who simplistically emphasized a theory of comparative advantage which delegated Latin America to being primarily an exporter of primary commodities.

The Depression and World War II have not been forgotten. Protection is being depended upon to bring about the increased acceleration of industrial development. The desire of the Latin Americans to reduce dependence on external purchasers of the Region's raw material through import substitution is easy to understand and did bring about some immediate results. Internal demand for manufactured goods which normally had been satisfied through imports was to be met by domestic production. Protection was extended to domestic businessmen to establish manufacturing operations. Foreign capital was getting away from areas that depended on export markets to the more profitable manufacturing operations geared to internal demand. The process also provided considerable amounts of technological know-how and managerial ability.

Agricultural interests have since the turn of the 20th century opposed excessive protection of manufacturing operations. This resulted from the increase in the prices of manufactured goods which was traced to increases in domestic production costs and possible reduction in the ability to compete in world markets. Political groups in Latin America have opposed this approach on the basis of increased prices and the resulting detrimental impact on the people. Protection was defended. strongly by labor groups, by economic nationalism, and by economic ideology. Thus primary goods lost some of their economic importance and political strength. Workers in protected industries who were now the recipients of high wage levels offset negative views of other workers in the labor force.

Protection devices continue to attract intellectual interest. For example, in the early 1960's nominal tariff levels on manufactured goods were 11.5 percent in the United States, 11 percent in the European community, 6.6 percent in Sweden, 16 percent in Japan, 30 percent in Taiwan, 9 percent in Brazil, and 144 percent in Argentina.[7] *This protection did not bear the expected fruit. Industrial development did not expand as rapidly as was hoped and external trade continued to decline. Rather than looking internally for trade policy corrections the culprits of the piece were sought externally. Blame for the inadequacies in the performance of the Latin American economy was geared to international markets which presumably were beyond the control of Latin American governments.*

Latin American Economic Development Dilemma

Latin America as a whole has reached a level of economic performance that locates it somewhere between the advanced industrialized nations and the developing group in Africa and Asia. There have been improvements in Latin America during the past 30 years both in terms of economic advances and social welfare improvements. Latin America's gross national product increase during the last three decades has approximated an annual rate of four percent which is higher than that of most of the industrialized nations with the exception of Japan, West Germany, and Yugoslavia. Commercial agriculture in the Region has been enhanced thus improving nutrition levels. Protein consumption is relatively high in comparison with income, health services have expanded reducing infant mortality, and life expectancy has increased. Communications have been vastly improved, illiteracy has been greatly reduced, water is now much more readily available, and electricity consumption has shown a significant expansion.

Compared to less developed regions, Latin America's perormance in the last three decades is very good. Latin America, however, does not tend to compare itself with underdeveloped nations, but to the advanced industrial areas. Because of this, rather significant economic advances tend to be viewed with dissatisfaction and result in frustration. Politically the far left leans toward revolution as the only way to bring about a higher level of economic development. The moderate middle-of-the-road center feels uneasy in terms of which way to proceed. The right is inclined to the posture that growth has not been adequate enough to relieve social pressures that tend to lead to a destruction of the existing order.

Much of the above indicated dissatisfaction can be traced to the inward oriented economic development policies of Latin American nations. A more external looking approach would have permitted the lower income groups in Latin America to have cheaper economic goods and in greater amounts. Greater emphasis on the exporting of primary materials would have undoubtedly resulted in a smaller indebtedness and dependence on foreign aid. The Region would have had greater bargaining power in the international arena and a larger share of the world's international trade. Economic integration would have been enhanced and thus political unity as well. Many economists feel such an approach would have brought about higher growth rates than have been achieved in Latin America and may have propelled the Region beyond the current semi-development stage. Overall, there have been enough economic forces generated in Latin America so that major breakthroughs in development in the coming decades can be reasonably expected.

Latin America economically stands ahead of other developing areas of the world. The average per capita income in the Region in the early 1970's exceeded $600 which was approximately one-third of the average income of individuals living in industrialized countries. This figure is three times as high as that of other developing nations. There are exceptions to this progress notably in the Northeastern part of Brazil, Upper Peru, the Caribbean, parts of Mexico, and in areas in Central America.[8] Life expectancy is higher than elsewhere in the developing regions. Per capita consumption is 2,000 calories per day, an amount hardly ever approximated by other developing areas. Medical facilities, levels of education, percentage of school age children in schools, and the number of students in higher education institutions per 100,000 population all exceed those in the developing world.

Latin America's level of development tends to approximate nations such as Italy, Greece, and Spain rather than African and Asian countries. In terms of culture, social aspects, and economic organizations, Latin America is closer to the economically developed nations rather than to the developing Third World. The Iberian culture was firmly implanted in the Region. Along with many undesirable feudalistic economic aspects of the Spanish and Portuguese systems there was the positive dimension of the new subject being treated as equals under the law. Ethnic fusion was relatively successfully accomplished in Latin America. During the latter part of the 1800s a large number of immigrants of non-Iberian origin moved into Latin America with a minimum of disturbance. Today, racial problems in Latin America are minimal compared with those in Africa, Asia, and the United States. With the exception of the Mexican Revolution, internal strife has been relatively minor. Thus, in these above mentioned respects Latin America is considerably ahead of the other undeveloped areas of the world.

Latin America has more internal consistency and a history of interaction with the advanced industrial areas of the world than do the majority of African and Asiatic nations. In Africa and Asia development problems are compounded by language differences, religious beliefs and varying ethnic groups. Overpopulation is a dilemma faced by many Asiatic nations which in general does not exist in Latin America. In African countries south of the Sahara national identification is made difficult at times by boundaries that were based on administrative decisions during the colonial period which did not fit the territorial boundaries of tribal or ethnic groups. Thus, in some of these nations there are mutually hostile groups interfering with internal cohesiveness in economic development matters. Latin America has a much larger percentage of its people integrated into market economies than do Africa or Asia. The percentage of wage earners in non-agriculture pursuits in Latin America is higher than those in Asia and Africa. This is an indication of economic activities that are not based on subsistence but result from industrial and commerical organizations. *Thus, a strong case can be made that Latin America as a whole has more in common with the United States, Europe, and Japan than it does with Africa and the majority of Asiatic nations.*

United States — Latin America Relations

United States-Latin America relations are currently undergoing great change and considerable uncertainty. Part of this is a result of the changing role of the United States in the world economy. The United States economic system was shaken when it awoke to the fact that it no longer dominated the world economic scene. This was brought home by deficits in the United States balance of payments, deterioration in the dominant role of the dollar in international trade, and the declining competitive ability of many American products in international markets. Faced with these difficulties, United States economic policy is focused on the effort to expand exports. Coupled with this situation is the difficulty of a rising inflationary level at home. Thus, to overcome the balance of payments deficit problem far more liberal trade agreements were made with Europe, Japan, and other industrialized nations.

The above indicated developments brought about a deterioration of goals, ambitions, and hopes of the Alliance For Progress. The disappointment arose from both Latin America and the United States with the objectives of the Alliance. Latin Americans frequently felt the economic interests of the United States and their region were at odds. Retaliation took the form of directing external relations to industrialized nations other than the

United States. This resulted in suspicion and concern both on the part of the United States and Latin America. Ties were made with advanced industrialized nations other than the United States because the current arrangement within the Americas was too narrow. The opinion was that it would be to the advantage of Latin American nations to expand their economic horizons. Some Latin Americans, however, have been hesitant to destroy past institutional arrangements which gave them a United States orientation. Latin American nationalism is one of the key barriers to harmonious United States relations with its southern neighbors. These manifestations are revealed not only in economic and political realms but also in cultural and intellectual activities.[9]

Post World War II United States policies towards Latin America were to a great degree based on a concern for national self-interest. The Cold War was in full sway and in an effort to thwart communistic expansion the United States entered into a number of alliances and supported this activity with foreign aid. In the years immediately after World War II, United States-Latin American relations were greatly affected by the United States' view that Latin America was less threatened by Cold War aspects than other regions of the globe. Latin America, on the other hand, developed and pursued a policy of morally justifying transfers of resources from developed nations to the Region in order to offset economic pressures brought about by deterioration in Latin American terms of trade. Foreign temporary inflows of capital were viewed as a way to get out of the vicious circle of poverty and launch Latin America into a period of rapid and self-maintained economic growth. By the latter part of the decade of the 1950s considerable amounts of short and medium term external capital had been accumulated by Latin America. These moves were made to force the United States to provide assistance to its Southern Neighbors. To further enhance their cause some Latin Americans did not present a completely accurate picture of their region. They described their areas as being poverty ridden, very much underdeveloped, and with hideous social inequalities.

The revolution in Cuba once again focused American attention on Latin America. The Inter-American Development Bank was created in 1959 with the membership consisting of the United States and 21 Latin American nations. This agency was to serve as a multilateral manager of funds which would come primarily from the United States and assist the economic and social development of Latin America. In 1960 the United States pledged $500 million for social development activities in Latin America and in 1961 the Alliance For Progress was launched. Expectations were high, both in Washington and South America, that significant advances would be made in developing the nations of the South. In the United States comparisons were made between the Alliance for Progress and the Marshall Plan in Europe. The implementation of the Alliance for Progress was basically between the United States officials and individual Latin American nations. In return for aid Latin nations were encouraged to alter and impose new tax structures, make land reforms, and improve health facilities. However, inadequate emphasis was placed on directing these funds to improving the capital base of the Latin nations and not enough attention was given to the expansion of exports from Latin America. This situation resulted in Latin America experiencing a deficit in the balance of payments on its current account in trade with the United States. The deficit in the current account, however, was generally offset by massive transfers of capital into the public sectors of these nations.

Between 1961 and 1970, $11 billion in the form of both medium and long term financing was extended to Latin America by the United States.[10] Part of the difficulty for Latin America with the United States current account was that the service payments for investment income, royalties, patents, and transportation more than doubled during the decade of the 1960s. Latin America's exports to the United States expanded very slowly during the decade and the Region's portion of the United States market declined. Imports into Latin America from the United States, on the other hand, expanded, representing 42 percent of all imports in 1968 compared with 45 percent in 1960. Latin America did not properly identify the change in United States import needs. The North American Giant's needs were increasingly in the form of manufactured items and less in primary products. Demand for tropical fruit products in the United States expanded very slowly, and in some areas, for example the per capita consumption of coffee, showed a slight decline. Latin American primary products from the tempered zone had to compete with home grown goods which in some cases had the advantage of protection. Only Brazil, Mexico, and possibly Colombia have shown any tendency to take advantage of changing market opportunities in the United States.

United States foreign trade policy worked to the detriment of its Latin neighbors. Quota restrictions were placed on items such as cotton, meat, and dairy products. Other foodstuffs were subject to a number of regulations whose primary purpose appeared to be to discourage their importation. Zone tariffs were put into effect and negatively influenced the ability of some Latin nations to sell agriculture products. By the middle of the decade of the 1960s an annual per capita income rate increase of two and one half percent was being realized in most of Latin America. Considerable overall improvement in economic and health conditions could be noted. Latin American governments attempted to promote favorable economic advances in Latin America themselves rather than to rely on external assist-

ance such as the Alliance. Accusations against the Alliance ranged from that
of being paternalistic to a form of Yankee imperialism. The increasing
seriousness of the Vietnam War and internal social economic problems
within the United States once again caused the Northern Giant to direct
much of its efforts away from Latin America. The Alliance was accused of
being unrealistic in its objectives and putting too much dependence on
Latin America's economic development on external sources. Part of the
difficulty is that:

"Latin Americans regard their Northern Neighbor with both admiration and dislike. They respect her free political system and the
dynamism of her enterprises but have antipathy for the brash asser-
tiveness of her individual citizens, and for the apparent neglect of
spiritual values in her pursuit of material rewards."[11]

Specifically, what has accounted for the gradual exclusion of Latin
American exports from the United States market which resulted in
America's share of total United States imports decreasing from 24 percent
to 11 percent from 1960 to 1970? The Third World as a whole declined
from 40 to 25 percent. The United States market purchased approximately
40 percent of total Latin American exports during the 1960s and the figure
declined to 30 percent by 1970. For the Third World as a whole comparable
figures were 22 and 13 percent. Latin America's share of total exports in
the United States during the decade of the sixties decreased from 17 to 13
percent.[12] These changes were the result of a more rapid expansion between producers and exporters of industrial goods than between manufacturing areas and exporters of industrial raw materials and foodstuffs.
Latin America's share of the United States market relative to other parts of
the Third World worsened.

*In spite of the above indicated trade shifts, the United States is still the
chief economic partner of Latin America. Furthermore, the United States
market must be considered indispensable if Latin America is to develop as a
manufacturing center and engage in export activity.* Between 1960 and 1969
this sector expanded at a rate of 17 percent annually and of this amount, 14
percent was represented by United States purchases. In 1969 the United
States purchased 30 percent of Latin America's manufactured exports. The
United States is also significant when specific items are analyzed, such as
cotton fiber, rods and spindles, iron tubes, adding machines, and other
electrical equipment. Much of the future development in this area depends
on activities and policies of United States owned international firms operating in Latin America.[13]

*It should be noted that while United States sales to Latin America have de-
creased in relative proportion to total sales, they increased in absolute terms
from $3.5 billion in 1960 to $5.7 billion in 1970.* These sales exceed those to

Africa and Asia. Specific United States exports are very much dependent on Latin America. For example, in 1968 the Region purchases of chemical products in the United States totaled $620 million which compared very well with the total European Common Market purchases of $750 million. During the same year Latin America obtained $2.2 billion in machinery equipment from the United States, which surpassed the $2 billion of exports in this category to the European Common Market. During the 1960s Latin America provided the United States with 42 percent of its total imports of 14 basic primary products. These products represented 32 percent of total worldwide United States imports during 1961-65 and declined to 23 percent in 1966-70. They represented 80 percent of total United States imports from Latin America in 1961-65 and 76 percent in 1966-70.[14] The economic interdependence of the United States and the Latin American nations is unquestionable.

While the absolute amount of investment capital going from the United States to Latin America increased during the 1960s, it decreased in relative terms. For example, in 1950 direct investments amounted to 32 percent of the total while in 1968 the figure had been reduced to 16 percent. During this period Canada and the European Common Market became relatively more important to Latin America than the United States. United States investments in developed countries between 1950 and 1968 expanded from 45 to 67 percent of the total. Increases in direct investments in Latin America were financed primarily by undistributed profits and local funds rather than by the influx of new external capital sources from abroad. During the sixties, Latin America's exports to the United States increased by 19 percent while payments on the United States investment in the region jumped by 39 percent.[15]

Direct investments from the United States were crucial to the economic development of Latin America. Government capital from the United States accounted for 80 and 50 percent respectively of foreign public financing during the first and second halves of the 1960s. These figures exclude funds channeled through international loan agencies. Many of these funds in the last few years have been direct to Mexico and Brazil. Latin American growth, because of insufficient domestic capital and foreign aid, remains heavily dependent on foreign investment with its accompanying political conflicts.[16] These transfers of funds are less important to the United States than to Latin America. This is true whether one relates the amounts to the gross national product of the United States or to its involvement with developed nations. *Nevertheless, the contribution made to the United States balance of payments by this favorable balance with Latin America is a major factor for the North American Nation. From 1961 to 1965 this contribution averaged approximately 10 percent and increased to about 25 percent of the favorable United States balance in its goods and services account during the second half of the sixties.* Thus, Latin America has been instrumental in helping relieve United States balance of payments difficulties.

In summary, a study of trade and financial relations between Latin America and the United States lead one to the conclusion that the economic ties between these areas in the post World War II period have weakened. Nevertheless, these two regions are indispensable to each other. The United States is the major commercial buyer and seller and the chief source of capital, both public and private for Latin America. On the other hand Latin America plays a critical role as supplier of some basic products to the United States, and the Region is a major purchaser of several categories of United States industrial goods. Additionally, economic exchange with Latin America helps to alleviate United States balance of payment difficulties.

Possible Future Developments

A major future question is whether the developed nations will continue to expand with horizontal integration. This would mean economic agreements among the United States, European Common Market, Japan, the Russian bloc, and perhaps China. The possibility of vertical integration by economic blocs exists. If the horizontal approach is further expanded, the undeveloped and semideveloped areas will increasingly suffer. A vertical integration movement might conceivably place areas such as Latin America in more favorable economic light worldwide. In terms of United States-Latin America relations, a worldwide horizontal effort will weaken these ties while a global vertical integration approach would tend to strengthen them.

A significant question mark in the future will be the role of multi-national corporations as agencies to bring about economic relationships between the Third World (including Latin America) and the developed nations. The major concern is whether the multinational corporations will tend to reduce or increase economic conflict between regions. Multinational corporations, because of their international emphasis, will be more flexible than traditional business firms. This is evident by their agreements with communistic countries and countries in transition to Communism. These firms tend to compete with others of a similar kind in other nations. This tends to increase the possibility of integrating them into the domestic economy and directing their efforts to meet overall domestic social and economic goals. These corporations, while very powerful, differ from traditional organizations that were geared to exporting raw materials to the manufacturing areas of the world.

Multinational corporations may be a new stage in the development of capitalism. Their importance cannot be denied as they in 1971 produced

$300 billion which approximated the total value of world trade during that year. The influence of American private enterprise is greater in Latin America than in any other region of the world. At times these business interests take precedence over the interest of the United States as a country. In the future the United States will have to give more attention to matters that affect the nation as a whole as opposed to individual businesses. This effort may be facilitated by the multinational corporations with their international type orientation.[17]

During this period of low profile or "benign neglect" on the part of the United States, Latin American has diversified its international economic relations toward Europe, Japan, and the socialist nations. More emphasis has been placed on increasing economic and political exchange within the Latin American Region. Interaction with Third World nations has expanded because of some overlapping in foreign investment needs, commercial policy formulation, and primary products exchange. These changes have probably resulted from the deterioration of the bipolar world which surfaced after World War II. Changing Cold War attitudes have greatly modified considerations of economic security and economic exchange. *Part of the change in United States-Latin American economic relations is a function of world-wide changes that were brought about in the shuffle of closing military, political, economic, and cultural gaps involving new forms of coexistence between the Communistic and Capitalistic worlds. Thus, the movement has been away from bipolar confrontation toward multipolar coexistence.* Hemispheric security from the viewpoint of United States interest has been enhanced. Latin American police and military forces have been expanded and have the potential to suppress and control internal disorders. This situation has brought a new power dimension on the scene for the United States. When difficulties arose in obtaining military equipment from the United States, Latin Americans purchased the equipment from Europe and even started manufacturing these items at home, particularly in Brazil and Argentina.[18]

The Soviet Union and other Communist bloc countries such as China may pose a possible future threat to Latin American primary products by competing in United States markets. United States diversification of economic interests reflects itself in investment patterns. In essence while worldwide United States foreign investments expanded from $12 billion in 1950 to $65 billion in 1968, those in Latin America increased only from $4.7 billion to $11 billion. During this period Latin America's relative importance as a source of attracting United States investments declined from 40 percent of all United States private foreign investments to 17 percent.[19] Another development in Latin America is the continual replacing of the landed oligarchy group, which was involved in the exporting of primary commodities, by individuals aligned to the new transnational manufacturing interests of the United States and other advanced nations. This group has a new concern for economic, social, and political matters involving private and public sector groups in the United States and Latin America. These latter groups include international financial institutions and those engaged in foreign aid programs.

This new industrialist group arising in Latin America, in dealing with multinational corporations that engage in manufacturing in Latin America, is going to expect that continuation of this type of activity will be dependent on the United States making its markets available with a minimum of trade barriers to the products of these firms. Thus as Latin America goes through major internal changes resulting from import-substitution and industrialization, its relations with the United States will be affected. Some of these nations are moving rapidly toward socialization of their economies, which is likely to lead to conflict with the United States and multinational firms operating in these nations. Multinational corporations will by necessity produce different political pacts between the corporations and local power groups. To implement their policies United States corporations will have to diversify their investments and help develop their base of operations in foreign countries by helping to expand the local market. Furthermore, increasing worldwide competition will provide the new leadership group in Latin America with increased bargaining power.[20] The possibility exists that these multinational corporations may increasingly attempt to engage in their own formal private diplomacy by creating transnational alliances functioning through international financial arrangements.

Efforts have been made to modify the economic framework among the Americas. The Inter-American Economic and Social Council established in 1963 coordinates the positions of Latin American members of The Organization of American States on economic issues. In May 1969 a joint Latin American position was stated regarding economic cooperation between the States and Latin America. In essence this stressed the importance of trade rather than aid and focused attention on barriers to trade in manufactured items as opposed to those impacting primary commodities. In 1969 the Special Committee for Consultation and Negotiation (CECON) was established. This body was created for the purpose of negotiating trade and other commercial matters between Latin America and the United States. *Emphasis was on a common position among the Latin American countries for new forms of inter-American cooperation in the economic and social fields. The purpose of this organization was to enhance the bargaining of the Latin American nations by permitting them to function as a bloc.* CECON officially stamps the seal of approval on this approach. This organization does not look at economic exchange as being of an inter-American nature, but as being United States-Latin American relations. A reality has thus been acknowledged — there is a diversion of interests on the part of the United States and Latin American countries on some basic fundamental issues of trade and international finance.[21]

The United States is generally supportive of these new positive types of firm approaches by Latin America. It is now realized by the North American nation that if Latin America is to make significant progress, Latin America must take the initiative in assuming the majority of the burdens. The United States posture has changed from one of activist involvement to that of providing needed support at the proper times. This new approach has been interpreted on the part of some Latin Americans as demonstrating a declining interest on the part of Washington in their affairs. Old accusations that the United States cares little for and understands less the problems of the Latin Americans have been resurrected.[22] The United States, for example, has not responded satisfactorily in reducing trade barriers to Latin American exports of semimanufactured goods. Much of this is the result of uncertain economic conditions in the United States which have led to protectionists attitudes. In August 1971 the United States imposed a 10 percent surcharge on all imports and made no concessions to Latin America in this broad application. The United States would probably stand to benefit by increasing imports from Latin America. Reduction in the restrictions on Latin American imports of goods and services into the United States would tend to enhance the development of Latin America in its current stage of semidevelopment.

Problems in striving toward bringing about freer trade will be encountered in the United States. Trade unions, because of high levels of unemployment, are no longer supportive of the free trade mentality as in the past. Multinational corporations are also under attack from trade unions because they are "exporting jobs." It is unlikely that as long as the American economy is operating below capacity one can expect a change of attitude on the part of the strong labor bloc. Another obstacle in the path of increasing Latin American exports to the United States is the question of whether Latin Americans can diversify their exports and make them more attractive on the United States market. Latin America needs to organize a strong and forceful lobby in the United States to promote its case.

From a causal point of view United States direct investments in Latin America have had a negative impact on the Region's balance of payments during the 1960s. Much of this however, is caused by remittances from Venezuela as a result of disinvesting of oil company properties in that nation. Overall, investments from the United States, including profits that are reinvested, have been higher than the income derived from these investments. However, the balance in Latin America's favor is relatively small. Foreign investment should be viewed from an overall balance of payments concept and not simply from a cash flow perspective.[23] There is an increase in the flow of United States investments into manufacturing in Latin America. For example, in Mexico, Brazil, and Argentina between 60 and 70 percent of United States investments are now in the manufacturing area. This change has resulted in a negative balance of payments problem because the shift has come from primary commodities that are exported to manufacturing industries that are produced for domestic consumption. One can expect the situation will change and manufacturing activities in Latin America will increasingly consider the export dimension. A major problem in United States-Latin American relations will be in the area of take overs of domestically owned firms. In these politically related activities the United States must attempt to cope with the disillusionment with democracy. A common viewpoint is that:

"Democracy in Latin America has proven to be very fragile and ineffectual. Democrative government (or for that matter the authoritarian governments of the past) has demonstrated scant capacity to develop Latin America, to alter the traditional patterns of the past, or to propel Latin America into the future. The most striking characteristic of the 1960s was the growing disillusionment with democracy."[24]

The major development coming out of the recent changes is that while the United States and Latin America will continue to be closely involved, because of their strong economic ties and geography, there will be a new emphasis. *Involvement will be more in the area of economic relations such as trade, foreign investments, transfers of technology, and finance rather than in internal development policies which are more and more being viewed as the domain of Latin American countries themselves.*[25] Also the North American Nation is coming to the realization that:

"Socio-economic development, however construed, does not appear to create political democracy, though there may be a loose, positive correlation between the two phenomena."[26]

The United States role in Latin America will also be increasingly looked upon by the Latin Americans in light of their relations with the total industrialized world as opposed to an Inter-American System. Latin Americans must continue to seek external financial resources to bring about the needed rate of economic advance. They must not only export more, to obtain funds so that the Region's potential can be realized, but also forcefully encourage intra-Latin American trade. The United States needs to assist Latin America to become a strong economic entity along with other industrialized nations. An economically strong Latin America with interests more closely tied to those of developed nations, as opposed to those of the Third World, would be in the best interest of both the United States and Latin America.[27]

Summary and Conclusions

United States economic relations with Latin America have undertaken a new phase during the past decade. Although economic exchange between the two regions has increased in absolute terms there has been a considerable decline in the relative importance of Latin American imports into United States markets and in the role of Latin America as an area of United States investments. The situation has resulted from an increase in the relative importance of manufactured items in the export trade of the United States and the relative decline of primary commodities as the chief source of trade in international activity. The rise of the European Common Market, Japan, the Socialist bloc, and the economic advance of the Third World also have contributed to the decline in the role of Latin America in United States foreign trade. From a Latin American point of view the development of the European Common Market, intra-Latin American trade, the Socialist bloc, and the Third World nations also have contributed to directing some of Latin America's foreign trade away from its Northern Neighbor.

Animosities have arisen as a result of the decline in the relative importance of trade between these two regions. Latin Americans bitterly complain about the restrictive trade policies of the United States. They blame this action on a lessening United States interest in and concern with Latin America in the face of the phasing out of the Cold War. United States policy makers on the other hand defend these policies in terms of domestic economic problems which have spilled over into a deteriorating position for the United States in international markets. Rapid inflation, a persistent high level of unemployment, and a weakening of the dollar in international financial centers has prompted strong efforts to attempt to strengthen the balance of payments position of the United States. Latin Americans in general have failed to adequately adjust their export mix to meet the changing market needs of the United States. The rise of the multinational corporation which is oriented towards manufacturing rather than to traditional investment in primary commodities increases the likelihood of a new industrial leap in Latin America. It is likely that these new firms will increase and direct their efforts to producing in Latin American countries not only for domestic markets but also for export.

In this year of the United States bicentennial one finds many points of common interest existing between the two areas. There is, as previously stated, the economic interdependence that is indispensable if the Americas are to maximize their economic well-being. The current important reappraisal of United States-Latin American economic relations reflects changing world conditions. The key to future relationships will be whether the advanced nations develop more horizontal integration or whether the world will break off into blocs which would be vertically integrated and relate to other blocs. If the latter situation takes place, one can expect United States-Latin American economic relations to begin assuming increasing significance. However, the United States will increasingly be dealing with Latin America as a whole rather than with individual nations formulating separate policies. Should the bloc concept develop, the interdependence between these two blocs will become more pronounced.

A new economic arrangement is evolving between the United States and Latin America. At the moment it is painful and will continue to be so for some time. This change promises to place the two areas on a more equal and healthy basis in their relationships. During this transition policy makers, inhabitants of the Americas, and other interested parties should not be blinded by present tensions. Policy makers in particular should not overlook the past with its long history of beneficial interregional relationships, fail to analyze the present objectively nor neglect to view the future with faith and hope for a more mutually satisfactory economic arrangement among the Americas.

Notes

1. I am indebted to James E. Price for his assistance with the preparation of this manuscript.

2. Adalbert Kreiger Vasena and Javier Pazos, *Latin America; A Broader World Role* (London: Ernest Benn Limited, 1973), p. 23.

3. Cleona Lewis, *America's Stake in International Investments* (Washington D.C.: Brookings Institute, 1938), pp. 575-607.

4. Vasena, and Pazos, *op. cit.,* p. 25.

5. *Ibid,* p. 28.

6. *Ibid,* p. 30.

7. Ian Little, Tibor Scitovsky, and Maurice Scott, *Industry and Trade in Some Developing Countries; A comparative Study* (London: Oxford University Press for the OECD, 1970), pp. 162-163.

8. Vasena, and Pazos, *op. cit.,* p. 37.

9. R. Ross Stanley (ed.), *Latin America in Transition, Problems in Training and Research* (Albany, New York: The University of New York Press, 1970), p. xiii.

10. Vasena, and Pazos, *op. cit.,* p. 93.

11. Harold Blakemore, *Latin America* (London: Oxford University Press, 1973), p. 103.

12. Anibal Pinto in Julio Cotler, and Richard R. Fagen, (eds.) *Latin America and the United States: The Changing Political Realities* (Stanford: Stanford University Press, 1974), pp. 100-101.

13. *Ibid,* p. 103.

14. *Ibid,* p. 104.

15. *Ibid,* p. 109.

16. Stephen Clissold, *Latin America, New World, Third World* (New York: Praeger Publishers, 1972), p. 255.

17. Pinto, *op. cit.,* p. 114.

18. Osvaldo Sunkel, "Commentary on Pinto," in *Colter and Fagen, op. cit.,* pp. 117-118.

19. *Ibid,* p. 119.

20. Luciano Martins, "The Politics of U. S. Multinational Corporations in Latin America" in Colter and Fagen, *op. cit.,* p. 403.

21. Vasena, and Pazos, *op. cit.,* p. 97.

22. Graham H. Stuart, *Latin America and the United States* (New York: Appleton-Century-Crofts, Inc., 1955), p. 8.

23. Vasena, and Pazos, *op. cit.,* p. 8.

24. E. Bradford Burns, *Latin America, A Concise Interpretative History,* (Englewood Cliffs: Prentice-Hall, 1972), p. 232.

25. Vasena, and Pazos, *op. cit.,* p. 100.

26. Richard Graham, *New Approaches to Latin American History,* Peter H. Smith and Richard Graham (eds.), (Austin: University of Texas Press, 1974), p. 253.

27. Vasena, and Pazos, *op. cit.,* p. 103.

CONTRIBUTIONS OF HISPANIC SCIENTISTS IN THE UNITED STATES

Alfredo Giner-Sorolla

El fin del hombre es hacer ciencia, catalogar el Universo para devolvérselo a Dios en orden.

M. Unamuno (Amor y Pedagogía)

Science should not be considered as a book-keeping of Nature but as the greatest of human adventures.

P.B. Medawar (The Art of the Soluble)

I consider science primarily as an intellectual adventure, the search of truth for truth's sake.

S. Ochoa (Quoted from Grande-Covián)

The Dynamics of the Emigration of Scientists

Civilizations usually receive impetus at crucial moments of their history from genetic and cultural intermingling and like many plants, they require cross-fertilization in order to achieve a further advance in their development. The emigration of scientists and scholars throughout history is not an infrequent phenomenon and is motivated by the search for a more fertile soil in which to develop their potentialities. Quite often the scientist may place himself, because of his vision and broad ideals, in conflict with established institutions of his native land compelling him to abandon a hostile or barren environment. Political, religious and ethnic persecutions have frequently been concurrent factors in the emigration of talented individuals, the beneficiary being the country which allows free expression of their ideas or beliefs. The inquisitive mind of a scientist requires broader views which motivates him to cross the boundaries of his native surroundings in the quest for a more favorable cultural climate.

Interestingly, the emigration of scientists and scholars in both the ancient classical and modern world has consistently followed the same westward flow as the dissemination of the ideas and doctrines of civilization. From the fertile crescent and ancient Egypt, civilization shifted to Greece and Rome and from there spread to the whole of Europe and later to the

123

Americas. Crucial to the development of western thinking was the emergence of Athens as both a political and cultural center of Hellenic civilization and the simultaneous, first-recorded emigration of philosophers and scientists from the Aegean Islands and the Ionian coast. The further expansion of culture as a result of this emigration of scholars and their influence upon Ptolemaic Egypt and the Roman Empire is well-known. The Middle Ages were witness to a widespread wandering of scholars; the westward trend of emigration continued with the arrival of Arab and Hebrew scholars at the caliphate in the Iberian peninsula. Later, during the Renaissance, the flow continued as Italian builders, engineers and artists emigrated to France inciting new technical and stylistic perspectives, which had reached a dead point by the exhaustion of artistic forms caused by the Gothic period.

From the time of the discovery of the American continent, quite a few scholars and scientists, mainly from England and Spain, were attracted by the accounts of the new flora, fauna and mineral wealth of the New World. We had to wait until the period between 1933 and the start of World War II, and then again from 1945 to the present to witness a significantly massive flow of European scientists to the United States. In the middle 1930's, as the United States emerged from the effects of the depression and started economic recovery and technological expansion under the New Deal, there was an exodus of many outstanding intellectuals from Europe, mainly those escaping from persecution in Nazi Germany.

We can pinpoint the start of large-scale emigration of Spanish scholars and scientists to Europe and America to the upheaval of the Spanish Civil War and its aftermath; only a few individuals left before this period. Although most of the refugees settled in countries of Hispanic America, some of them found their way into the United States. The main influx of scholars and scientists, especially from Spain to the United States, began in the early 1950's after the establishment of the scientific exchange program between the United States and Spain. Relatively few Spaniards have settled here during the present or last century in comparison to the amount of Northern Europeans or, in recent times, the Asians. The proportion of Spanish scientists to the total number of Spanish immigrants is, however, very high as compared to the ratio of scientists to professionals coming to the United States from any other country.

The scope of an article makes it impossible to give a comprehensive survey even in summary form of the work of all the Hispanic scientists in this country. Omissions, therefore, are unavoidable due to limitations of space. I shall deal not only with outstanding Hispanic scientists but also with other established scientists and the younger, recently arrived investigators, as they hold a definite promise for future fruitful realizations. The ad-

vancement of science results from the work of towering and singularly gifted individuals and also from the quiet, imaginative and patient toil of a
great number of dedicated investigators.

The lines of investigation which have attracted most of the Spanish scientists to work in the United States are mainly those related to problems of
the life sciences: virology, neurology, molecular biology, biochemical
evolution, enzymology, biomathematics, immunology and genetics. To a
more limited extent, in the number of individuals, there have also been important contributions to the fields of physical sciences, especially nuclear
physics, cosmic rays and thermodynamics.

Ramón y Cajal and the Growth of Spanish Science

*It is necessary in fact, if we would enroll ourselves with the civilized
peoples, that we cultivate intensively the deserts of our land and brain thus
rescuing by prosperity and mental vigor all those national riches that have
been lost in the sea and all those talents which have been lost in ignorance.*
S.R. Cajal

A portrait of Ramón y Cajal with the above words in Spanish occupied a
prominent place in almost every primary school across Spain the first
decades of this century. Parallel to the impression that Cajal made upon so
many Spanish students during his lifetime was the impact that this great
master of the Spanish school of neurology made on the world of science. I
believe it is appropriate, before I proceed to discuss the individual contributions of Hispanic scientists, to remember what this impact was that Cajal
made on his colleagues in the United States and, conversely the impression
that young America made on him. In this manner, I wish to pay tribute to
the great personality of this man who so decisively contributed both to the
growth of Spanish science and, indirectly, to the emigration of Spanish
scientists to the United States.

It was Cajal's visit to the United States, and those to English and German
universities, which prompted him to utter his lofty thoughts on the need for
quality education and research. Cajal showed admiration for the well-
established American universities and hospitals, and had phrases of praise
for the excellent services of the libraries. During the year following the
Spanish-American war, which was called in Spain "the disaster of '98," and
which caused in Spain a wave of self-deprecation among the people and a
natural, although transient resentment, Cajal quite remarkably was invited
to lecture in the United States, along with other European scientific cele-
brities, at a commemorative symposium at Clark University. He was over-
whelmed and surprised at such an invitation coming from a country which

only months before had been in armed conflict with Spain. One of his biographers[1] has described his arrival in New York and his admiration for the "stern fiber of the Anglo-Saxon race which impelled laborers to activity even under the blazing sun and heat of a New York summer." In a different context his biographer remarked the sad feelings of Cajal "that barriers of language and custom have turned medical men to other countries, and Spain has seemed out of the current of scientific advance"[2].

At the end of the 19th century, Cajal decided to undertake the exploration of the brain because at that time the histology of the nervous system was one of the most important and rapidly developing fields in biomedical research. This was facilitated by the availability of more powerful optical microscopes and the introduction of new staining techniques. One of the motivations for this interest was the belief that mental diseases were caused by a pathological condition of the nervous cells; therefore, an intense search was undertaken for the elucidation of the structure of the brain and a possible correlation between morphological abnormalities and mental disturbances.

The genius of Cajal has been the source of inspiration and stimulus to generations of Spanish scientists. Not only the example of his work and life, but the writings in which he left the imprint of his wisdom and his deep scientific spirit constitute a most valuable legacy. Many of us have been stimulated and have found food for thought by reading his "Rules for Scientific Research" or "Tonics of the Will" and have enjoyed his lively and often profound "Conversations in the Café," where the views about the society of his time and the thoughts about his concept of the world are expressed. Undoubtedly, the influence of Spain's first scientist upon the present and future generations of Hispanic scientists, an example to be proud of, will be a lasting one.

The Pioneering Work of Durán-Reynals

There was no significant emigration of Spanish scientists to the United States in the present century until the third decade with the arrival of a young virologist, Durán-Reynals. He probably had no premonition whatsoever that he was to be the first Spaniard who held an official position in the field of science in America when he joined the Rockefeller Institute in 1929. In time, Durán-Reynals was instrumental in bringing to the United States other young Spanish scientists who, like him, became part of American science Notable among these scientists were Dr. Jordi Casals and Dr. Jordi Folch-Pi, whose achievements in their respective fields of virology and neurochemistry are later discussed. This flow of Spanish scientists continues to this day and its origins can be traced to the one man who first revealed to Durán-Reynals the road he was destined to travel.

Francisco Durán-Reynals was born in Barcelona in 1899. While in Medical School Durán-Reynals had come under the influence of Dr. Turró, a brilliant bacteriologist who fired the imagination of his medical students with the great discoveries which in his lifetime had radically changed the fields of Medicine and Biology, especially in the area of bacterial infection.

The same year of his graduation, in 1925, Durán-Reynals received a scholarship from the "Junta de Ampliación Estudios" to study abroad. After two years in Paris, he decided to come to the United States because he sensed that American science had a quality which he wanted to see for himself and, specifically, New York, which was perhaps unique among cities.

At the Pasteur Institute in Paris, Durán-Reynals had become a virologist and his main subject of investigation was to identify the factors responsible for the different effects of viruses. His contribution in this field involved two lines of research:

The first, started at the Pasteur Institute and finished at the Rockefeller Institute, concerned the effect of certain substances on local lesions induced by viral infection. Durán-Reynals reported in the late twenties the discovery of a substance which is abundantly present in the testes of mammals and which he called, because of its effects, the 'spreading factor'[3,4]. Durán-Reynals found that the effect of the spreading factor could also be obtained with bacteria and with poisons and that it involved a phenomenon widespread in nature. Thus, he demonstrated that highly virulent bacteria secrete this spreading substance to facilitate invasion of the tissues, which was later characterized as an enzyme called hyalorudinase.

The second line of investigation pursued by Durán-Reynals at Yale University Medical School concerned the role of viruses in cancer. By the time Durán-Reynals began these studies, there was evidence that viruses could induce cancer in animals, but the meaning of this evidence was obscure and poorly understood because of the resistance, which prevailed, to the idea of viruses being related with this disease. Thus, it was generally believed that virus-induced cancer was an atypical event involving extremely rare, probably aberrant viruses. Durán-Reynals demonstrated that cancer is only one of the effects of infection with viruses which in any respect do not posses a single property which distinguishes them from other viruses. In 1945, Durán-Reynals published a review on these observations[5] and cautioned that close attention should be paid to the most common viral infections in man as a possible cause of human cancer. His last contribution to this problem, shortly before his untimely death in 1958, involved results indicating that infection in animals with one of the viruses most widely present in man increases, very significantly, the susceptibility of these animals to the cancer-inducing effects of chemical carcinogens.

When Durán-Reynals first published his observations, opposition to the virus theory of cancer and to these observations was adamant and impervious to all evidence. This attitude continued for some years in spite of significant contributions in the 1950's which clearly supported Durán-Reynals' concepts. Advances in virology also have supported Durán-Reynals' concepts, and the evidence substantiating his findings has become overwhelming. The tide began to turn shortly after he died, and in the early 1960's, the opposition (practically overnight) became silent. Since then the role of viruses in cancer has turned out to be a major subject of investigation in cancer research. Knowledge in this field has progressed enormously in the last few years, and so far all of Durán-Reynals' postulates have proven to be true.

J. Folch-Pi

The quality of a scientist is frequently attributed to his ability to develop new techniques or improve existing ones in order to open new frontiers. Suffice it to mention how improvements on Golgi's staining methods helped Cajal to unravel the structure of the nervous system or later helped Ochoa to isolate and use enzymes for the mapping of the genetic code. The prestigious medical scientist, Jordi Folch-Pi, is similarly an innovator in the field of study of the composition of the nervous tissue. Folch-Pi came from Barcelona at the instigation of Durán-Reynals to work first at the Rockefeller Institute and later at Harvard Medical School, where he is Director of Research of the McLean Hospital. Under the influence and inspiration of Cajal, he set to work on the exploration of the biochemistry of the brain and nervous system. Professor Folch-Pi has made outstanding contributions to the field of Neurochemistry, in which he is the world's most renowned figure; suffice to say that his citation index, that is, the yearly number of references by other scientists to his work, is among the highest in the country.

The most important aspects of his research are: First, the isolation and characterization of phosphatidylserine, one of the most widespread phospholipids in the animal kingdom[6]; second, the identification of inositol as a component of animal phospholipids[7,8,9]; third, the discovery of a new type of lipid-protein complexes (proteolipids) which are constituents of the neurons[10]; and, finally, the creation of very efficient methods for the extraction and purification of all types of lipids which are used in laboratories throughout the world[11,12].

Folch-Pi believes in the excellence of Spanish scientists, although he notes the absence of tradition and lack of interest in science in the past in Spain. This is in contrast to the long-standing and profuse support for

science and technology in the United States. A noticeable change, Folch-Pi
notes, in the right direction has been made in Spain, especially in Madrid,
with the creation of new and well-equipped research centers[13].

Jordi Casals

An intensive work on virology from the standpoint of identification,
classification of the arboviruses (arthropode-borne viruses) and arena
viruses has been made by Dr. Jordi Casals, who came to the Rockefeller
Institute in 1936 upon the advice of Durán-Reynals, and is now at Yale
University School of Medicine. Dr. Casals' main objectives have been the
development of serological techniques applicable to these viral agents in order to classify them in related groups and diagnose them in human infections[14],[15].

Casals can be considered a pioneer in the development of methods for
detecting immunological responses to viruses and for determining antigenic
similarities among groups of viruses.

R. Lorente de Nó

A disciple of Cajal, Lorente de Nó, also from Aragón, studied the
organization of the cerebral cortex and the physiology of the peripheral nerves. He did most of this work at the Rockefeller Institute where he has
been active since 1936. He is now Professor Emeritus at the University of
California.

The Post-Spanish Civil War Emigration of Scientists

As a consequence of the Spanish Civil War and shortly thereafter World
War II, a stream of Spanish refugees, among them many intellectuals, settled in Hispanic America and some of them in the United States.

The post-war period was characterized throughout the world and particularly in the United States in an upsurge of scientific research, in a prominent
way in the biological sciences. The application of analytical tools such as X-
ray diffraction, amino acid analyzers, radioactive labeling and chromatography has led to the birth and development of the new science of
Molecular Biology. This discipline is exploring the intimate processes of life,
growth, replication and biological heredity at the molecular level.

Severo Ochoa

It is within the field of Molecular Biology that the figure of Professor
Severo Ochoa, born in Luarca, Asturias, stands out for his breakthroughs

in Enzymology and Molecular Biology, which were made mainly since his arrival to the United States. Professor Ochoa had made a deep imprint both in America and Spain, testified by the number of brilliant disciples who have made outstanding contributions to Science.

In his scientific career, Ochoa had as mentors the figures of Ramón y Cajal (although not in a direct form), Juan Negrín, Teófilo Hernando in Spain, and Meyerhof in Germany; he also worked in England with Peters. After his stay in England, Ochoa was invited to work in the United States in 1940 with the Coris in St. Louis. He then moved to New York where the bulk of his work was done at New York University where he was Chairman of the Department of Biochemistry. The work of Ochoa in this country can be classified into three main groups of research problems culminating in the discovery of crucially important enzymes which have contributed considerably to the development of Biochemistry. The first type of problem concerning the enzymatic mechanisms of carboxylation and decarboxylation of α-ketonic acids was catalyzed by the 'malic enzyme.' Ochoa demonstrated the identity of the process of carbon dioxide fixation in green plants and in animal tissues[16].

In the second type of investigation, Ochoa studied the enzymatic mechanisms of the citric cycle (Krebs cycle), which was connected with the work above described. Only one enzyme of the Krebs cycle was known and isolated by 1942; the key reaction of the cycle, namely, the condensation of a two-carbon unit, the active acetyl group, with malate to yield oxalacetate and this to citrate, was discovered by Ochoa and Stern in 1949, who isolated the 'condensing enzyme' responsible for this reaction[17].

In the third group of investigations Ochoa and Grunberg-Manago, in 1951, discovered polynucleotide phosphorylase, an enzyme isolated from *Azotobacter vinelandii,* a soil bacteria which has the unique capacity of synthesizing organic nitrogen compounds from atmospheric nitrogen[18].

This was the first enzyme able to synthesize long-chain polynucleotides, thus being a precursor of the nucleic acid polymerases, the enzymes which catalyze the formation of ribonucleic acid (RNA) polymers. This fact was discovered from the observation by Ochoa that when the enzyme was added to a solution containing the nucleotides (the whole subunits of nucleic acids) of the four bases which exist in RNA, they formed a pattern which to all appearances was RNA. Up to that time only a living cell could make this complex compound and, therefore, this discovery represented a breakthrough which has been qualified as the most significant discovery in Biochemistry since Wohler in 1826 who described the synthesis of a biological substance, urea, from inert materials[19]. Ochoa's former student, Kornberg, in a parallel study synthesized deoxyribonucleic acid (DNA) from the corresponding nucleotides and, as a consequence, they were awarded the

Nobel Prize in 1959 "for their discoveries of the mechanisms in the biological synthesis of ribonucleic and deoxyribonucleic acids."

The availability of polynucleotide phosphorylase permitted Ochoa to carry
out detailed studies on the elucidation of the genetic code. The genetic
material in the cell bears, in a coded form, the precise specification for the
biosynthesis of different kinds of protein molecules required for its
existence and replication. The genetic code is like a "dictionary" in that the
cell translates the "four-letter language" of nucleic acid (the four
heterocyclic bases) into the "20-letter language" of protein (the twenty
amino acids)[20].

In recent years Ochoa, at the Roche Institute for Molecular Biology, is investigating the initiation, elongation and termination processes of the
polypeptide chain and the isolation of the different factors involved in the
protein synthesis of eukaryotic cells[21].

Among Ochoa's disciples and co-workers in Spain and America are M.
Salas, E. Viñuela, P. Lengyel, W. Szer, S. Wang, C. Nombela, and J.
Sierra. The present generation of Spanish scientists have, in the figure of
Ochoa, not only an example of a great investigator but also the promoter of
studies on the intricate problems of protein biosynthesis, both in the United
States and in Spain. On the occasion of his 70th birthday, in 1974, Ochoa
was honored with a homage which took place both in Barcelona and in
Madrid in the form of an International Symposium and concluded with the
dedication of a Center of Molecular Biology bearing his name and in which
the work he initiated will be continued and expanded.

In the opinion of Grande-Covián "Ochoa's ability to maintain his enthusiasm and devotion to scientific research even through the most difficult periods of his life seems to me a distinctive mark of his personality..." For Ochoa "science is primarily an intellectual adventure: the
search of truth for truth's sake; an endeavor to a better understanding of
Nature, regardless of the practical advantages which may be derived"[22].

Ochoa is a Spanish investigator who occupies a prominent position in the
world of science and who has adapted perfectly well to American scientific
life where he is one of its outstanding protagonists. He once said that "a
researcher is never satisfied by achieving and finding the goal of his work,
because science is inexhaustible"[13].

Santiago Grisolía

A scientist from Valencia, Professor Santiago Grisolía, now at the University of Kansas Medical Center, was attracted by the work of Ochoa and
has been dedicated since 1945 (date of his arrival in America) to the field of
Enzymology. Among his many contributions to this branch of science is the

discovery of the catalytic effect of N-acetyl glutamate on the biosynthesis of the amino acid citrulline in 1953. These studies culminated in the finding of carbon dioxide fixation and the demonstration that citrulline was indeed an intermediate in urea synthesis[23,24]. Other important investigations clarified the necessity of the integrity of cells and the direct fixation of carbon dioxide on ornithine, thus demonstrating the enzymatic formation of an intermediate compound containing carbon dioxide, ammonia and high energy phosphate and the coupling of adenosine triphosphate to synthetic reactions. The early discovery of the catalytic role in acetyl glutamate led to the understanding of the urea cycle and the synthesis of pyrimidines.

After nearly 30 years of research, Professor Grisolía has established proof of the existence of carbonyl-phosphate, a compound which has a half-life of the order of half-second, which may help to clarify the intermediate mechanism of many other carbon dioxide fixation reactions. Contrary to the view generally accepted, Professor Grisolía showed that substrates or components necessary for enzymatic activity had either no effect or inactivated enzymes, also that acetyl glutamate activated and then inactivated carbamyl phosphate synthetase. This phenomenon was then shown to occur with many other enzymes and led also to the discovery of *cold lability* and the concept of elastoplasticity. Another very important discovery by Grisolía consisted in the isolation of the enzyme carbamyl phosphate phosphatase, which has the smallest molecular weight of all known enzymes. He also investigated the degradation of pyrimidines (heterocyclic components of nucleic acids) in animal tissues as well as their incorporation into nucleic acids, demonstating single handedly the existence of all the enzymes involved in the pyrimidine metabolic degradation pathway.

In the opinion of Professor Grisolía, enzyme regulation, in particular protein turnover, consists essentially of nutrition at the molecular level.

John Oró

Within the field of Molecular Biology in its projection to both space and time, we have to consider the personality of Dr. John Oró, from Lérida, who since 1952 has been working at the University of Houston where he is Professor of Biophysical Sciences. His many scientific contributions encompass diverse fields, most of them centering on the elucidation of the problem of the origin of life on Earth.

In my view, the most important discovery of Dr. Oró has been his demonstration in 1959 of the prebiotic synthesis (that is, in conditions resembling those of primitive Earth) of the main basic components of nucleic acids from simple substances (ammonia, hydrocyanic acid and water) which are postulated to have been present in the primordial Earth.

These constituents have been detected in the atmosphere of Jupiter and other planets. Oró observed that after a few days of heating a solution of hydrocyanic acid in aqueous ammonia, several components of nucleic acid (adenine among them) were spontaneously formed. In addition Oró analyzed the intricate stages of this synthesis, which are quite different from the known biosynthetic pathway and isolated its many intermediary compounds[25,26].

A contribution to the exploration of objects from outer space, that is, meteorites and lunar rocks, was made by Dr. Oró, the latter analysis within the framework of a NASA program after the return of the Apollo missions. This was done mainly with the help of the modern methods of gas chromatography and mass spectra. The data from the moon rock analysis have yielded some interesting carbon and nitrogen compounds which are not of biogenic origin or even indicative of any kind of prebiotic synthesis in the harsh conditions of the lunar environment. These compounds are thought to be formed by a peculiar reaction of the ionized species of solar radiation, the so-called solar wind, on the moon surface[27,28].

The projection of analysis into the remote past has been carried out by Professor Oró with sediments of the Precambrian period, dating back to 3 billion years before the present, in which he detected aliphatic hydrocarbons of the isoprenoid type (among them, pristane, a cancer-promoting substance), thus indicating the possible origin of cancer from living organisms (plants or bacteria)[29].

Meteorites, objects which may have originated in the solar nebula, that is, the body from which the solar system evolved, have been a more distant origin. Analyses carried out by Dr. Oró have shown that organic compounds as complex as aliphatic and aromatic hydrocarbons were present.[30] Since the possibility of contamination by terrestrial organic matter has been excluded, it has been inferred by Oró that these compounds may either represent residues of prebiotic synthesis or remains of organic and/or living matter from outer space. Interestingly, some of the hydrocarbons are of the polycyclic type, which are known to induce cancer in animals and men, suggesting, according to Oró, that the occurrence of aromatic polycyclic hydrocarbons in meteorites may be indicative of the cosmic occurrence and remote existence of carcinogens. Parallel to these investigations, Dr. Oró has contributed to the study of the universal and growing problem of contamination of the environment by analyzing air and dust samples, which have revealed a great number of hydrocarbons[31].

A most interesting experiment, in which Dr. Oró has recently contributed (as a member of a special task force with NASA), is the design and construction of the Viking Mars landers, which were launched in 1975 to land on Mars. This artificial satellite carries a gas chromatograph and a mass spectrometer (a real feat of miniaturization) for the identification of organic compounds, water and volatile constituents in the atmosphere and surface of Mars. The results of these experiments are yielding a distinctive picture of the composition of the red planet and its possible significance in regard to the problems of the origins of life in the Universe.

The above-described prebiotic synthesis by Oró of molecules so decisively involved in the process of life can be considered a breakthrough in Biopoesis, the fascinating new field of science dealing not only with the search for the origins of life but also with the investigation of producing life by synthetic means. In work done in 1975 at the NASA Ames Research Center, Dr Oró and colleagues have synthesized with very simple ingredients (aqueous solution of hydrocyanic acid and ammonia), and in very mild conditions, microspheres of polyamino acids resembling cells. In Oró's opinion, the possibility of creating a living being from artificial biogenic components in the form of a self-replicating nucleic-acid-protein complex is a feat which will be accomplished in a not too distant future.

In recent times, Professor Oró has become interested in the possible application of the extreme sensitivity of gas chromatography and mass spectra methods to the problem of early diagnosis of human cancer. These studies consist of the determination of the pattern of normal and abnormal constituents in blood serum and urine of animals and humans. In this manner, both the early stages of the induction of cancer and the progress of a given therapy could be determined.

Dr. Oró has brought together a team of collaborators, on which he has left the imprint of his imagination and enthusiasm for research from biophysics to problems of outer space. Among these collaborators, he has trained scientists who have now returned to Spain - for example, Dr. Gibert and Dr. Gelpí. Other co-workers include Drs. Kimball, Nooner, Stephen-Sherwood, and Zlatkis. Professor Oró has also been instrumental in the creation of the Institute of Fundamental Biology in Barcelona, one of the most active in the country, and recently in the creation of the Institute of Biophysics and Neurobiology, where the attempt will be made to continue the line of research initiated by Cajal, particularly in studying the relationship between structure and function at the molecular level and at the level of neurotransmitters, work which has been started by a team headed by Dr. Gelpí.

We have in Oró an enthusiastic man of science, an investigator gifted with a most fertile imagination, and who has decisively contributed to two of the most fascinating research problems of the present century: the breakthrough in the artificial synthesis of components of nucleic acids with its relevance to the problem of the origin of life on Earth and the exploration of its existence in the Solar System.

H. Fernández Morán

Development of new tools for research is as essential as new methods for the advancement of science. Professor Fernández Morán, a Venezuelan from Maracaibo, now at the University of Chicago, a very dynamic and highly imaginative researcher, has introduced two important instruments: the super-conducting electronic microscope and the diamond knife. With the first instrument, a very stable image of high resolution of molecular structures can be obtained by the supercooling effect of liquid helium. In this manner, a major drawback common to all electron microscopes, the "thermal noise" or heat generated by the electric current in the electromagnets that focus the image, could be eliminated. Fernández Morán has spent many years improving this superconducting electronic microscope. His reward has been the possibility of seeing crystal structures as small as two angstroms.

With his powerful microscope, Professor Fernández Morán is exploring the ultrastructure of the brain and nervous system, undoubtedly attracted as many Spanish biomedical investigators by the most challenging complexity of these organs of the body. He declared that "as a practicing physician who was depressed by the utter futility of seeing patients die of brain tumors despite all our efforts, I turned to basic research with the desire to learn more about these tumors".[32]

The second instrument developed by Professor Fernández Morán, the diamond knife, is the sharpest cutting instrument in existence. This tool could be used to separate intact glucose molecules from its polymer glycogen or slice the DNA macromolecule and restructure it. Similarly, an ultramicrosurgery could be developed which may in the future be a technique for genetic engineering.

Fernández Morán has proposed a hypothesis of how living forces act; he believes that living systems possess a "mometum order" which canalizes the flow of energy and in which cooperation of the functions of the chemical components is found. "Possessing momentum order, the whole all becomes greater that the sum of its chemical components. It becomes alive."[32]

Josep Segarra

Following the tradition of the school of Cajal, Dr. Josep Segarra, a neurologist from Barcelona, came in 1953 to Boston to work initially under Denny Brown. Dr. Segarra's contributions to the field of neuropathology have been the determination of the vascular syndromes underlying profound changes of consciousness[33] pioneering investigation into the demential states due to thalamic lesions and the isolation and description of a new degenerative cellebellar disease[34]. He is now involved in the study of experimental iatrogenic carcinogenesis, which will determine the possible induction of brain tumors in those patients under long-term medication.

A. Giner-Sorolla

My home town is Vinaroz and I obtained my Ph.D. at the University of Barcelona. Since 1954 I have been working in experimental cancer chemotherapy and carcinogensis (the process of tumor formation) at the Sloan-Kettering Institute in New York. In one of my lines of research I have found that minute chemical alterations in the structure of some nucleic acid components yield substances with marked biological activity as anticancer agents in experimental animals[35]. These substances act as anti-metabolites, blocking the growth and proliferation of cancer cells. Other types of agents we are investigating may exert their anticancer activity by an enhancing of the immune response. These are conjugates of serum proteins with anticancer drugs and also certain thiazole derivatives.

In addition, I have been involved in problems of environmental and iatrogenic (medicinal drug-induced) carcinogenesis and their prevention. We are trying to determine the direct and transplacental cancer-inducing effect in experimental animals of certain components of nucleic acids which are found in minute amounts in all living cells. These components, by interaction with nitrites in the intestinal tract, may form nitrosamines which are potent carcinogens. In a parallel study, we are investigating the effect of several widely-used drugs on the induction of tumors in the nervous system in mice. The studies on the prevention of these tumors will consist of determining the effect in animals of the presence in the diet of certain reducing substances (ascorbic and retinoic acid among others), which may inhibit the formation of nitrosamines in the gastrointestinal tract[36].

In collaboration with Dr. C. López, we are developing new arabinosyl nucleosides, some of which have shown a potent inhibitory activity against herpesvirus infection (herpesvirus being presumably associated with some types of cancer). We are seeking with these agents a concurrent anticancer effect as already obtained with their ribosyl analogs. We are also focusing our research on the observed potent enzymatic inhibitory effect of one of these substances against adenosine deaminase. In this manner an increased therapeutic activity of these nucleosides may be obtained[37].

The study of the emergence of carcinogens both before the appearance of the first living organism (protocarcinogens, i.e., "carcinogens before cancer") and during Evolution has attracted my attention for some time[38]. I am especially looking for a chronological correlation at different stages of the evolutionary process between the emergence of a particular carcinogen in the environment and the appearance of animals susceptible to their attack. The maximum of interaction of chemical carcinogens and animals during Evolution took place in all probability during the Mesozoic (about 100 million years ago). At that time the abundance of plants containing carcinogens may have caused poisoning and tumors in pandemic proportions in reptiles and could have been a factor in their extinction.

It is claimed that about 90% of all human cancers are caused by chemicals of natural or artificial origin. A parallel, therefore, could be drawn between the possible lethal effects of the emergence and abundance of natural carcinogens in the geological past (as well as those massive outbreaks of cancer recently observed in livestock fed with meal accidentally contaminated with carcinogens) and the effect that man and animals may experience from exposure to the ever-increasing number of carcinogens of this technological age[39]. I believe that the monitoring of the global effect of this injurious environment and its control, which are part of my present research efforts, constitutes one of the most formidable problems which both scientists and society have ever faced.

Francisco J. Ayala

An intensive work in the field of genetics has been carried out by Professor Francisco J. Ayala, who came from Madrid, in 1962 obtained his Ph.D. at Columbia University, and is now Professor in the Department of Genetics at the University of California at Davis. In experiments carried out with *Drosophila,* he has studied the influence and response of insect populations to several challenging environmental factors: density, limitation of space and food availability. Professor Ayala had found that these challenged populations evolve genetically to become adapted to these environmental factors. In addition, populations with greater initial amounts of genetic variation (either by crossing strains from different localities or be irradiation) evolve and grow faster[40,42].

A special interest in Dr. Ayala's studies is in the humanistic and ethical implications of Biology, in particular Evolution and Genetics. He has an impressive list of publications starting with religious and social problems. His production and meteoric career contain a remarkable combination of old Castillian characteristics and rigorous genetic research.

Josep G. Llauradó

A Professor of Biomedical Engineering, Josep Llauradó, from Barcelona, is now at the Medical College of Wisconsin. He is working in the fields of compartmental analysis of electrolyte distribution in tissues, extrarenal effects of aldosterone and digital computer simulation of physiologic functions.

For a long time it was thought that cells were impermeable to sodium and potassium ions because of the high concentration of sodium and low concentration in potassium outside the cell in relation to the inside. The cells manage to keep sodium outside, but both alkaline cations can cross the cell membrane from the inside and also leave the cell. This dynamic equilibrium is maintained by several forces (osmotic, diffusion, hydrostatic pressure and active transport). For these studies, Professor Llauradó is using radioactive tracers or auxiliary chemical substances and takes advantage of the digital computer simulation program[43].

Carlos López

A young virologist from Ponce, Puerto Rico, Dr. Carlos López, is working on those types of viruses which contain DNA. His accomplishments include the isolation and characterization of a new number of the virus group (progressive pneumonia of sheep, similar to that previously studied by Durán-Reynals)[44], at the Rocky Mountain Public Health Laboratory. He later worked with R.A. Good at the University of Minnesota on herpesvirus infections in immunodeficient and immunosuppressed patients[45], Dr. López, now at Sloan-Kettering Institute, is trying to understand what role the immune system plays in resistance to virus infection. He has found that the cellular type of immunity was responsible for this resistance. He has carried out extensive studies in certain types of inbred strains of mice which are excellent tools with which to investigate the cellular deficit associated with these infections[46]. Dr. López anticipates that these studies will lead to the possibility of pinpointing genes and gene products responsible for resistance to herpesvirus infection. These viruses are of importance as they may be associated with the induction of cancer.

Jaime Miquel

Dr. Miguel, a biologist from Valencia, presently at NASA in the Ames Research Center in California, has been active in the field of gerontology, that is, the process of aging and its possible implication in the development of cancer. According to him, the influences of the brain on every tissue of the body makes the study of the aging of the central nervous system the basic element of research in gerontology. The presence of arteriosclerosis in humans is an obstacle to the study of "normal aging" of the brain. Since rodents do not suffer from arteriosclerosis, rodent brains at varying ages have been used by Dr. Miquel to study different signs of aging in the nerve cells[47]. In addition to rodents, *Drosophila melanogaster,* the fruit fly, which already rendered great services in the hands of Morgan in discovering the principle of the gene, is also being used in these studies[48]. The similarity between cytoplasmic degeneration in these invertebrates and mammalian nerve cells of rodents suggests the existence of common structural features of aging. The effect on the aging process of either the absence or presence of vitamin E was also studied by Dr. Miquel. He found that vitamin E does not alter the age-associated degeneration. In the *Drosophila,* the aging process was studied by determining the percentage of fluorescent lipopigments present in the cytoplasmic volume.

Roberto Segura

A young researcher from Valencia, Dr. Roberto Segura, came in 1970 to the University of Kansas and now is at Cornell Medical College. His field is neuropharmacology, the study of the effect of different chemical stimuli at the level of the neuromuscular junction[49]. He is also involved in the study of the effect of malignant tumors of the same junction. Dr. Segura is investigating the nature of a factor that he believes is released by the tumor and would cause the degeneration of nerves and muscles, accounting for the observed weakness of cancer patients[50].

Osias Stutman

There is a growing interest in the field of Immunology, derived in part by recent developments in the elucidation of the structure and function of antibodies and a greater knowledge in the cellular immune response. Dr. Osias Stutman, from Buenos Aires, collaborated with the Nobel laureates Houssay and LeLoir. He came to Minnesota Medical School in 1967 where he worked with R.A. Good. He is now at the Sloan-Kettering Institute investigating among other problems the ontogeny of immunological function (both T-cell and B-cells, thymus and nonthymus-dependent), their involution and role in the development of tumors[51],[52]. He also "tries to understand the immunity against tumors, their characterization and mechanism." The importance of these studies is based upon the recognition of the existence of an immune response in the body against cancer and the need to increase this response as an effective therapy[53].

M. García-Muñoz

In the field of Physics, I would like to mention the figure of Dr. Moises García-Muñoz, an astrophysicist from Valencia, who was working on the Spanish Atomic Commission and is now at the Enrico Fermi Institute for Nuclear Studies at the University of Chicago. Dr. García-Muñoz is working towards the goal of obtaining the isotopic composition of cosmic rays. This knowledge is essential for the solution of the problem of their origin, confinement and propagation[54]. For this research, Dr. García-Muñoz has used experiments on satellites and space probes, which have led to the discovery of low energy galactic helium and has carried the first measurement of the cosmic ray lifetime using artificial satellites[55].

It is generally accepted that cosmic rays originate from concentrated matter; therefore, it is natural to assume that the detection in cosmic rays of primary antinuclei would imply the existence in the Universe of concentrated antimatter. The analysis of cosmic rays could, therefore, supply direct evidence about the occurrence of concentrated antimatter in the Universe undergoing parallel processes of stellar evolution and nuclear synthesis[56].

Alberto Sirlin

An outstanding Physicist, Professor Alberto Sirlin, came from Buenos Aires in 1959 and has since been in the Department of Physics at New York University. His activities have led him to participate in numerous institutions around the globe as a Visiting Professor, mainly at the CERN Nuclear Studies Center in Geneva. He has been interested for many years in the study of the weak and electromagnetic interactions of elementary particles, which in recent years has been a trend towards a unified theory (unified gauge theory) of the weak and electromagnetic interactions. Sirlin has also been working on aspects of extended solutions of relativistic field theories[57,58].

According to Professor Sirlin, four fundamental interactions (or forces) exist in the Universe: strong interactions, such as nuclear forces between neutrons and protons, which keep the atomic nucleus together; electromagnetic interactions, which dominate the forces between atoms (all chemical and perhaps biochemical reactions are included here); weak interactions of β-decay of the atomic nucleus; and, finally, gravitational interactions, which dominate the Universe at the cosmological level. Sirlin is studying the elementary particles which are involved in the first three types of interactions and which have been unified in the gauge theory. He has predicted that this theory can be confirmed experimentally[59].

J. Gómez-Ibáñez

Since 1942 Dr. Gomez-Ibañez has been at Wesleyan University where he is now Professor of Chemistry. The thermodynamics of solutions, the physical properties of macromolecules and the critical states of matter have been his main field of research[60,61]. He has been actively involved in educational problems, especially the promotion of the teaching of chemistry in Hispanic America[62].

C. Villar-Palasí

Work on glycogen metabolism and the mechanism of action of cyclic adenosine monophosphate has been the main research topic of Dr. Villar-Palasí, who came to this country in 1957 and is presently Professor of Pharmacology at the University of Virginia School of Medicine. Professor Villar-Palasí has carried out investigations on the hormonal effects on the glycogen metabolism[63] demonstrating that a pyrophosphorylase was responsible for glycogen synthesis instead of the previously formulated phosphorylase. Villar-Palasí has made the important discovery that the degree of dependence of the enzyme synthase kinase on cyclic adenosine monophosphate was increased by insulin and found a plausible mechanism for the inotropic effect of epinephrine. This work is being extended to the effect of diverse hormones on heart and other types of muscle.

David Cardus

The application of mathematics to biology and medicine has entered a new era with the advent of electronic computers. To create a bridge between the science of numbers and the art of healing has been one of the main endeavors of Professor David Cardus since his arrival to the United States in 1957.

Professor Cardus was born in Barcelona, where he graduated from Medical School. After a period of research on respiratory physiology in several centers in Spain, France and England, he came in 1957 to the Department of Physiology, Lovelace Foundation in Albuquerque. Since 1960 he has been in Houston where he is currently Director of Research and Director of the Biomathematics Division of the Department of Rehabilitation of Baylor College of Medicine.

The main scientific contributions of Dr. Cardus can be classified into three fields: First, the physiology of exercise, which was the reason for his coming to the USA to work in the space program before the foundation of NASA. He participated (in cooperation with Dr. Luft) in the basic physiological studies which led to the selection of the first seven astronauts.[64] Second, his mathematical background, quite unusual in a physician, led Dr. Cardus to the development of computer techniques for the study of the various physiological functions. In this manner, he has been a pioneer in the introduction of the computer in biomedical science. His interest in the field of biomathematics is attested by his publication of a book on mathematics for biomedical investigators.[65] He has, among others, developed mathematical models of heartbeat frequency responses to exercise and recovery.[66] In addition, he has been involved in the application of computers to the rehabilitation of patients with ischemic heart disease.[67, 68] Third, he has devoted much effort to the question of the concept of health. Dr. Cardus has been proposing for years the urgent need for a medicine based on the concept of health in contrast to all the present thinking and focusing of "health" systems upon disease: "There is some degree of logical inconsistency in using the terms "health systems" when the actual concern is disease and not health."[69, 70] Cardus has stated that an up-to-date concept of health should be based on the study of human performance in response to a variety of physical and non-physical factors. In this manner, according to him, human performance can be described in three possible dimensions: 1) the capacity to perform determinate functions, 2) the optimization with which these functions can be performed taking into consideration the state of the organism, and 3) the adaptability of the organism to environmental changes.

Cardus feels that up to the present, progress in medicine has been to a great extent more the result of sanitation and preventive measures than the eradication of disease. There is, according to him, a need for the identification of the attributes of health in man so as to understand human behavior and his aspirations for a better life in this time of ever-increasing industrialization.

I have had the opportunity to observe the keen interest of Dr. Cardus in humanistic and social problems. His dedication to research on health problems is matched only by his devotion to tasks such as the Institute of Hispanic Culture of Houston, of which he is Chairman of the Board of Directors. I have heard him stating that the scientist to be a true scientist must be involved in the social problems of his time. David Cardus has given this example of dedication in his work as a medical scientist and in his enthusiasm for furthering Hispanic ideals and culture in the United States.

The Impact of Hispanic Scientists in the United States

Science does succeed by a burst of activity of individuals within the framework of a social organization which allows full use of this activity.

Well-run societies make good science, but not necessarily vice-versa. The infusion of new scientists from Spain and Hispanic America to the scientific community of the United States is an enterprise in which the Hispanic culture is taking a new fulfillment.

In evaluating the impact of scientists on human knowledge and, in our case, that of Hispanic investigators on American science, one has to consider the diverse fields of discovery.

A summing up of the main directions of research shows in the first place the fruitfulness of the work by Hispanic scientists in the field of biological and biomedical sciences. This is exemplified in the work of the disciples and followers of Cajal, such as Lorente de Nó, Folch-Pi, Fernández-Morán, Miquel and others in their research on the structure, function and composition of the nervous system. This type of work is of utmost value to clinicians, from histologists and neurologists to psychiatrists. The importance of this contribution is revealed by the enormous problem of mental disorders which increasingly afflict the United States and the world.

In the field of virology, I have shown how the pioneering figure of Durán-Reynals developed the concept, now recognized as entirely valid, that the most common viruses can induce cancer. This concept is of capital importance for the understanding and treatment of this disease, the second important cause of death in the United States. The possibility of viruses as a cause of cancer, with or without the concurrence of carcinogenic substances, has contributed to the current vigorous upsurge in the study of immunology and the search for an immunotherapeutic remedy against cancer, be it in the form of a vaccine or by activation of the immune response of the body as a primary defense against the disease. Working in this field the young Hispanic scientists, López and Stutman, are developing promising new techniques.

The research on enzymes and nucleic acid components which attempts to unravel the vital processes of protein biosynthesis and nucleic acid metabolism has constituted a most significant scientific contribution by Ochoa, Grisolía and others. These studies have a possible application to the understanding of cellular mechanisms leading to cancer.

The exploration of the Solar System is among the greatest feats of the present century from the manned landing to the probes into the planets. I have referred to the contributions of Oró, to the decisive breakthrough of prebiotic synthesis and the development of analytical procedures to search for biogenic elements and compounds in the Moon and Mars. I also wish to remind you of the outer space exploration searching for the composition and origin of cosmic rays made by García Muñoz and the role of Cardus in the selection of astronauts in the space program. In this manner Spaniards have been contributing to the epic of the exploration of new worlds as they were previously present in the discovery and settlement of America.

I would like to mention some institutions whose activities have been pivotal for the renaissance to Spanish science and for the two-directional flow of scientists between the United States and Spain. In the first place, I should mention the "Junta de Amplicación de Estudios" founded earlier in the century to promote studies abroad by Spanish scientists and scholars. This "Junta" was an outgrowth of the "Institución Libre de la Enseñanza" created by Giner de los Rios, a pioneer of the yet unfinished tasks of a "Europeanization" of the Spanish educational system. Other organizations which have been helping the development of research in Spain are the Cajal Institute and the Rockefeller Foundation. Since 1939 the "Consejo Superior de Investigaciones Científicas," the Fundación March and the Fulbright scientific assistance programs have sparked and stimulated to a greater extent the scientific exchange and collaboration which has contributed in part to the flourishing of a multifaceted Spanish school of science in the United States.

Conclusion

I have succinctly examined the main aspects of the impact and contributions by scientists from Spain and Hispanic America in basic and applied science. I would like finally to discuss one of the rewards that most of the scientists from the Hispanic countries obtain by working and settling in the United States. In addition to a more fertile soil, they experience the feeling of breathing a current of fresh air, away from certain traditional views centered around nebulous and rigid absolutes. The mainstay of the scientific endeavor is the free use and acceptance of critical analysis and the harmony and synthesis of conflicting views. This atmosphere and spirit is found in the United States, and it is absolutely essential for the efficient development of any scientific enterprise. The Hispanic scientist in the United States has been attracted by this atmosphere and taken full advantage of it for the furthering of his goals.

Two opposite conceptions of science are summarized in the quotations with which I prefaced this article. The prevalent American (or in broader sense, Anglo-Saxon) concept of the quest for truth consists in viewing the scientific endeavor as a never-ending struggle and an always-evolving process, and not a simple accumulation of data. Science is not a goal to be attained by cataloging the Universe but by an unending adventure, a search never satisfied with the possession; to use an expression of Don Quixote: "The road is always better than the inn."

It will remain for sociologists and historians to investigate and pass an ultimate judgement about the unique phenomenon represented by the emigration of a large number of Spanish scientists to the United States in recent times. So far as I know, no other country can match the extent of its contribution of science in the United States so proportionately high in relation to the size of its scientific community as has been done by Spain. I would also dare to say that the quality of this contribution runs parallel to its quantity. It has not been my purpose to discuss this fact, which has been debated frequently in publications among which I could mention the incisive analysis by Gómez Gil. I would like to point out, however, that this phenomenon leads to the reflection about its causes, the peculiar idiosyncrasy of the Spanish scientist and above all the unusual historical circumstances of the recent decades.

In summary, a two-way, mutual impact has been operating between the contributions from the highly imaginative and valuable work of a large number of Hispanic scientists in this country and the beneficial influence that the American scientific spirit has brought about in most of us. These accomplishments should be present in our minds as incentives to face the challenge of the future.

Acknowledgments

The work by the author referred to in this article was supported in part by the National Cancer Institute Grant CA-08748. I am indebted to the scientists discussed in this article for data on their contributions and especially to Dr. M.L. Durán-Reynals for helping me with the biographical sketch of her late husband. I thank Drs. D. Cardus, A. Gómez Gil, R.W. Moss, J. Oró and J.M. Segarra for valuable discussions and suggestions. I gratefully acknowledge the skillful editorial assistance of Mrs. P. Higgins in the preparation of this article.

References

1. Cannon, D.F., "Explorer of the Human Brain: The Life of S.R. Cajal," Schuman, New York, p. 195, 1949.

2. Penfield, W., *Arch. Neurol. and Psychiatry, 16;* 231-220, 1920.

3. Durán-Reynals, F., Exaltation de l'activité du virus vaccinal par les extraits de certains organes. *C.R. Soc. Biol. 99:* 6-7, 1928.

4. Durán-Reynals, F., The effect of extracts of certain organs from normal and immunized animals on the infecting power of vaccine virus. *J. Exp. Med. 50:* 327-340, 1929.

5. Durán-Reynals, F. and Shriegley, E.W., Virus infection as an etiologic agent of cancer. *A.A.A.S. Conference on Cancer.* 1-23, 1945.

6. Folch-Pi, J., The isolation of phosphatidyl serine from brain cephalin and identification of the serine component. *J. Biol. Chem. 139:*973, 1941.

7. Folch-Pi, J. and Wooley, D.W., Inositol, a constituent of a brain phosphatide. *J. Biol.*

*Chem. 142:*963, 1942.

8. Folch-Pi, J., Brain cephalin, a mixture of phosphatides. Separation from it of phosphatidyl serine, phosphatidyl ethanolamine and a fraction containing an inositol phosphatide. *J. Biol. Chem 146:*35, 1942.

9. Folch-Pi, J., Brain diphosphoinositide, a new phosphatide having inositol metadiphosphate as a constituent. *J. Biol. Chem. 177:*505, 1949.

10. Folch-Pi, J. and Lees, M., Proteolipids, a new type of tissue lipoproteins. Their isolation from brain. *J. Biol. Chem. 191:*807, 1951.

11. Folch-Pi, J., Ascoli, I., Lees, M., Meath, J.A. and LeBaron, F.N., Preparation of lipide extracts from brain tissue. *J. Biol. Chem. 191:*833, 1951.

12. Folch-Pi, J. and Lees, M. and Sloane Stanley, G.H., A simple method for the isolation and purification of total lipids from animal tissues. *J. Biol. Chem. 226:*497, 1957.

13. Gómez Gil, A., "Cerebros españoles en los U.S.A.," Janés, Barcelona, 1971.

14. Casals, J., Arbovirus infections *Serol. Epidemoil.* 99-117, 1973.

15. Casals, J., Arena viruses. *Yale J. Biol. Med. 48:* 115-140, 1975.

16. Ochoa, S., Biological mechanisms of carboxylation and decarboxylation. *Physiol. Rev.* 31:56-106, 1951.

17. Ochoa, S., Enzymatic mechanisms in the citric acid cycle. *Adv. Enzymol. 15:*183-270, 1954.

18. Grunberg-Manaho, M., Ortíz,D.J. and Ochoa, S., Enzymatic sythesis of nucleic acid-like polynucleotide. *Science 122:*907-910, 1955.

19. Riedman, S.R. and Gustafson, E.T., "Portraits of Novel Laureates," Schuman, New York, 1963.

20. Ochoa, S., Synthetic polynucleotides and the genetic code. *Fed. Proc. 22:*62-74, 1963.

21. Nombela, C., Nombela, N.A., Ochoa, S., Safer, B., Anderson, W.F. and Merrick, W.C., Polypeptide chain initiation in eukaryotes: Mechanism of formation of initiation complex. *Proc. Nat. Acad. Sci. 73:*298-301, 1976.

22. Grande-Covián, F., "Severo Ochoa" *I.C.S.U. Rev. World Sci. 5:*147-158, 1963.

23. Grisolía, S. and Hood, W., *In* "Biochemical Regulation Mechanisms in Eukaryotic Cells." E. Kun and S. Grisolía, eds., Wiley, New York, 1972.

24. Grisolía, S., Wagner, R., and Mayor R., eds. "The Urea Cycle," Wiley, in press.

25. Oró, J., Mechanism of synthesis of adenine from hydrogen cyanide under possible primitive Earth conditions, *Nature 191:*1193-1194, 1961.

26. Oró, J. and Kimball, A.P., Synthesis of purines under possible primitive Earth conditions. *Arch. Biochem. Biophys.* 96:293-313, 1962.

27. Oró, J., Flory, D.A., Gilbert, J.M., Reynolds, J.M., Lichenstein, H.A. and Wikstran, S., Abundances and distribution of organogenic elements and compounds in Apollo 12 lunar samples. *Proc. 2nd Lunar Sci. Conf. 2,* 1913-1925, 1971.

28. Oró, J., Personal communication.

29. Oró, J. and Nooner, D.W., Aliphatic hydrocarbons in pre-Cambrian rocks. *Nature 213:*1082-1085, 1967.

30. Olson, R.J., Oró, J. and Zlatkis, A., Organic compounds in meteorites, II. Aromatic hydrocarbons. *Geochim. Cosmochim. Acta 2, 31,* 1935:1948, 1967.

31. Gelpí, E., Nooner, D.W. and Oró, J., The ubiquity of hydrocarbons in nature *Geochim. Cosmochim. Acta 2, 34,* 421:475, 1970.

32. Lewis, R.S., "Humberto Fernández-Morán, "Men of Science," 382, 1972.

33. Segarra, J.M., Cerebral vascular disease and behavior. Arch. Neurol. *22:* 408-418, 1970.

34. Boller, F. and Segarra, J.M., Spino-pontine degeneration. *Eur. Neurol. 2:*356-373, 1969.

35. Giner-Sorolla, A., Burchenal, J.H. and Bendich, A., Hydroxylaminopurines: Synthesis, physiochemical properties and bioligical activity. *In* The Purines, Theory and Experiment. E.D.

Bergmann and B. Pullman, eds. The Jerusalem, Isreal Academy of Sciences, pp 478-503, 1972.

36. Giner-Sorolla, A., Longley-Cook, J., McCravey, M., Brown, G.B. and Burchenal, J.H., Nitrosaminopurines and nucleosides, synthesis and biological activity. *J. Med. Chem. 16*:365, 1973.

37. López, C. and Giner-Sorolla, A., Arabinosyl-N^6-hydroxyadenine: A new potent antiherpesvirus drug. *N.Y. Acad. Sci., Abstr. Meeting*, p. 31, February, 1976.

38. Giner-Sorolla, A. and Bendich, A., The emergence of carcinogens during the evolution of living systems. *In* Cosmochemical Evolution and the Origins of Life. J. Oró, ed., Vol. *2*, 315:323, Reidel, Dordrecht, 1975.

39. Giner-Sorolla, A., Los carcinógenos químicos: Productos naturales. *Afinidad* (Barcelona) *32*, 141-156, 1975.

40. Ayala, F., Genotype, environment and population numbers. *Science 162*: 1453-1459, 1968.

41. Ayala, F., Competition between species. *Am. Sci. 60*:348-357, 1972.

42. Ayala, F., Biological Evolution: Natural selection or random walk? *Am. Sci. 62*:692-701, 1974.

43. Llauradó, J.G., Digital computer simulations, an aid to the study of arterial wall Na Kinetics. *J. Appl. Physiol. 27*:544-550, 1969.

44. López, C., Eklund, C.M. and Hadlow, W.G., Tissue culture studies of the virus of progressive pneumonia. A slow infectious disease of sheep. *Proc. Soc. Exp. Biol. Med. 138*:1035-1040, 1971.

45. López, C., Simmons, R.L., Mauer, S.M., Nagerian, J.S. and Good, R.A., The association of renal allograft rejection with virus infection. *Am. J. Med. 56*:280-289, 1974.

46. López, C. *Nature 258*: 152, 1975.

47. Johnson, J.E., Jr. and Miguel, J., Fine structural changes in the internal vestibular nucleus of aging rats. *Mechanisms of Ageing and Development 3*: 203-324, 1974.

48. Miguel, J., Tappel, A.L., Dillard, C.J., Herman, M.M. and Benson, K.G., Fluorescent products and lysosomal components in ageing *Drosophila melanogaster. J. Gerontol. 29*:622-637, 1974.

49. Segura, R., Effect of glucocorticoids on the neuromuscular juction in normal population and in *Myastenia gravis. Neurology*, in press.

50. Segura, R. and Ziegler, D., Dermatomyosites and cancer. *Dis. Nerv. Syst. 34*:284-288, 1973.

51. Stutman, O., Hemopoietic origin of B cells in the mouse. *In* "Micro-environmental factors of immunity." Jankovic and K. Isakovic, eds., New York, pp 19-26, 1973.

52. Stutman, O., Timo y desarrollo inmunológico. *Medicina* (Buenos Aires) *31*:610-625, 1975.

53. Stutman, O and Good, R.A., Immune response and neoplasia. *Adv. Biol. Skin. XI*:357-385, 1975.

54. García-Muñoz, M., Cosmic ray charge composition ($Z \lesssim 28$), Proc. 13th Int. Cosmic Ray Conference, Denver, Col. Vol. *5*, pp. 3513-3568, 1973.

55. García-Muñoz, M. and Simpson, J.A., Galactic abundances and spectra of cosmic rays measured on the IMP-4 satelite. Proc. 11th Int. Cosmic Ray Conference, Budapest, *Acta. Physiol. Sci. Hung. 29*, Suppl. 1, 317-323 and 325-330, 1970.

56. García-Muñoz, Mason, G.M. and Simpson, J.A., The isotopic composition of galactic cosmic ray lithium, beryllium and boron. *Astrophys. J. 201*: L145-L148, 1975.

57. Sirlin, A., Role of strong interactions and the intermediate boron in the radiative corrections to weak processes. *Acta. Phys. Aust., Suppl. V*:354-390, 1968.

58. Beg, M.A.B. and Sirlin, A., Gauge theories of weak interactions. *Annu. Rev. Nucl. Sci. 24*:379-449, 1974.

59. Sachs. A.M. and Sirlin, A., *Muon Physics,* Vol. *II:*49-81, Academic Press, 1975.

60. Gómez-Ibáñez, J.D. and Shieh, J.C., The excess free energy of mixtures of cyclohexane and *n*-Hexadecane. *J. Phys. Che. 69:*1660, 1965.

61. Gómez-Ibáñez, J.D. and Wang, F.T., The excess Gibbs energy of mixtures of cyclohexane with *n*-Eicosane and with two other *n*-Alkanes. A relation of congruence. *J. Chem. Thermodynamics 3:*65-117, 1969.

62. Gómez-Ibáñez, J.D., Chemical education activites in Ibero-America. *J. Chem. Educ. 41:*586, 1964.

63.Villar-Palasí, C., The hormonal regulation of glycogen metabolism in the muscle. *Vitam. Horm.* New York *3:*65-117, 1969.

64. Cardus, D., Quantitation in Biology and Medicine. J. Chron. Dis. *19:* 319-324, 1966.

65. Cardus, D., "Introducción a las matemáticas para médicos y biólogos "(Introduction to Mathematics for Biomedical Investigators). Barcelona, Editorial Vicens-Vives, 1972.

66. Cardus, D. and Zeigler, R.K., Heart-beat frequency curves. A mathematical model. *Comput. Biomed. Res. 1:*508-526, 1968.

67. Cardus, D. Compreshensive testing in ischemic heart disease. Proceedings of the International Federation for Information Processing. Hanover, Germany, October 11-15, 1971.

68. Cardus, D., Fuentes, F. and Srinivasan, R. Cardiac evaluation of a physical rehabilitation program for patients with ischemic heart disease. *Arch. Phys. Med. Rehabil. 56:*419-425, 1975.

69. Cardus, D. Towards a medicine based on the concept of health. *Preventive Medicine 2:*309-312, 1973.

70. Cardus, D., Implicacions médiques d'una nova aproximació al concepte de salut. (Medical implication of a new approach to the concept of health). Anales de Medicina, Academia de Ciéncias Médicas de Cataluña y Baleares, pp. 507-537, 1973.

ROLE OF HEALTH IN INTERNATIONAL RELATIONS

Hector R. Acuña

I am pleased and honored to have been invited to the Bicentennial Symposium, sponsored by the Institute of Hispanic Culture of Houston, during this year of historic celebrations for the United States of America.

The Pan American Health Organization, which I am honored to serve as Director, has been associated with the international health activities of the United States for almost half the period covered by the bicentennium of independence.

As we approach the year 1977, we are nearing the 75th Anniversary of the Pan American Health Organization. This means the completion of seventy-five years of service to international public health activities in the Americas. The Organization has grown during this period from a small international entity to a rather large and complex structure.

Allow me now to give you a little bit of history as to the origins of PAHO. At the beginning of the century, a spirit of hope and expectation was prevailing throughout the Americas, with the signing of new state treaties and the expansion of commercial relations. However, those years were clouded with the constant threat of epidemics which the individual countries fought and suffered, generally alone since quarantine restrictions were arbitrary and ineffective, thus interrupting travel and commerce.

It was in Mexico, my country of birth, that in January of 1902 eleven American Republics met, at the Second International Conference of American States, to discuss peaceful arbitration and commercial relations. Quarantine and sanitation policy was formally adopted. In December of that year, a permanent Executive Board, known as the International Sanitary Bureau, was established in Washington, D.C. with the following objective: "To lend its best aid and experience towards the widest possible protection of the public health of each republic in order that diseases may be eliminated and that commerce between said republics may be faciliated."

Changing its name later to the Pan American Sanitary Bureau, in 1947 it became the executive arm of the Pan American Sanitary Organization which in turn became the Pan American Health Organization in 1958. And so, PAHO was born; the world's oldest international health body. Its Secretariat, the Pan American Sanitary Bureau serves, since 1949, as the Regional Office of the Americas for the World Health Organization.

The Constitution of the World Health Organization was ratified on April 7, 1948. WHO is a specialized agency of the United Nations, carrying out programs in the field of health. It operates under the review of the General Assembly and the Economic and Social Council, but retains autonomy in matters of membership, program, personnel and finance. It now has 145 full and three associate members. Its budget is supported by contributions effected on a quota system from Member States, based on the United Nations scale. Additional funds for technical assistance are provided by several other UN organizations, notably UNDP, UNICEF, UNFPA, FAO and WFP. It works in close collaboration with bilateral organizations such as AID and CIDA in programs of mutual interest. In the last six years, the development banks, principally the World Bank and the Inter-American Development Bank, have been very much involved in this Region in developing programs with a large health component.

Health is regarded as one of the fundamental rights of every human being. Governments have responsibility for adequate health services and other social measures. Health we recognize as "a state of complete physical, mental and social well-being and not merely the absence of disease or infirmity."

As the Director-General of WHO stated last February at the United Nations, "We have learned from bitter experience that, in development, the economic and social factors must be inextricably linked, and that seeming progress on one side cannot be well founded without support and reinforcement from the other. Economic measures have a very direct bearing on health, and health measures in turn must make a direct contribution to development. But too often, we have seen economic growth accompanied by social stagnation, if not outright social deterioration and tension."

The emphasis of WHO has been towards the developing countries, though it continues to have a responsibility to assist and advise developed countries where degenerative diseases, mental illness, virus diseases, carcinoma and social disorders are pressing problems.

Likewise, PAHO plays an important role in international health. The Pan American Health Organization is responsible for drawing up, in collaboration with its 27 full members and 3 associate members, a plan of international cooperation for health activities within the budgetary allocations approved by its Directing Bodies. Surinam is now in the process of becoming the 31st member of our Organization, after gaining its independence in 1975. In the Americas, with a mosaic of cultures and problems, planning a composite and harmonious program of technical cooperation is no easy task. For this reason, its health situation should be examined within the context of socioeconomic development.

While our experience has shown that the health sector itself is capable of achieving substantial advances in specific areas, the problems prevailing in Latin America and the Caribbean are such that new solutions and multisectorial approaches must be adopted, if a real impact is to be made.

This is indeed the approach that PAHO is following in its cooperative efforts to help the Member Governments in dealing with their existing health problems, particularly with the extension of the coverage of health services to underserved populations.

During the last decades, there has been a continuous economic growth in most countries, leading to a 5% annual increase in their gross national product, while the population is augmenting at the annual rate of 3%. Despite these achievements, it is evident that economic growth has not automatically ensured an equitable distribution of income and improvement of living conditions. One outstanding feature of recent socioeconomic developement in the countries of the Americas, is the lack of balance between the "needs" and "expectations" of a constantly growing population and the limited capacity of the national economies to satisfy them.

The peoples of the Americas have now a more clear consciousness of their rights. Consequently, all population groups expect to attain the living standards of the developed world which have so far been enjoyed by only small groups in the developing countries. They also claim the right to participate actively in the decision-making processes and to define their real needs, thus having a direct bearing on their own destiny.

The lesson to be learned is that developing countries cannot hope to solve their problems by following the patterns of economic growth that made prosperous the developed countries, due to the social cost unbearable in a world shaken by a revolution of human rights and rising expectations.

The population is by far the greatest source of wealth in Latin America and the Caribbean, and represents their present and future potential. Changes in its total numbers, distribution, age structure and life expectancy are of primary importance for the provision of health services.

In 1930, the population of the United States and Canada surpassed that of Latin America by 24 million. By now the total Latin American population of 300 million is 25% higher than that of the two before mentioned countries, and it is estimated that by the end of the century it will be twice as much, reaching the impressive figure of over 650 million people.

In most of the Latin American countries, the proportion of population growth in rural areas is still higher than that of the urban areas, although it tends to decrease since it is estimated that by the year 2000, around three of every four Latin Americans will live in urban areas. This increasing migratory flow to the cities results mainly from poor living conditions and lack of working opportunities in the rural areas. People are attracted by the mirage created by modern mass communications which stimulate and widen their expectations. However, only a few of them are able to reach a higher standard of living and the rest agglomerate themselves in slums and shanty towns, aggravating the already existing problems in the major cities.

The population of Latin America is young considering that 43% are under 15 years of age and 20% are women of child-bearing age. These groups represent 63% of the total population.

Life expectancy flunctuates between 60 and 65 years, and in some countries it has reached levels comparable to those of developed countries. Problems originating from this situation begin to show their implications in health care, demanding new types of services and facilities.

Differences in the health situation exist among countries, as well as within regions and communities in each country, which determine a variety of health needs. However, health problems in Latin America as a whole are essentially due to communicable diseases and poor environmental conditions. These are aggravated by a very low per capita income in most of the countries which prevents the population from having an adequate diet. The combination of these factors results in high mortality and morbidity rates that mostly affect vulnerable groups, such as women and children.

Although modern health technology is used to combat diseases, its benefits have not yet reached all population groups in Latin America. An appraisal of the situation, carried out at the beginning of the present decade, showed that approximately 40% of the total population had no access to health services. This is particularly affecting population groups living in rural areas or in the outskirts of large cities.

Health services, on the other hand, as a result of traditional approaches and concepts, are mostly oriented to the individual care of the sick, with little regard for the health needs of the community. This is the result of a legacy of systems and approaches designed and implemented in the past by the countries of today's developed world. For the most part, they have remained unchanged in Latin America.

Health care services, both of preventive and curative nature, are provided in the various countries through governmental institutions, as well as through the various countries through government-subsidized and private agencies, which assume responsibility for segments of the population.

The dramatic rise in the cost of supporting a health-care establishment has been the main reason for the provision of health services rapidly becoming a major source of debate. The Governments and the people are understandably concerned over the prospect of spending 8%, or more, of their gross national product on health services. Investments of this magnitude inevitably give rise to questions concerning the relationship between value and expenditure, that is, the benefit against the use of scarce resources. On the other hand, when access to needed medical care is left under individual responsibility, far more is the preoccupation with acute cases and with a way to cope with the increasing cost of these services.

In spite of the efforts made by the countries of the continent to increase the number of physicians, dentists, nurses and other health personnel, they are in short supply. The number of graduates from universities and training schools, has not kept pace with population growth. Although between 1960 and 1969 the number of doctors increased about 41% in Central America, the effect of this tremendous effort was neutralized, in a significant proportion, by the population increase, that for the same period was about 32%. As a result, the ratio of the doctors to population remained nearly static.

The Ministers of Health, well aware of the situation which I have just described, adopted Ten-Year Health Plan for the Americas when they met in Santiago, Chile, in 1972, which defines priority lines of action, establishes objectives and areas of major interest, and identifies basic strategies for the Region as a whole.

The central objective of the Ten-Year Health Plan is the extension of health service coverage to underserved populations, starting with the provision of primary health care with community participation. With this purpose, the Plan gives priority to four fundamental programs.

First, the reduction of morbidity and mortality caused by the most prevalent communicable diseases and the eradication of malaria in areas with approximately 75 million inhabitants. Second, programs of maternal and child health, designed to reduce mortality in these vulnerable groups. Third, intensification of programs to reduce grade III protein-calorie malnutrition by 85% and grade II by 30% in children under five years of age. Fourth, environmental sanitation programs which, during the decade will provide water and sewage services to more than 80% of the urban population and 50% of the rural population. This also includes water, air and soil pollution control.

Specific regional goals were developed for each program area, in addition to which our Organization has promoted the development by each country of its own national goals in the light of their cultural patterns and their social and economic development, clearly stating their objectives and the structural changes needed to achieve them. As an Organization concerned with the transfer of technical skills and with suitable programs in human resource development, we have endeavoured to build and increase the capability in planning and programming of each Member Country, thereby ensuring optimal use of their own resources and external assistance. We are commited to the concept that greater community participation is essential in the development and, more particularly, in the implementation of comprehensive national health plans and programs.

The implementation of the Ten-Year Health Plan calls for a new concept of international solidarity. The developed countries must learn how to assist the developing countries without attempting to impose solutions on them. The solutions required today must be those which the affected population is capable of implementing with its own resources.

In addition, technological advances should be adapted and not simply adopted and new and more efficient and effective technical and administrative solutions should be developed, in order to maximize the potential of utilization of the scarce financial resources, bearing in mind a cost-effectiveness approach.

Within these approaches, the countries of the Region are trying to meet their real community needs for coverage. Active, conscientious and well-informed participation of the community in the identification of their real needs and expectations and in the design of appropriate solutions is a basic component of the newly adopted strategies for health care in the Region.

From this, it clearly follows that coverage of health services has a new dimension within the Ten-Year Plan, in which a multisectorial approach is essentially required. In practical terms, this implies a complete redefinition of the roles of the health professionals, whose education has been rooted in the traditionalism and authority of scientific disciplines. It would be necessary, in the first place, to critically review the training programs in order to overcome their limited vision of the problems and to eliminate prejudice and traditional teaching so as to facilitate the development of new forms of rendering services, on the basis of a team-approach through which auxiliary and technical personnel should work side by side towards a common goal.

Decision-making opportunities are being developed where highly knowledgeable and talented health professionals should be available to contribute ideas, experiences and creative and innovative thinking. International technical cooperation agencies must also support the countries in this endeavour.

The Pan American Health Organization is currently undergoing a reorganization, by developing a new approach to our program of work. This is of utmost importance since our Organization needs to be structured in such a way that it can adapt readily and quickly to the rapidly changing Region that we serve. This reorganization involves changes in the functional structure of PAHO; its headquarters and its Area and Field Offices.

There are many organizations and agencies providing assistance in the field of health, and one of our major tasks is the coordination of these efforts so as to optimize the effect on the health of the peoples of the Americas. We have Representatives in all independent countries of the Americas; they are responsible for programming and coordinating the technical cooperation to our Member Governments. They strive to maintain good working relations with international and bilateral agency representatives in the countries they serve to ensure collaboration and integration of all technical cooperation in the health field.

As an international organization, we must continuously assist our Member Countries in the formulation of their national policies, so that social legislation necessary to strengthen public health services in tandem with socioeconomic development can be realized.

We are concerned and committed to assist countries in bringing primary health services to all their citizens. We are conscious of the problems that exist and we seek to solve them in partnership with our Member Countries by providing the human and financial resources needed to increase coverage, thereby improving the quality and expectations of life.

In closing, I would like to quote what Thomas Jefferson very appropriately said nearly 200 years ago, and that still remains valid today, "knowledge indeed is a desirable possession, but health is more so."

A CAJAL PILGRIMAGE

Hebbel E. Hoff

The Spanish Heritage: Exploration

The accomplishments of the people of Spain and their influence on world history are readily apparent; to place them appropriately in the context of Spanish culture and the Spanish character is quite another matter, however much it is clear that accomplishments spring from culture and character, and culture and character are forged in the fires of accomplishments and failures. A European country, and facing the Atlantic, Spain is only partially isolated by the Pyrenees, and its age-old native population of Cantabrians and Iberians early fell under the influence of the Celts who left such a great heritage of general culture and a few words that are still meaningful; *cerveza* comes readily to mind. Then came the Vandals, the Visigoths, and later the Frankish armies under Charlemagne; they too all made their biological and cultural contributions. Again only one need be mentioned: the encounter of Charlemagne's rear guard with the Basques, who fiercely resented any intrusion into their independence and sped Charlemagne's army across the pass at Roncesvalles, leaving a legend to be transmuted with the years into one of the great Gothic epics. It can be no happenchance that the same region gave birth to another of the great Gothic quartet in the story of the Cid; both proclaimed the Visigothic ideal of the leader and those who chose to follow him, and the loyalty with which the leader and the followers served each other. No doubt but that from the Visigoths came the unqualifiable definitions and ideals of loyalty, honor, and the values of a man's word, and the idea of consensus in settling both private and public issues. Still later came associations with the houses of Burgundy, Flanders, Bourbon, Hanover, and Habsburg; much of Spain's present history has its roots in these. For years Spain was a merchant in the northern countries, and the great trade in wool from the flocks on the Meseta flowed through merchants of Burgos and shippers of Bilbao to weavers in Ghent and Bruges to provide a financial backbone for Spain and much else like the flamenco.

But while the northern visitors were still peacefully at home in their nor-thern climes and still painting themselves blue with woad, Spain was re-

157

ceiving infusions of the high culture of the Mediterranean through Phoenicians and Carthaginians trading for tin and mercury and silver, and the ships of the thalassocratic Greek states came to establish trading posts that were miniature Greek cities like Ampurias, a Greek emporium. Finally came the Romans just before the beginning of the Christian era to conquer the whole of Spain. They established the city of Caesar Augustus, transformed through the centuries to Zaragoza on the Ebro, the river that gives the Iberian peninsula its name. Zaragoza became the center of a Roman province unparalleled in its peace and prosperity from olive oil, wine, and minerals, where the good life was lived for centuries as perhaps the only idyllic period in Spanish history. From then on Spain was firmly Christian and even in the extremity of the furthest extention of Moslem power enclaves of Christians remained. Nowhere was the conflict with non-Christians more lasting, more bitter, or more determined, and nowhere has the Christian Church had a greater and at times more uncompromising influence on the lives of the people.

With the Romans came the Shephardic Jews, this branch of Jewry taking its very name from the country. The Visigothic rulers were subjecting them to the fiercest of persecution by the first quarter of the sixth century; thereafter they had their varied vicissitudes, accepted by the early Moorish invaders and taking part in the great cultural development of this period. Maimonides may be recalled as the greatest of Talmudic scholars and a truly great philosopher and physician who lived in Córdoba, until he and most of the other Jews in Spain fled before the wave of intolerance that had its origin in both Christian and Moorish parts of Spain; the Chartist monks and the Moslem sect of the Almohades both share the blame. Readmitted, the Jews again played their part in the development of Spain until a recurrence of intolerance, exclusively from Christian sources, led to their final expulsion by the Christian Queen and King, Isabella and Ferdinand.

Great as was the Jewish contribution to the culture of Spain, and it was indeed great, their genetic contribution may well have been equally great or even greater; there are suggestions that may be as much fact as fiction that even Ferdinand himself bore Jewish blood through his grandmother who seems to have been affiliated with important *converso* families.

Even more can be said of the Moslems, largely North Africans from the Maghrib, who occupied Spain to a greater or lesser degree from 711 to 1492. After an easy conquest there was an interval of peaceful interrelations among the Christians and Moslems until the eleven hundreds. Then, possibly as the result of the intensification of the Reconquista and the growth of Christian and Moslem intolerance, the detente fell apart. After the final success of the Reconquista with the fall of Granada, the Moors too, insofar as they were identifiable, were expelled from Spain. The cultural heritage the Moors left to Spain and to all Europe was immense; their genetic contribution can have been no less.

All in all Spain must be considered as one of the great melting pots of the world rivaling, in its mixture of peoples and cultures, the United States itself. There developed a rich and varied culture with subgroups such as the Basques and the Catalans who retain identity in language and customs in a way that is found in no other modern European or American state.

The past is present in Spain to a degree that is also unique. Worship of the bull may go back to Egypt and Mesopotamia; it was well established in Crete as related in the legend of the Minotaur, and young men and women were sacrificed to it. There must have been a very early Cretan influence in Spain to judge from the Paleolithic cave paintings in eastern Spain in the neighborhood of Lérida, and the worship of the bull may have followed these early contacts. However it may have first come to Spain, the culture of the bull remains, most obviously expressed in bullfighting. But so does sacrifice of young people to the bull; a sacrifice hedged around with different expressions and transmuted in its form, but in all likelihood a survival of the old Cretan bull ritual. Recent newspaper accounts of this year's festival of bull running in Pamplona record another death in this most dangerous game; some twenty or more have occurred in recent years. Counting from the time of the cave paintings in Altamira, Spain has thus perhaps the oldest and most complex history of any country in Europe, and her people have perhaps the greatest genetic and cultural complexity of any of the people of Europe.

Out of this vast genetic and cultural reservoir have come so many advances in art, in literature, and in almost every type of human endeavor as to defy description. One characteristic stands out in bold relief—that of exploration. The energy and the drive that sparked and nourished the Reconquista developed the energy and determination; Spain's long maritime history in the Mediterranean and the Atlantic developed the sailors and the ships; the firm association with the Church transmitted the ideas of early cartographers such as Nicolaus of Cusa who had mapped much of Europe and had no doubt that the world was spherical, and Ferdinand's confidant and treasurer, the *converso* Santangelo, scraped together the money to send Columbus off on his first voyage. Thereafter there was no let up in the voyages of discovery and exploration. The West Indies, México, Perú, Florida, and the Philippines were explored and occupied; a New World was discovered that radically changed the center of gravity of the known world, and the Spanish language came to be spoken by more people than any other language. Gold and silver were found too, and the history of Spanish discovery and exploration is written in the gold and silver of churches wherever Spanish is spoken.

The outlet for discovery of the physical world soon became constricted by the ambitions and military power of other countries and in due time was shut off entirely. It was a sad time for Spain as the plate fleets were plundered and in time ceased to sail, and as the wealth and initiative shifted northward and westward it seemed that the old spirit of discovery and exploration had ceased to be a prime attribute of the Spanish character.

This was by no means so; if the old outlets had closed up, the spirit of discovery and exploration remained, lying dormant, until people with more than usual genius recognized their gift and applied it with the same spirit of adventure as the explorers of the great days. Such a one was Santiago Ramón y Cajal, one of the very greatest explorers of a much greater unknown than the New World (Figure 1). His explorations were carried out in the nervous system, his discoveries mapped and described its structure in a completely new way that has given impetus and insight into nearly a century of continued exploration. It is fitting to observe that his discoveries, like those of the explorers of Spain's heroic days, were written in silver; silver laid down in the walls of the elements of the nervous system so that the microscopist could for the first time see clearly and trace unmistakably the form and course of these elements.

Cajal's Heritage: Father and Country

Among the great four founders of modern neuroscience Cajal was unique by virtue of his very Spanishness. Pavlov, born just the year before Cajal, was able to go to university in St. Petersburg, — the intellectual, scientific, and artistic capital of Russia — spend two profitable years with Ludwig in Leipzig, and return to a University appointment in Physiology. Freud, born some six years later, suffered in his academic career because he was Jewish, and after good training in research with Brücke and Meynert, he had to forsake research and academic preferment for the practice of Neurology. Nevertheless, the freedoms permitted the Jews in Vienna, even as little as they were, opened the way for a vast and explosive expansion of the Jewish society, and Freud, like Pavlov, was raised in the light of great traditions and was among the élite of a great and burgeoning society of high intellect. So too was Sherrington, raised in the home of a physician foster father who if not rich was well enough off to send him to a good school and to Cambridge where he vigorously played the games of the élite of the young Englishmen and was recognized for the great qualities he was to display in his studies of the nervous system. At Cambridge he established almost filial relations with such great scientists as Michael Foster who constantly watched over his career.

Figure 1. The statue of Santiago Ramón y Cajal on the landing of the main staircase in the School of Medicine in Zaragoza. The lofty and somewhat severe expression of the great scientist is illuminated by a secret smile as though he were perhaps thinking of the escapades of his youth. Above at the level of the second story ceiling he is flanked by statues of Hippocrates and Archimedes representing the Art of Medicine and Science. Surely no other scientist has been as artistic in his work or has more effectively directed both art and science to the same end. All these photographs are black and white reproductions of selections from some seven hundred remarkable color photographs taken by Mr. Jerry Chastain who was a companion on this pilgrimage.

As a young physician-pathologist he knew Marcel Ruffer among others, and together they began to develop diphtheria antitoxin in a horse in Sherrington's care, and as the horse came to be ready to yield a good titer of antitoxin, Sherrington heard of the severe illness with diphtheria of his nephew. Bleeding the horse by lamplight and preparing the serum in the small hours of the night, Sherrington went by early train to the bedside of his nephew in the country where he found the boy almost *in extremis*. The antitoxin-bearing horse serum which he injected reversed the course of the disease, and the young patient lived to be the first patient in England to be treated and treated successfully with the first antitoxin made in England. Sherrington began early to take his holidays in Switzerland and was one of those Englishmen who made Switzerland the center for mountain climbing and winter sports that it has become.

Cajal's father, on the contrary, was the son of a modest farmer in the town of Larrés (Figure 2), who was forced to leave the farm because of the rights of older brothers to the land, and was apprenticed to a nearby village surgeon, where he learned the trade of barber and blood-letter. Fired by the ambition to become qualified as a medical doctor, he devoted almost every energy and every resource to this end year after year. He accomplished his ambition by painful stages that lasted throughout most of his early life, beginning when he went to Barcelona to study for his first diploma while supporting himself by working as a barber. "Refraining from all pleasures, submitting to a regimen of unbelievable austerity, and without an income other than his salary and tips at the barber shop my father obtained the coveted diploma of a surgeon with first class standing in all subjects ... There in his quiet and obscure struggle for spiritual and physical nourishment, breathing that atmosphere of indifference and coldness that surrounds the talents of the unprotected poor, my father learned the terror of poverty and the rather exclusive worship of utilitarian science" is how Cajal remembered it. With a wife whom he had known in Larrés, and a growing family, the father practiced in the small towns of the province of Huesca in Aragón from 1850 to 1856 always studying for new examinations while taking care of his family and patients. He had but a single recreation which he pursued with a passion that went far beyond its utilitarian value; to see the patients scattered through his district, he rode daily through a wild and wooded countryside abounding in game, and he became an ardent hunter. Rabbits and birds came often to the pot in his first home in the little town of Petilla de Aragón where he first began to practice. Only when his family was almost fully grown did he finally obtain the coveted title of physician and surgeon.

In his early poverty, in his father's ambitions for his family, and in his struggles and sacrifices to further these ambitions, Cajal resembled much more two great earlier scientists in France: Claude Bernard and Louis Pasteur. Both were sons of sergeants in the armies of Napoleon; Pasteur's father had been awarded the ribbon of the Legion d'Honneur as a soldier. No one became a sergeant in *those* armies without being the kind of man these men were: brave, determined, persevering, and above all, loyal. After

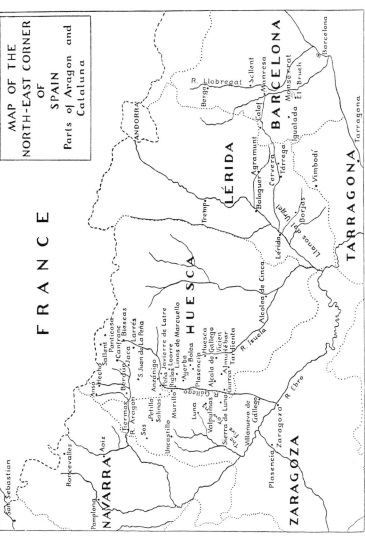

Figure 2. A map of the Cajal country. It is largely the province of Huesca in Aragón, bounded by the Aragón river on the north and west, the Isuela on the east, and the Ebro on the south, with the Gállego its main north-south axis. To the west are Pamplona and Roncesvalles; Altamira and Santiago de Compostela are off the map at the left. The strategic position of Zaragoza at the confluence of the Gállego and the Ebro is obvious.

This map is from Cajal's autobiographical *Recollections of My Life* (Trans. Craigie and Cano), Philadelphia, The American Philosophical Society, 1937, xi + 638. It is the principal source of information about Cajal's life, and the source of all the quotations in the text of this article.

Napoleon's fall these brave men were impoverished and dishonored; they saw in their sons a way to assert their own worth, and their sons recipro- cated with love, respect, and zeal to justify their fathers by their own contri- butions to science. So too Cajal loved and respected his own father, and we can see in him too the determination to justify by his own work his father's efforts and sacrifices.

But most people in Spain were poor, and Spain itself was desperately poor and at the very nadir — or very close to it — of its national fortunes. But this poverty had as its background a breathtakingly beautiful country, and at every hand were magnificent reminders of the glories of the great days of Spanish history. Luna was the old town of the Luna family; it was given to the first Luna as a reward for his services in the Reconquista, and from it the family spread to become at one time one of the greatest land owners in Spain holding power both at Court and in the Church. Among the many great Lunas was Pedro, who was elected Pope by the Cardinals at Avignon in 1394, only after many vicissitudes to be deposed as a perjurer and schismatic in 1417. Before that he had retired to the stronghold of Peñíscola in 1415, from whence he maintained his claim to the apostolic seat until his death in 1422. In the Cathedral de Seo in Zaragoza, which he had enriched, there hang today, as they did in Cajal's time, the six great tapestries that had hung in the Palais des Papes in Avignon, and in his isolated castle at Peñíscola. The new moon of the Luna arms is still part of the insignia of St. Andrew's University in Scotland, to which he gave its charter.

At Jaca, where many of Cajal's relatives lived, were great medieval works of art in the churches; in Sos was the baptismal fount (Figures 3 and 4) of Ferdinand who had lived there before his marriage to Isabella (Figure 5), and some very great church art (Figure 6). At Huesca was the palace of the old kings of Aragón who had been at the spearhead of the Reconquista, and the wall before which the great Ramírez I was killed by a Moorish arrow still encircles the city. Every hill seemed to have its smaller or greater castle such as the great frowning pile of the fortress of Aragón, blackened by the fire that destroyed it, though never conquered by the enemy. The Castle of Loarre, rising from its isolated rocky base like only a few in Europe, was nearly intact except for the loss of screening walls. Off to the west the great- est art treasure of all lay hidden, awaiting discovery only some forty years after Cajal's birth: the Paleolithic cave at Altamira with its wonders of the artistic spirit of man some twenty thousand years ago (Figure 7).

If there were castles and paintings, and tapestries, and great names to conjure with, there were also great legends. The legend of St. George and the dragon had grown in Aragón; Catherine of Aragón seems to have brought it to England where St. George became that country's legendary figure. Legend also had it that St. James the Apostle had walked across

Figure 3. "The site of the ruins of the Casa de Sada in which Ferdinand the Catholic was born. Completely restored by Don José Manuel Pardo de Santayana y Suárez.
   In gratitude for the best King of Spain, Sos del Rey Católico, March, 1957." (From the brass plaque on the building.)

Spain, stopping in Zaragoza to confer with the Holy Virgin, to end his days on the Atlantic coast, where he was buried. His reputed burying place at Santiago de Compostela became one of the most sacred shrines for pilgrimages in Europe, and the legend of St. James continued to grow until he became one of the great champions of the Reconquista, unseen until the Christian forces were in dire need when he revealed himself and rallied them to greater exertions in battle. The scallop shell badge of the pilgrim was a frequent decoration of the churches along the pilgrim's way. *The Song of Roland* and the story of the Cid told of events that had happened in that very country, for the Moorish host in *The Song of Roland* lay in Zaragoza and may well have marched up the Gállego, crossed to Verdún on the Aragón and reached Roncesvalles from there. The Cid too knew Zaragoza.

   Such was the heritage of the young Cajal. Often only too aware of the relentless poverty of his family and his country, inspired beyond measure by the evidences of the one-time greatness of Spain that lay around him, the love and respect for his father so manifest throughout his life became transmuted into a love for Spain, into a most painful sympathy for her present

Figure 4. The balcony of the room in which Ferdinand was born. It is to the right rear of the building as viewed from the front, as in Figure 3. The balcony overlooks the city gates through which Ferdinand's mother rode when labor pains had begun as she was at the front with her husband. The tower was rebuilt by Ferdinand who "adopted" the city.

Figure 5. Ferdinand's baptismal fount in the shape of a lotus flower and of Moorish origin. It is to be found in the Church of St. Esteban, the upper and newer of a pair of churches built one above another. The ribs of the vaults of this church are richly decorated with scallop shells to indicate that it was on an old pilgrim's route to Santiago de Compostela.

state after such a glowing past, and a determination to do whatever he could to help restore her to the preeminence of her great days by his science. We can feel certain that in his genetic inheritance from strong Aragonese stock and on the influence of his childhood in such an environment, with such a father and in such a country, the foundations of his greatness are to be found. This is the reason for a pilgrimage to the scenes of Cajal's formative years in Aragón that culminated in his establishment as a young teacher of Anatomy in Zaragoza, where the determination and sacrifice of his father had brought him some years earlier to complete his medical studies and where his career began.

The Fine Structure of the Nervous System: The Neurone Doctrine

One of the most fruitful generalizations in medicine has been the Cell Theory. Given clear definition by 1840, it stated that all organized beings, whether plants or animals, are aggregates of individual living units, the cells. Each cell leads a double life within the organism. First of all is its own

Figure 6. The remarkable crypt of the lower 11th century Church of Santa María del Perdón with one of the most precious Madonnas in Spain not yet protected by a museum. Later a somewhat newer Madonna with a typical Aragonese beauty was placed above in St. Esteban. Both are a golden blonde. The paintings on the walls are from the 14th century.

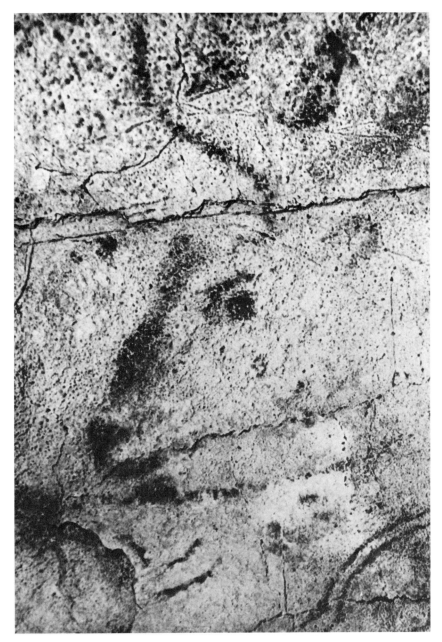

Figure 7. There are many single creations among the paintings on the ceiling of the inner cave at Altamira that would be worthy of any master, but this gentle deer is my favorite.

individual life, absorbing the oxygen and foodstuffs from the body fluids that it needs for its nourishment and giving off the waste products of the nutritional process to the surrounding fluid. In a very real sense the cell is born, it grows and develops, it may often reproduce, and it ultimately dies. At the same time every cell carries out some function to maintain the organism of which it forms the building blocks. Some cells are able to contract; they are often bound together to make the body's contractile tissue, muscular tissue, and this tissue is the essential component of all contractile organs such as skeletal muscles, the heart, and the muscular component of the intestines. Other cells are grouped together to form glands, such as the sweat glands, the salivary glands, the digestive glands. These form secretions like sweat and saliva or tears that are discharged on the body surface or into the gastrointestinal canal. The analogy is frequently drawn between the individual cells in their private and public functions and individuals in our human society. Like the cells, individual men and women lead their own private lives; they feed themselves, take care of their private needs for clothing and shelter, are born, reproduce, and die. Like the cells they too have a public life in which they carry out some function for the good of the society, and often at the direct behest of the society. Here too the principles of division of labor apply; some people are farmers, some doctors and lawyers, but in all their manifold complexity, they are designed to maintain a healthy society. It is not far-fetched then to speak of the ''body politic'', or to call an organism ''a society of cells''.

The influence of the Cell Theory on medicine in the last half of the nineteenth century was immediate and without parallel in the history of medicine. There is no doubt that this doctrine turned medicine onto the right road and continues today to influence the progress of medicine. Whole new sciences sprang up: histology, microbiology, cellular pathology, embryology, biochemistry, and cell biology. Together they changed the face of medicine and paved the way for the great advances of the twentieth century.

But in the remarkable advances that were being made everywhere in medicine, the nervous system fared badly; the impetus that the Cell Doctrine gave to other studies, old and new, failed to reach the nervous system, and studies in this area remained unproductive.

The reason was clear; most of the cells of the body were readily delineated by microscopic study, even of naked tissue, and could be studied profitably even in such crude preparations. Soon scientists began to stain thin slices of tissue with natural and later synthetic dyes, and each particular dye permitted better allover studies and made it possible to study the finer parts of the cell itself. Today, application of reagents makes it possible to identify a whole panorama of intracellular components, specifically stained because of the chemical reaction between the intracellular components and the dye in very much the same way that the development of color in chemical solutions makes it possible to determine the chemical components of the body fluids.

The nervous tissue, on the contrary, resisted effective staining with the dyes that stained other tissue. Within the nervous system, particularly the grey matter of the brain and spinal cord, cells could for certain be seen, but they were imbedded within a feltwork of nerve fibers, and no connection could be made between nerve cells and nerve fibers. In the end most workers came to view the nerve fibers seen in such an indecipheral confusion and profusion in the grey matter as the main working structures in the nervous system, while the cells served mainly to nourish and support the nerve net.

In the years centering upon 1885, Camillo Golgi invented the technique for staining the nervous system with silver which proved to be the key to the microscopic structure of the nervous system. Silver salts appeared to be absorbed particularly well by the surfaces of cells and fibers within the nervous system. Once absorbed along the outer surface of the cell or fiber, they could be reduced to a fine black precipitate that outlined the surface of the nerve cell and fibers as no dye had ever done. Golgi may not have developed the process as fully as he might, or he may not have had the requisite skills in microscopy; he may even have failed to see what his slides really did show because of preconceived opinions. Whatever the cause, Golgi clung to the old theory of the importance of the intercommunicating nerve net or syncytium of earlier students.

Golgi's work attracted the attention of young Santiago Ramón y Cajal, then in his thirty-fifth year, when he was Professor of Anatomy in Valencia, and he too began making preparations of the nervous system by the silver impregnation method. He had been interested in photography from his teens; he was already an experienced photographer, and in Spain in those days it meant that he had learned to make his own photographic dry plates by mixing silver salts in gelatine in the dark room and pouring the solution over glass plates to dry and harden for use at a later date. His own plates were as good as the best that could be imported from Germany, if not better, and had Cajal been commercially minded, he could have established a productive photographic industry in Spain.

Looking at his own slides, taken from grey matter wherever it was found, Cajal found that the rich nerve net of earlier investigators did not form a continuum from one fiber to another. Wherever fibers were found they were alone and separate from all others. The so-called nerve net was not a network at all; independent fibers in great profusion were simply packed together like the individual fibers in felt. Only at one site were fibers continuous with any other structures and that was at the nerve cells. Here the nerve cells were seen to be the point of origin of two types of fibers: (a) Some nerve cells gave rise to a single fiber that passed out of the nervous system to muscle fibers, where it branched profusely and innervated a group of several hundred muscle fibers each of which was innervated by branching of the original fiber like a bunch of grapes each suspended by a twig from one of the several branches of the single stem. At the ending of each nerve twiglet in a muscle fiber there was no continuity of the protoplasm of the nerve fiber into that of the muscle fiber. Other fibers of the same kind took a course within the central nervous system by way of a longer or shorter course in the grey or white matter to some other part of the nervous system to end around other nerve cells. Here too the fiber did not communicate with the material within the cell, its protoplasm, and here too the rule was *contiguity* and not *continuity* from cell to cell; (b) The other type of fiber was of somewhat different structure; it remained wholly within the grey matter of the nervous system, was shorter than the other fibers, and many of these root-like fibers were connected to a single nerve cell.

Looked at from this viewpoint, the fibers of the white and grey matter of the nervous system were, each and every one, processes of a particular nerve cell and were dependent upon that cell for their life. The nerve cell was therefore the essential unit of the nervous system, establishing contact with other cells within the nervous system and with muscles and glands outside it via the single fiber or axon it gave off, and receiving communication from other cells via its other outgrowths, the dendrites. Some years later Waldeyer hit upon the name of the *neurone* for this fundamental nerve cell with its protoplasmic processes, its many *dendrites* by which it received information from other cells, and its single *axon* usually heavily branched, by which the nerve cells establish contact with other nerve cells and with muscles and glands or other structures.

In the end, then, the beautiful silver-stained slides that Cajal made established the Neurone Doctrine as firmly as the Cell Theory as a whole, and the neural sciences were thereafter free to develop as fully as those concerned with the other cells of the body. By this work Cajal established himself as one of the four great masters of the knowledge of the nervous system, who are almost wholly responsible for bringing the study of the nervous system into the twentieth century. We have named the other three: Sherrington, the great student of the functions of the nervous system; Pavlov, who conceived of the "conditional reflex", and Freud, who made psychiatry a subject for scientific study. With his study of the fine structure of the nervous system Cajal not only joined them as their peer, but in many ways provided the structural basis for their own great contributions and for the great developments in the knowledge of neurosciences that have followed.

Figures 8 and 9 reproduce Figures 1 and 6 of Cajal's famous Croonian
Lecture of 1894, which more than any of his writings introduced him to
English and European scientific circles, for many of his earlier reports had

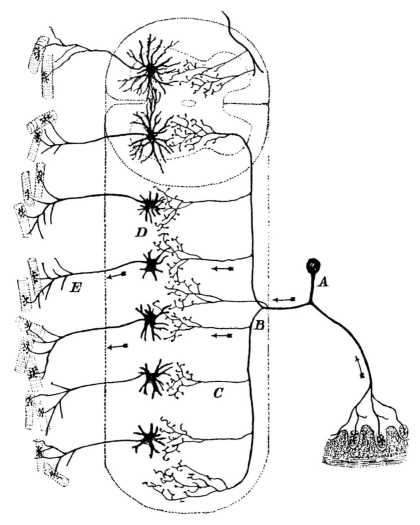

Figure 8. Figure 1 of Cajal's Croonian Lecture showing the simple two neurone arc of the
stretch reflex or knee jerk. The cell body of the afferent neurone outside the spinal cord in the
dorsal root is labelled (A). Its entering fiber branches freely (B) as it enters the spinal cord;
some even reach as far upward as the medulla. Others (C) cross the cord to the ventral horn of
the grey matter and establish contact with dendrites and the cell bodies of motor neurones (D)
each of which sends a single axon (E) out via the ventral root to the skeletal muscle fibers.
Each fiber branches freely and innervates a considerable number of individual muscle fibers.

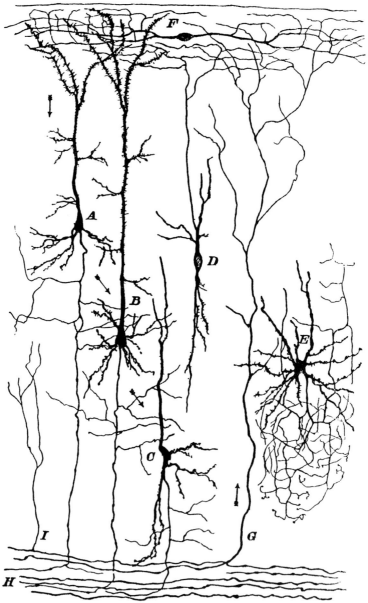

Figure 9. This is Figure 6 of Cajal's Croonian Lecture and shows something of the complexity of the cerebral cortex. A and B are pyramidal cells whose axons descend the spinal cord to control the action of the motor neurones depicted in Cajal's Figure 1. C is a polymorphous cell, E, a Golgi cell, and F, a special cell of the molecular layer of the cortex. D is a cell whose axon ascends to the molecular layer. H is the bundle of white matter consisting of the fibers of cells in the cerebral cortex and elsewhere. The cortex is richly supplied with axons originating elsewhere; G is an example.

been published in local medical journals with a restricted circulation. Figure 8 shows the simplest of all nervous pathways: a two neurone reflex pathway through the spinal cord. This consists only of an afferent neurone bringing messages in from the body and contacting a motor neurone whose axon leaves the body to innervate appropriate muscles. We now know that this sort of simple pathway is used in reflexes like the knee jerk that is familiar to everyone. Figure 9 shows the arrangement of incoming, intercommunicating and outgoing fibers and neurones in the cerebral cortex. The giant Betz cells can be identified with their outgoing axons which pass down the spinal cord in the pyramidal tracts as important elements in the mediation of voluntary muscular action.

Petilla de Aragón

Santiago Ramón y Cajal was born on the first of May, 1852, in the hamlet of Petilla de Aragón, (Figure 10), a tiny enclave of the nearby province of Navarra somehow left behind as a part of Navarra in the changing

Figure 10. The tiny hamlet of Petilla de Aragón, despite its name a small section of Navarra, totally surrounded by Aragón. Cajal's birthplace was in ruins five years ago; now it has been restored but is without furniture or occupants. It is the unpainted stone building somewhat to the right of the middle of the single line of houses that constitute the village.

fortunes that finally settled the borders of the two kingdoms. Remembering nothing of his life in Petilla, for the family soon moved to Larrés and then to Luna where they stayed until 1856, Cajal made a trip to his birthplace in the early years of the twentieth century, probably in 1904 or 1905. His route lay along the old, old road from Jaca to Pamplona that Marsilia may have taken on his foray from Zaragoza to attack Charlemagne's rear guard at Roncesvalles, but he turned south at Verdún y Tiermas finding only a bridle path through precipitous mountains nearly obliterated by a flash flood a few days earlier. One of the poorest towns in upper Aragón, Petilla had no connections with the nearby villages of Sos and Uncastillo. It is situated upon a spur of the neighboring range of mountains crested by vertical sickielike peaks and the ruins of a feudal castle. The town was still desperately poor, and many houses, including his birthplace, were in ruins and inhabited by what Cajal called "nomadic beggars". Saddened by the sight of such desolation and poverty, Cajal left vowing never to return nor did he ever again visit his birthplace, so painful were the reminders of his father's struggles and the sad state of Spain.

Today one cannot take the direct route Cajal followed from Verdún. There is a great dam on the Aragón river and impounded waters make the old direct route impassable. It is necessary to go further west, cross the dam itself, and turn back, following well maintained black-topped roads. Irrigation from the reservoir and the reforestation of past years have changed the face of the countryside. Still green in July, ample crops of wheat were ripening in the fields, and the little brook of Cajal's time was a clear stream of good size. On the main street of the village, facing the brook across a well-built stone parapet was the house in which Cajal was born, now restored but empty and lonely. As the dark evening clouds gathered over the village, one could understand Cajal's melancholy at visiting a place in an almost indescribably romantic setting of natural beauty but which yet oppressed his heart by the dark threatening peaks behind the village and the unhappy sentiments it evoked.

Valpalmas

After two years at Petilla, Cajal's family moved to Larrés for a year and then to Luna where they stayed until 1856. There young Santiago began to show a penchant for mischief that was to characterize his whole boyhood; vigorous, daring, and resistant to discipline, he was also enterprising, adventuresome, inventive, and a natural leader of the other boys in every sort of devilment. Today he might well have been labelled as a hyperactive child, and treated. Playing one day on the threshing floor on the town common in Luna — threshing floors were one of the favorite meeting places for the boys of the town — young Santiago had the idea of beating a horse, which promptly laid him unconscious with a terrible kick on the forehead. Young Santiago recovered only after several days of anxiety for his parents, but apparently drew from the experience the decision that such sport was worth the blows that invariably followed, usually from his father. Looking back on the episode in his riper years, Cajal wrote that "this was my first mischief; we shall see later that it was not my last."

While living in Valpalmas from 1856-1860, young Santiago began his formal schooling at the age of six, and, more importantly, his informal tutoring with his father, who began to teach him French, choosing for his schoolroom an abandoned shepherd's cave not far from Valpamas. Here father and son were free from interruption and distractions and worked to such good effect that by the age of eight, Santiago had a good command of French, could write well enough to serve as his father's secretary, and had a good idea of geography and arithmetic. Figure 11 shows such a shepherd's cave with ample evidence of long inhabitance by shepherds and their

Figure 11. A shepherd's cave close to Valpalmas, no doubt like that where young Santiago and his father went whenever possible to study French, Spanish, and arithmetic. It was by following a dog that ran into a much similar cave guarded by an outcropping of limestone that the cave in Altamira was found.

charges with the smoke-covered walls above fires that may well have been lighted there for centuries. These caves seem not to have been Paleolithic dwellings, at least no drawings or paintings have been found in this area, but the region lies between the caves in Altamira and the later ones around Lérida, and there is little doubt but that they have sheltered man as long as he has lived in this part of Spain.

In Valpalmas Santiago began to develop an abiding love of nature; all the hours he could find away from his studies he spent in exploring ravines, springs, rocks and hills, admiring the colors of sunrise and sunset and spring and fall. He collected birds' nests, birds' eggs, and the birds themselves. He watched with fascination the moment of hatching, the growth of feathers, the first awkward attempts to fly, and the final soaring flight away from his observation.

Here too, Santiago began to develop with clearness a patriotic fervor for his country and an understanding of its great past. Here also he experienced his first natural disaster; in the midst of a thunderstorm the village priest was imprudent enough to climb the belfry to toll the bell. A bolt of lightning struck him dead and left him hanging over the wall. The lightning then passed down through the schoolroom, shattering the ceiling and leaving the school mistress senseless. At Valpalmas, also, Santiago saw his first eclipse of the sun; his father's lucid explanation allayed his irrational fears and helped make this eclipse of 1860 a brilliant revelation for his youthful intelligence.

Ayerbe

In 1860, Santiago's father was appointed to the medical practice in Ayerbe, much larger and richer than any of his previous charges. Situated on the road from Huesca to Jaca, Ayerbe has a unique double town square, separated by the opulent former residence of the Marquises of Ayerbe (Figure 12). A double-peaked hill rises just behind the town with its ruins of an ancient feudal castle on one of them. Santiago was a stranger in Ayerbe; although Valpalmas was only a few miles away, the conventional dress was different and there was a special dialect jumbling French, Castilian, Catalán, and ancient Aragonese words and phrases. But Santiago soon accommodated to these distinctions, and while making solitary excursions to the mountains, rivers, and to romantic hilltop castles, he also set about becoming the leader of the very boys who at first had called him a foreigner. In spinning tops, tossing quoits, games of tag, running races, jumping and fighting, he more than held his own, but he really achieved leadership in throwing stones at lamps, plundering orchards, scaling the roof tops of houses, and handling the cudgel, bow and arrow, and especially the sling. He wrote that ''I contrived to join in and surpass the escapades,

Figure 12. The former residence of the Marquises of Ayerbe is now the town hall, and the square on this side is the Plaza Ramón y Cajal. Here young Santiago outdid himself in boyish pranks and began to exercise his strong artistic interest, which was so poorly appreciated by the itinerant painter whom the elder Cajal asked to serve as a referee of the quality of his early paintings.

knaveries and rascalities of the boys of Ayerbe so much that I quickly had the honour of figuring in the *Index of Bad Companions* drawn up by the God-fearing fathers of families."

"About that time", Cajal wrote later, "if my memory does not deceive me, my artistic instincts began or at any rate showed a great increase. When I was about eight or nine years old, I suppose, I already had an irresistible mania for scribbling on paper, drawing ornaments in books, daubing on walls, gates, doors, and recently painted façades, all sorts of designs, warlike scenes, and incidents of the bull ring. A smooth white wall exercised for me an irresistible fascination. Whenever I got hold of a few cents I bought paper or pencils; but, as I could not draw at home because my parents considered painting a sinful amusement, I went out into the country, and sitting upon a bank at the side of the road, drew carts, horses, villagers, and whatever objects of the countryside interested me. Of all these I made a great collection, which I guarded like a treasure of gold."

His utilitarian father, having at first forbidden what he considered a non-profitable pastime relented enough to submit Santiago's art treasures to an itinerant plasterer and decorator, temporarily in Ayerbe to repaint the church walls damaged in a recent fire. This "dauber of walls" left no doubt of his unfavorable opinion and Santiago's father placed a complete interdiction on further painting. There followed a long and silent struggle with the father, but by hook or by crook Santiago continued his drawings; once some caricatures of the school master gained him a sentence to the school's dark closet reserved for punishment.

In this darkened cell he discovered for himself the phenomenon of the pin-hole camera and the camera obscura. Noting that narrowing the aperture gave a sharper image, he made one of the proper size in a slip of paper which he attached over the original hole and began to make drawings of the scenes the camera obscura brought to him. We can probably discern in this event the beginning of Cajal's lifelong love of photography and of his great work in staining the nervous system.

Jaca: Escuelas Pías

Don Justo, as Santiago's father was called, was more than worried by the artistic turn his son had taken, especially after the unfavorable pronouncement on its quality by the peripatetic house painter, and he soon took steps to see that his son's interest should take a more utilitarian turn. He must have had the idea in mind for some time, and indeed he calculated with some nicety his own future move to Zaragoza, when his son should be ready for medical school. Now, feeling that a knowledge of Latin was a prerequisite for a medical education, he sent Santiago to Jaca, where an uncle lived, to attend the Escuelas Pías (Figure 13) run by a group of Esculapian fathers, an order having its origins in France. The school partook in some ways of a disciplinary school for incorrigible boys; it taught by sheer memory and employed the simplest of physical disciplines: frequent beatings and week-end incarceration on bread and water. Young Santiago accepted the former with equanimity and evaded the latter by divising pitons by which he could climb down from his cell into the college garden and over the twelve foot wall to the fascinations of one of the great old cities of the past with its wealth of art, its great traditions, and its spectacular setting with the Aragón river nearby, the great needle-like projections of Los Mallos (Figure 14) and the huge Sphinx-like mass of Uruel nearby (Figure 15). The Pyrenees were near enough to give an abundant snowfall in winter — today the old Jaca is almost completely overlain by the hotels, shops, and other appendages of a modern center for winter and summer sports — and Santiago helped build fantastic snow forts and castles with passages and tunnels connecting their many chambers. Needless to say, Santiago learned very little Latin. (Let no one overinterpret these accounts

Figure 13. The door to the Escuelas Pías. Jaca is now a bustling winter and summer resort, and it was virtually impossible to obtain a good photograph because of the incessant automobile traffic. In the back is the play yard, now cemented over and serving largely as a basketball court. To its left is the 12-foot stone wall that young Cajal climbed to reach the corner of the Calle de las Escuelas Pías and Calle de Sancho Ramírez, and gain his freedom for the weekend.

Figure 14. Los Mallos (The Mallets), a formation of needlelike vertical rocks, of the typical Aragonese red. It was a constant attraction to Santiago, and a source of danger as well as excitement.

Figure 15. The frowning reddish mass of Uruel; a gigantic Sphinx when seen from a somewhat greater distance.

of the detention rooms in the schools in Ayerbe and Jaca. Nearly 100 years later an article in the *Houston Post* dated December 11, 1977, described a not unsimilar detention room in Iowa under the headline: " 'Slammer' helps maintain discipline at school".)

Huesca

Recognizing finally that Santiago would learn no Latin and little else besides at the hands of the Esculapian fathers, Don Justo determined to send his son to the Institute of Huesca; the main classroom was the audience chamber of the old kings of Aragón and to the left of the front wall was the door to the famous "bell chamber" of Ramiro II, El Monje (Figure 16). Here he stopped the unrest of his nobles by arranging the heads of the principal plotters in a circle on the floor and hanging the head of the ringleader by his hair with a rope tied to a hook at the crown of the vaulted ceiling and calling the rest of the nobles to see his "new bell". Before the walls of Huesca the redoubtable Sancho Ramírez, father of El Monje, died leading the attack on the city in the course of the Reconquista.

Huesca had been a principal city long before that; it was the Osca of

Figure 16. The throne room of the ancient Kings of Aragón and the classroom of the Institute of Huesca when Cajal was a student. To the left is the doorway down to the famous "bell chamber" of Ramiro II, "El Monje". By good fortune this room will soon house the main lecture room of a new School of Medicine in Huesca.

Roman Days, and it was filled with the art and the romance of the great old days; young Santiago breathed it all in with growing maturity and appreciation of the feast spread before him. His masters at the Institute were of a different cut than those at the Escuelas Pías in Jaca, and he began to make progress on his studies.

At twelve years of age, filled with wonder and pleasure at the new intellectual vistas opening up before him, he was still much of the boy he had been. Treated with disdain by some of the students, he was the butt of much derision for an oversize overcoat his mother had cut down from one of his father's, leaving an ample margin for future growth. (It seems to be a practice of mothers everywhere to do this when altering hand-me-downs, and they all seem to be singularly deaf to the objections of the recipient, as all of us who have borne this embarrassment can attest.) Picking on the ring leader of this treatment, Santiago attacked him with all his strength but was ingloriously defeated. Trying time after time he was time after time defeated, until, embarking on a systematic course in exercise, he finally defeated his tormentor after some three years of defeat. They became good friends thereafter.

There were expeditions along the beautiful Isuela, and few birds escaped bow and arrow and the slingshot with which Santiago was particularly expert. They played the old games of boyhood on the city threshing floor which overlooked a road entering at a city gate far enough away so that they could stone horses, carters, police, and other passersby and be long gone by the time their victims had made the circuit and reached the threshing floor. Now, as then, the city wall cannot easily be scaled at that point.

Nearby was the great castle palace of Sancho Ramírez, Loarre (Figure 17), unconquered and undamaged; one of the most beautiful in Europe, standing on its own pinnacle of rock as do only four or five more in the whole of Europe. There was ample opportunity for all kinds of dangerous games, climbing all over the castle, or reclining on an abutment high above the ground dreaming brave dreams of past greatness and future glory. Not far distant were the ruins of the great fortress of Aragón (Figure 18).

These dreams soon came to be expanded; back in Ayerbe for the holidays, and following his usual habit of exploring the roofs of neighboring buildings, he came upon a window to the attic of a neighboring confectioner's house. Entering, he found it a storehouse for the confectioner's supplies of dried fruit, nuts, and other materials, but to his surprise he found a store of books that were totally new to him. These were *The Count of Monte Cristo* and the *Three Musketeers* by Dumas, *Notre Dame de Paris* by Hugo, *Gil Blas de Santillana* by LePage, *The Voyages of Captain Cook*, *Robinson Crusoe*, and *Don Quixote* to name those known in all countries by

Figure 17. The Castle of Loarre attracted Cajal time after time, even when grown, to climb over the battlements and to look down from its towering heights. It is now being restored; the old screen walls are being rebuilt and the rooms renewed. The old well near the central tower still provides an ample supply of pure water for construction.

all young people, and many, many others. Denying himself the immediate pleasure of sampling the tempting store of the confectioner's stock, and thus arousing his suspicions, Santiago borrowed a book at a time, always returning it to the exact place and gorged himself instead on the delightful books, forgetting completely the common occupations of everyday life. *Robinson Crusoe* was perhaps his favorite, for it was the story of a man who by his unaided efforts surmounted difficulties, dangers, and pitfalls to carve out his own unique paradise. It perhaps also fitted best his own individualistic nature, and his desire as well as the plain necessity to carve out for himself, and by himself alone, something of value in a different world.

Two other incidents of Santiago's school days at Huesca must be related, for they reveal the scientist that was all too greatly still overshadowed by the unrepentant mischievious boy who took long walks in the countryside, climbed difficult mountains and walked along the tiles of the houses at night, and who by day led a band of like-spirited companions on all sorts of adventuresome forays. Two photographers had installed themselves in the crypt of the ruins of the church of Santa Teresa and there Santiago spent hours watching the manipulation of silver iodide and bromide spread over

Figure 18. The threatening ruins of the Castle of Aragón blackened by the fire that destroyed it. As the Reconquista moved south, castles like this, which had withstood Moslem counterattacks, were left behind to the mercy of the elements and the ravages of fire.

glass in a thin film of wet collodion (Figure 19). Above all he was absorbed by the theory of development of the film in pyrogallic acid, which, absorbing oxygen, reduced the silver salts unaffected by light to metallic silver and so produced the negative plate. Throughout his life, Cajal was an ardent photographer, and later on he even began to make his own gelatine-bromide dry plates that were an improvement on the expensive imported plates. Such was the demand for these plates that with a little capital and a good partner he might have started an important new industry in Spain, but lacking both he returned to his other duties. If he failed to make a fortune, he did make his distinguished career in no small part because of his skills in handling silver salts and his meticulous attention to every detail of the delicate process.

Then in addition his father began to teach him osteology during his holidays in Ayerbe; together they collected the bones that lay everywhere in the poorly attended cemetery. Here Cajal found another great ability; in two months he had learned more names, relationships, and landmarks of the bones than he had learned of other subjects in years of schooling. Ob-

Figure 19. The church of Santa Teresa in Huesca, once in ruins but now rebuilt. By the change in color of the brick halfway up the door one can recognize the state of the ruins when two photographers occupied the crypt and young Cajal learned the first mysteries of the manipulation of silver salts. It may well be said that the foundations of his future greatness were laid in the old foundations of this church.

viously he was enchanted by the solid reality of the parts that presented themselves so vividly and unforgettably before his eyes.

But Santiago was slow to grow into maturity, and though he passed his first year in the Institute of Huesca, he only barely did so. Then followed a number of scrapes with police and carters on the road below the city wall in Huesca, while at another time he publicly caricatured a master of the Institute for his political beliefs. This led to a public stoning of the caricature by political opponents. His subsequent failure in the class this master taught was only to have been expected. Typical of this unhappy period, when he had not yet outgrown childish things and had yet to grow into manhood, was an occasion when he and his brother found a gold piece which was quickly converted into an enormous pistol and vast stock of ammunition. (I remembered when my brother and I were given twenty-five cents which we immediately spent on two pounds of gunpowder; the storekeeper kept it in a keg behind the counter and scooped it out like sugar or flour. For a whole day we engaged in all sorts of risky pyrotechnics and explosions from an ad hoc cannon constructed of a length of waterpipe stoppered at one end with a corncob.)

Frustrated and at his wits end, Don Justo withdrew his son from school for a year, apprenticing him to a barber and then to a shoemaker. The young Santiago learned his trades well and advanced rapidly as a shoemaker to the point that he was given the opportunity to make new shoes. He became friendly with both his new masters and so completely won them over that soon he was able to spend as much time as before on reading, drawing, and his own particular brand of incorrigible behavior. His father gave up trying to discipline him and sent him back to the Institute in Huesca. By now, however, Santiago had learned his lesson, adequately if not perfectly, and now he applied himself to his schoolwork and graduated with his class. There had been a last fling in which he and three cronies planned to run away to Zaragoza; they got as far as a neighboring village where the uncle of one of the boys fed them royally and gave them a good night's rest. In the bright morning light the romantic dream faded, and it seemed the best part of wisdom to submit to a more mature self-discipline and trudge back to Huesca. In Huesca he took out his frustrations in writing romantic poetry and a novel bearing unmistakable similarities to *Robinson Crusoe*. Before long he and his companions began acting out episodes from the novel along the Isuela, plastering themselves with mud and discharging arrows at imaginary attackers. The boys even dreamed of going one day on an expedition to find a desert island. As one of the four boys wrote later, Cajal continued to dream of finding his island, and he did; "in the central nervous organs, in the spinal cord and in the brain, is found in worthwhile fashion the Island of Cajal."

Figure 20. The medical school of Zaragoza where Cajal completed his medical studies. Nothing at all remains of the school itself at present, because the building was taken over by the Hospital of Nuestra Señora de Gracia when the new medical school was built. Napoleon's troops storm- ed Zaragoza and the spearhead of the attack was on the city wall to the left and behind the building. The pockmarks of stray musket ball and cannon balls can still be seen.

Figure 21. Zaragoza was itself on the pilgrim's route to Santiago. St. James was indeed supposed to have passed through the city on his westward journey. Appropriately, the Hospital of Nuestra Señora de Gracia is dedicated, as this old mosaic floor proclaims, as "Domus infirmorum urbis et orbis"; a "home for the sick of the city and the world". The much neglected small Church of San Juan de los Panetes was another asylum for hungry and needy pilgrims as the name implies. (Los Panetes were small loaves of bread given to pilgrims.)

Zaragoza

After completing the Baccalaureate at Huesca, Santiago's father took him to Zaragoza and enrolled him in the introductory year — the PCN of the French schools or Physics, Chemistry, and Natural Science in the Medical School (Figures 20 and 21). In the main the teaching was pedantic and didactic; the professor droning out the contents of notes long out of date. But the new spirit of experimental medicine had its early exponents, and one of these, Bruno Solano was already attempting to forge bonds between his professorate, the workshops, the laboratory, and the factory as Pasteur had done in France. Santiago's father's calculations worked out just right; having secured an appointment in the Provincial Medical Service, he

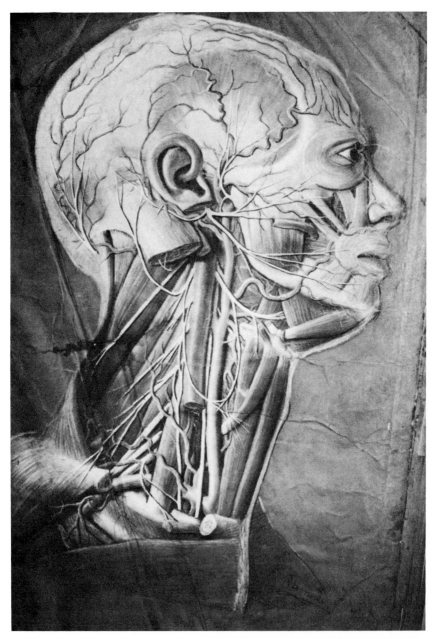

Figure 22. The external head and neck, dissected by Cajal and his father, and painted on canvas with pastels as one of a number of teaching exhibits by Cajal. This painting is signed: S. Ramón.

moved to Zaragoza with his family and in addition to his work in the clinics for the poor, he was given an appointment in Anatomy, and father and son began to dissect together. Now Santiago's skill at drawing stood the two in good stead, and Santiago prepared an ever growing portfolio of anatomical paintings done on canvas in pastel (Figure 22). The hope that these paintings might be published could not be carried out because of the backward state of graphic reproduction in Zaragoza. At the end of Cajal's second year

Figure 23. The Roman walls across the Ebro from the confluence of the Gállego. "Here in the year 24 A.D. the IIII Macedonian, the VI Victorix and the X Gemina (legions) founded the colony of Cesaraugustus." (From the marker at the site.)

in Medicine he was appointed as dissecting assistant. The appointment strengthened his growing interest in Anatomy and gave him the opportunity to make some money through private lessons in practical anatomy.

As had happened before, Santiago's early years at Zaragoza were not particularly happy; his old friends from Huesca were one or two years ahead of him and too occupied with their new enthusiasm to pay much attention to Santiago. Again he had recourse to solitary walks in the country along the Ebro and visits to the churches and museums with which the city abounded (Figures 23 and 24), for if in the old days Jaca and Huesca were in every way more important than Zaragoza, the city, now the capital of Aragón, was

Figure 24. At the edge of the city stands the great stronghold of Zaragoza, the Aljafería, built and rebuilt, added to and changed from before the Romans to after Ferdinand and Isabella used it as their palace; later it became the site of the Inquisition. Moorish designs and Roman towers are everywhere, but perhaps the most gorgeous single structure is the golden ceiling of Ferdinand and Isabella's throne room with its pineapple bosses. It is probably the finest ceiling in all of Europe. Perfectly symmetrical end to end and side to side, its inscription states that it was made in 1492.

clearly the new center artistically, intellectually, and industrially. During these years Santiago developed three new enthusiasms: literature, gymnastics, and philosophy. He wrote a novel on travels through the cardiovascular system on a red blood corpuscle; the preliminary draft with colored drawings adapted from the great German histologists was subsequently lost; others developed the same idea and not long ago an exciting film was made on the subject in this country.

After a few retrograde steps into the old pastimes of fighting and casting stones with his accurate sling, Santiago sublimated the old urges in a mania for body building, trading lessons in muscular physiology for a course in physical development. After a year of vigorous calisthenics, which indeed produced a remarkable muscular development, Santiago gave up the pursuit of large muscles, and thereafter came to feel that such excessive development was inconsistent with proper intellectual development.

Now for the first time Santiago fell in love with a young lady who lived in the Calle Cinco de Marzo (now the Avenida de los Requetés de Aragón) (Figure 25). As was the custom in those days he followed her home day after day, watched her balcony for hours, and idealized her as the supreme model of a goddess. He found that he was crossing the path of an engineering student who had much the same pretentions as Santiago. Fighting at fisticuffs with the engineering student followed, and Cajal won, but with the exaggerated chivalry of the very young, he agreed to let the young lady decide between them. In a few days however the engineer found that the young lady had a very considerable dowry and such was the innocence of the day that both young men renounced their suits lest they would be accused of fortune hunting.

Military Service In Cuba And Return To Zaragoza

In June of 1873, Cajal graduated with the title of Licentiate in Medicine, was picked up in the draft of that year, and began to serve as a common soldier. Studying for the omnipresent examinations for the Army Medicine Service, he was ranked sixth in a list of a hundred candidates and was one of thirty-two young physicians appointed as Lieutenant. For eight months he was brigaded with troops stationed at Lérida, whose function was to protect the frontier districts from depredations by the Carlist rebels. In eight months of marching and counter-marching they never once established contact with the rebels.

At the end of this period a number of Medical Officers was chosen by lot to go to Cuba, where the independence movement had flared up again, and

Figure 25. The former Calle Cinco de Marzo, now the Avenida de los Requetés de Aragón, along which young Cajal saw his first love. Along this street he would follow her home at a discreet distance, and below her balcony he would wait for hours. Along this street, he met his rival, the engineering student; both in the end renounced their dream goddess.

casualties were high. Along with this draft he was promoted to Captain. Arriving in Cuba he was appointed to care for a hospital with some 200 patients; most of them had malaria. The strategy for the subjugation of the rebellion was essentially to cut the island into three parts by two North-South roads carved out through the jungle, the *trochas militares*, bordered by palisades and barbed wire entanglements, with block houses every five-hundred meters and wooden forts at company strength every thousand meters. The East road absorbed several thousand soldiers; the West road eight or ten thousand. Usually three out of four soldiers were sick in the hospitals and the troops had a turnover time of only three or four months. In all, this campaign cost some 74,000 casualties by illness; most of them died, and the system of military roads and the concept of a static defense were abandoned. After more than twenty more years of being bled white, "to the last man and the last peseta", Spain was finally stripped of the last of its colonial empire in the Spanish-American War.

Cajal's own troubles were increasing. He had a debilitating attack of malaria, his pay rarely reached him, and his attempts to reserve meat, eggs, sherry and beer for the patients in the hospital were regularly frustrated, and most of these supplies were consumed by officers and male nurses. The Major in command would not listen to Cajal and attempted to bring him up on charges of insubordination, but the clear evidence of graft and other abuses that Cajal presented was such that the charges against him were dropped and the whole matter swept under the carpet. Mustered out of the service for illness, Cajal returned to Spain and Zaragoza where he received a temporary appointment in Anatomy which was increased in 1877 to Temporary Auxiliary Professor. In 1878 he took the examinations for his Doctorate in Madrid, and being told of the kind of questions he could be asked by kindhearted Madrid students he passed the examination by dint of a few days of hectic cramming. The lasting good of his visit to Madrid was an introduction to histology and microscopy which was to become his life work.

Illness And Recovery: A Life Work Begins

Not a little unlike his father, Ramón y Cajal was virtually obsessive in his dedication to science; his whole life rotated around his work. But like his father's passion for hunting, which was the only relaxation he permitted himself, Ramón y Cajal had a passion for the Café and the good company he found there. The sharp and brilliant interplay of intellects, the extempore epigrams, the well-turned phrases; in sum, the display of the lambent conversation of the very special genre of the Spanish Café — not at all to be confused with that of the Boulevard Cafés of Paris — fascinated him beyond measure. So much did he enjoy his evenings at the cafés with his friends that he felt so guilty at the time it took away from his work that he usually returned to his apartment to work still later into the night to make up for lost time.

It was in the Café de la Iberia, while playing a "strenuous" game of chess with a dear friend in the military administrative service, that he had a sudden and unexpected hemoptysis. Returning home in deep unquiet and retiring soon after a light supper, he was seized by an even more frightening hemorrhage with its sudden rush of bright red foaming blood — the almost certain sign of serious pulmonary tuberculosis. Soon there appeared the other signs of the dread disease: dyspnea, persistent cough, perspiration, emaciation, and high fever; he had seen the signs too often in the unfortunate soldiers he had treated in Cuba and too often in the patients at the clinic in Zaragoza to have any doubts about the diagnosis. In a profound depression, his hopes of contributing to the advance of Spanish Science in ruins, he could only anguish at the irremedial uselessness of his existence.

Here again his father proved dauntless, admitting no thoughts of defeat. As soon as Santiago was a little better, after two months in bed, his father sent him first to the old Roman baths at Panticosa, high in the Pyrenees, where the beginnings of a modern health establishment had been started in 1854, and where consumptives had already begun to congregate for their cure (Figures 26 and 27). Here, driven by the romantic mood of that century of tuberculosis, he gave himself over to the most gloomy thoughts, climbing the almost vertical cliffs that walled in the little resort with a view to die with his face to the stars at the pinnacle of the cliffs. But quite the opposite happened; as he broke the usual rules and resumed his old love of the exploration of nature, his hemoptyses diminished in frequency, his fever receded, and his lungs and muscles functioned better and better. Slowly the realization came that he was recovering his health and would live.

Soon Cajal stopped his medical regime totally; the medicines were abandoned; the details of regime disregarded; the highly reputed nitrogenated water was no longer drunk; he lived a normal life. He resumed his walks, his photography, his drawing, his long conversations, as though an endless life were in prospect; and so it was.

For a few weeks longer, Cajal and his sister lived in a few of the undamaged rooms of the "new" monastery of San Juan de la Peña (Figure 28). Napoleon's cannon had almost totally destroyed the rest, and along the façade of the adjoining church were waist-high bullet pocks where the infantry had attacked on the flank, or where guerillas had been shot.

Here in the peace of the high Monte Pano with its panoramic view of the rising ranks of the Pyrenees and its most distant peaks, Cajal found new

DILIGENCIAS Á PANTICOSA.

Las antiguas empresas de **ESTRELLA** y **PIRINEOS**, ofrecen á los señores viajeros sus espaciosos y elegantes carruajes, así como el personal, escogido y práctico en el terreno, por estar ejerciendo todo el año servicio hasta Jaca.

Se despachan billetes en Madrid, L. Ramirez, Alcalá, núm. 12, y en Huesca, Fonda de España.

Esta fonda, abierta al público desde el dia 15 de Junio, ofrece á los señores viajeros la ventaja de estar el local muy próximo á la estacion del ferro-carril, y además un edificio nuevo, como asimismo el mueblaje, buen trato, comodidad, aseo y economía.

Se sirven comidas á precio fljo y á la carta.   25   10-d

AGUA DE PANTICOSA.

Se recibe semanalmente del Establecimiento en la Farmácia de Rios hermanos. Coso, número 53.

Figure 26. In the year that Cajal developed tuberculosis, Panticosa, an old Roman watering place high in the Pyrenees was already recognized as a health resort and its water bottled for distribution. The railway extended only to Huesca and a stage coach had to be depended upon for the last and most difficult, but most strikingly beautiful, stage of the trip.

The advertisement reads as follows: Diligences (Stage Coaches) to Panticosa.

The old firms of Estrella and Pirineos offer travellers their spacious and elegant carriages as well as a select personnel with experience in the terrain so as to be able to maintain service as far as Jaca throughout the year.

Tickets are obtainable in Madrid from L. Ramirez, Alcalá No. 12, and in Huesca at the Fonda de España.

This inn, open to the public from the 15th of June, offers travellers the advantage of a location very close to the railway station, and in addition a new building as well as furnishings, good service, comfort, cleanliness, and economy.

Meals are served at a fixed price (table d'hôte) and á la carte.

strength, new enjoyment of life, new places to visit like the "old" monastery halfway down the steepest face of Monte Pano, sheltered from above by the overhanging cliff in the characteristic red of Aragón, and an impossible climb from below against any opposition at all (Figure 29). So it had remained a sheltered nest of Christian resistance without interruption, with its old Visigothic crypt, its gem-like early medieval cloister, and its undisturbed chapel where the oldest kings of Aragón were entombed.

Figure 27. Panticosa is a small town with precipitous cliffs ringing it around except for a passage-way for the headwaters of the Gállego and a road. A Roman watering place, it began to be recognized again as a health resort in 1854 and soon all the paraphernalia of a 19th century watering place were organized, and countless springs were identified as having separate curative powers. This old building, surrounded by lilacs in bloom, is perhaps the only one that exists from Cajal's time.

Figure 28. The "new" monastery of San Juan de la Peña after it was destroyed by Napoleon's cannon. On the front can be seen an intact roof covering some six rooms that were undamaged, and here Cajal and his sister stayed for a few weeks. A path to the left of the chapel leads to a remarkable view of the serried ranks of the Pyrenees, rising in orderly sequence. The Gran Hotel at Jaca still sends a good motherly cook to the monastery, and here we stayed for some three weeks as we traced Cajal's early life.

So it was that Cajal returned to Zaragoza in October of 1878, with renewed health, revitalized ambitions, and all his old energy, to throw himself wholeheartedly into his work in the dissecting room and his histological laboratory. He was appointed Director of the Anatomical Museum in 1879, and decided to get married. In his usual fashion, he had first seen his fiancée while out walking, and after much family opposition married her; their income was then some twenty-five to thirty-five dollars a month. Cajal's instincts were true to him; for him she was indeed the perfect wife. A friend used to say about his scientific career, "Half of Cajal is his wife."

In 1884 Cajal was awarded the Chair of Anatomy at Valencia after the usual competitive examinations. Here in 1885 came the great cholera epidemic that ravaged much of Europe, and his work on cholera opened before him a career in bacteriology and immunology. But it was too late for him to be distracted from histology: at the house of a friend in Madrid, Cajal had seen for the first time some of Golgi's own preparations of the nervous tissue stained with his new discovery, the silver impregnation

Figure 29. The old monastery of San Juan de la Peña hidden under the overhanging red cliff and atop another almost equally steep. At the left is the newer chapel. Then a fragment of the jewel-like cloister can be seen, and at the right there is a Visigothic chapel far under the cliff.

stain. A new world was revealed to his eyes, and he began to employ the Golgi method and to study it with all his great patience. The rest is history. These studies opened the way into the fine hidden structure of the nervous system. It is still one of the great "Open Sesames" to the study of the nervous system.

In France, Louis Pasteur had made transcendental discoveries that, like Cajal's, have been woven into the warp and woof of much that we know today about the biology of the cell; he was in addition a mighty catalyst for new work all over the world. In France he became a great hero of science, wearing the ribbon of the Legion d'Honneur for his contributions to France in Science just as his father had worn his for heroism in France's battles, and young scientists emulated him, became great in their own right, and made French Science great. We need only to mention the Curies, Pierre and Marie to make this point amply clear.

So too had Santiago Ramón y Cajal made the very greatest of individual discoveries. So also, like Pasteur, did the flame that he lighted attract the best minds all over the world to the study of the structure and the function of the nervous system; indeed in discussing the nervous system in any detail at all, Cajal's name is the first name that must be mentioned. But the climate of Spain was not propitious, and Cajal stands alone in his scientific greatness; the country has not yet produced his like in science. Can it be that all the great forces that produced Spain's proudest days, beginning with the cave painters in Altamira, have died out? Are the halcyon days of the Roman Spain, the times of devoted early Christians and their embattled enclaves in northern Castile and Aragón, the honor, loyalty, and power in war of El Cid Campeador, the genius of a Ramón Llull and of Miguel Servet, the drive for discovery of the Conquistadors, the heroism of the fighting men at Lepanto, and of the shipbuilders who built and the seamen who sailed the ships at Lepanto and to the New World no longer to be found in Spain? Cannot these energies and these visions be transmuted into the new tasks in a New World? Sir Charles Sherrington had some of the microscopic slides Cajal had prepared with his own hands, and generously let me examine them when I was one of his young students. No one can look at them, see the map of the New World of the central nervous system Cajal wrote out in a tracery of silver and believe anything else but that the old energy, the old vision, and the old love of exploration is still a part of the Spanish inheritance, that it will find its outlet, and that the world will again benefit from it.

Acknowledgment

These studies were supported in part from the National Institutes of Health, Grant No. R01 LM 00453 through the National Library of Medicine and from Special Fund 368-G07174, Baylor College of Medicine.

EPILOGUE: REFLECTIONS ON THE SYMPOSIUM

David Cardus

We are all aware that nations do not emerge from nowhere. Each nation has a cultural ancestry and a political birth. Many of the old nations are the spontaneous product of the ages. The United States of America are a volitional creation; they were born with a clear vision of what they wanted to be and set as the supreme goal the primacy of human freedom. Two hundred years later, the march toward that goal continues and as one looks at the distance covered and that still laying ahead, there are good reasons for satisfaction and insatisfaction. As compared to others, the people of this nation have achieved high levels of tenure in natural and civil rights. But there still remain obstacles to total fulfillment which are due, at least in part, to a slanted valuation of one class of cultural values versus others. Despite its notorious and, for some, disquieting diversity, there is only one human race. Despite its splendorous variation, there is only one human culture.

The recognition of natural and civil rights places predominant emphasis on the individual. But individual and cultural heritage are inseparable and promoters of new societies should keep in mind that in a multicultured society, social and cultural values should not be made antithetic. Failure to realize this frequently leads to social conflicts which pull much of the human energy which is needed to fulfill collective goals.

Studies of social values in the United States of America underscore the puritan role in the shaping of this nation, but there are non puritan antecedents and societal components with immanent cultural values that must be effectively incorporated into the building of a more real America.

As a fact, the multicultural make-up of America is not unique. Many nations are constitutionally multicultured. The particular feature is that this nation cannot afford a cultural integration by historical sedimentation. It must achieve it by a willful, rational process. The mutual recognition of Indian, Spanish, Anglosaxon, Black and Oriental traditions is not a simple matter of justice but the safest assurance that preset national goals can be achieved and higher goals can be contemplated.

The cultural background of the ethnic components of a nation determines a variety of human perceptions of the world in which we live. This symposium has focused attention on the Hispanic component. An analysis of the Hispanic past of America gives insight into the development and social role of institutions that exist still today. It helps also to better understand the complex behavioral relationships of a multicultured society. Those interested in the socioeconomic background of California may, for example, appreciate the importance of the Neve regulation in fostering social reform by balancing civil power against that of the missions as it can be derived from Campbell's investigations.

The Hispanic-American of Alta California must have imprinted in his soul the vital experiences of those early Hispanic settlers whose lives were so tightly linked to the ecumenical designs of the Spanish church. The men of Tortilla Flat, so well understood through Steinbeck's empathy, believe in the thaumaturgic power of Saint Francis and in the treasures of Saint Andrew's night. As much as an atavism in contemporaneous America this may seem, men and women of this spiritual make-up are part of America.

The political birth of the United States of America required external assistance. France's participation in the independence of the British colonies is an obligated chapter of all American history textbooks. But Spain played also a role that, except for some fact seeking erudits, has received little attention. And the same is true in regard to law; laws on water regulation, homestead and community property are laws brought by the Spaniards, laws still enforced in several of the states of America. These historical facts should be transmitted to all generations for they must become part of the conscious heritage of the American people.

Artistic creation is one of the highest expressions of human freedom. Through literature and the plastic arts man expresses his feelings and ideas to his fellow men. When art and literature are used as means of protest, the message may be irritating to established political powers and to the group or groups that constitute the cultural basis of such powers. When this occurs within a nation the aesthetical message expresses the anxiety of a marginated cultural minority.

The fulfillment of certain national goals is often dependent upon the availability of specialized manpower. Educational programs and scientific research are two examples. The United States of America have always had wide open doors to scholars and highly educated immigrants. Many of these have greatly contributed to the intellectual education of American youth. Much of this century's scientific achievement has resulted from the work done in this country by researchers who acquired their basic knowledge in other countries. Considering that Spanish is spoken by and taught to millions of Americans, the contribution of Hispanic teachers in the overall national educational effort is of considerable magnitude. Science and education are effective sources of human freedom; freedom from the prejudices that separate men; freedom from ignorance that undermines man's faith in his abilities to control the adverse forces of the environment.

As the confines of our planet become less misteriously distant we realize the necessity for considering every portion of it as part of a unity. Links among peoples are the intimate network of this unity. The potential usefulness of the varied cultural roots of the American people in the conduct of international affairs should not be underestimated. President Carter may not simply have succumbed to political pressures in making a black man the link with African nations but rather respond to an instinct inspired by his knowledge of human nature. Commonality in cultural background is likely to facilitate human communications. Hispanics and Orientals could play a role in the relations between USA and Asiatic and Spanish speaking countries.

As one contemplates the American panorama, the conviction grows that cultural heterogeneity is a benefit for a society that firmly believes that men are bound by a common destiny. It is, however, apparent that each cultural component of a society may sense the need for social change at different times. Resistance to change must be accepted with a spirit of comprehension for it depends on a strong adherence to the values of the past and to the uncertainty that changes can lead to a future of a better quality than the present. Differences in tempo in perceiving the need for changes may slow down the harmonious development of a society but they may also be conducive to choices that better represent man's intuition of how human life can be enriched.